Praise For

WITHOUT REMORSE

In unflinching language, Vonda Pelto escorts us into the claustrophobic bedlam of a giant jailhouse and lays bare the behavior of notorious serial killers. Pulling no punches, she allows us a voyeuristic look into their convoluted minds, and shares shocking personal experiences that will leave you reeling.

—Don Lasseter

Author, Journalist

Dr. Vonda Pelto's brutally honest book, *Without Remorse*, takes the reader on a forbidden tour behind the gates of the men's jail, a haunted house where Serial Killers live. But most powerful is the juxtaposition of Pelto's personal and professional life, with its conflicts between men and women, sex and violence, and intimidation and vulnerability.

—Carole Lieberman

M.D., M.P.H., Forensic Psychiatrist/ Expert Witness

Vonda Pelto scares me. This book is way too much fun. I hear she's the favorite pin-up on Death Row. Pour yourself a cup of warm arsenic and settle in for the ride.

—Brian Alan Lane

Bestselling Author, *Cat & Mouse: Mind Games with a Serial Killer*

I sentenced men like these from the bench. Dr. Pelto had to deal with sadistic killers who had no remorse for their actions. She does an incredible job of revealing the depths of the soul of these killers.

—Judge Donald McCartin

Retired Superior Court Judge "The hanging Judge of Orange County, CA, who sentenced nine men to death row

One hell-of-a-book! So well written that you feel as though you actually knew these killers. I felt like I was right there with Vonda I loved the book. *Without Remorse* shows a side to these killers that the general public never sees. It puts you right there in the jail with them. What this great book reveals is the two sides of these men, the dark side and the human side. How could these killers be so charming and yet, be able to murder and mutilate a follow human being?

—Jeff Hathcock
   Film Producer

Without Remorse is an incredible journey that only Vonda could undertake, with her eyes wide open and a determination that even the most horrendous killers of society couldn't break. This is a brilliant book!!!

—William L Fabrizio
   Producer and Screenwriter

This is a one-of-a-kind book by a one-of-a-kind author. Vonda L. Pelto has written a disturbingly factual account of her years as a unique psychologist in L.A. County's Men's Jail. She met with the area's worst serial killers to prevent them from wreaking havoc on themselves.

—Tedd Thomey
   Award winning columnist for *The Independent Press Telegram*
   Author of eighteen books and a successful Broadway play

Without
REMORSE

Without
REMORSE

THE STORY OF THE WOMAN
WHO KEPT LOS ANGELES'
SERIAL KILLERS ALIVE

Vonda L. Pelto, Ph.D

SEVEN LOCKS PRESS
SANTA ANA, CALIFORNIA

Seven Locks Press
P.O. Box 25689
Santa Ana, CA 92799
(800) 354-5348

Individual sales: This book is available through most bookstores or can be ordered
directly from Seven Locks Press at the address above.

Quantity Sales: Special discounts are available on quantity purchases by corporations,
associations and others. For details, contact the "Special Sales Department" at the
publisher's address above.

Cover & Interior Design Kira Fulks • www.kirafulks.com
Technical Support Robyn Saunders • www.robynsaunders.com

Printed in the United States of America

Library of Congress Cataloging-in-Publication Data is available from the publisher

ISBN: 978-0979585289

DEDICATION

To my loving husband Jim Lia,
my daughters Tera and Deanne,
my sons-in-law Richard and Nick
and my grand children:
Lauren, Ariel, Alex, Jeremy, Jake and Cassie.
I could never have finished this book
without your love and support.

ACKNOWLEDGMENTS

———◆◆◆◆◆———

Thanks to Pam and Jim Stewart, Kaaren Paratore,
Brian Alan Lane, Frank Gaspar, Barbara Briley Beard
and all my writing buddies at Long Beach City College
for reading my manuscript and giving me constructive suggestions.
Most of all, thanks to my publisher, Jim Riordan,
for laughing and crying with me.

CHAPTER 1

WHAT'S A NICE GIRL DOING IN A PLACE LIKE THIS?

I stepped through the portal slowly, cautiously, as if I were stepping into quicksand, and immediately froze. There was a deafening roar. Metal doors slammed, voices screamed out from unseen loudspeakers, and feet with chains attached to them dragged along the cement floors. The jail was ripe with the stench of stale cigarette smoke, rank body odor, feces, disinfectant, and burnt toast. And there was a heaviness to this foul, repugnant combination of smells that added to the oppressiveness of the atmosphere. Momentarily, I thought I would be sick.

"Stranger in Paradise" bellowed out from an unseen speaker system, and I worked hard to stifle a nervous laugh. *Elevator music in a men's jail? Totally insane!*

Looking around, I struggled to take in this alien world.

A loud clang sounded. The heavy steel door engaged and was grinding closed behind me. I was inside a men's jail! Me, a girl from Needles, California; a town of forty-five hundred people located on the edge of the Colorado River, where my father worked for the Santa Fe Railroad and my mother clerked for the JC Penney Company. My impulse was to turn and run out of there, but there was no escape; the gate had locked behind me.

I felt tentative and rubbed my sweaty palms along the sides of my skirt. My heart pounded against my chest wall so hard it felt like I had run a marathon.

Directly across from the gate where I had entered, six male inmates dressed in yellow jumpsuits sat along dingy, mustard-colored walls on backless wooden benches. Each man had a manacle fastened to his right ankle. Shackles ran from the steel ankle bracelets to metal cylinders that supported the benches anchored into the concrete floor.

Two of the inmates looked at the ceiling as if they were praying. Two others glared at me as if they had never seen a woman. One inmate mumbled and gestured wildly, responding to unseen voices inside his head. The inmate seated at the end of the bench had his jumpsuit unbuttoned to the crotch, urinating noisily into a Styrofoam cup. He faced the long hall, unconcerned that I stood only a few feet away.

I stayed motionless, turning my head to observe the mustard-colored hallway that extended in both directions, hoping someone would notice my hesitation and come to my rescue.

Half a dozen inmates dressed in blue jumpsuits scrubbed the walls with wooden bristle brushes, some on their knees, others stretching to reach the upper portions of the dirty hallway. The slamming of the gate alerted them to my presence. Wolf whistles followed, with someone shouting "New meat! Fresh pussy!"

I felt hot and slightly disoriented. *Vonda, get hold of yourself.*

Turning to the right about fifty feet away, a gate of bars stood in a closed position. Metal panels composed the ceiling with long fluorescent tubes providing bright, monotonous light that bounced annoyingly off the highly polished concrete floor. Intermittent metal doors punctuated the hallway, portals into the sheriff's administrative offices. The opposite end of the hall dead-ended about thirty feet away.

Voices reverberated down the austere, concrete hallway. I assumed they belonged to the inmates. Unexpectedly, a loud, coarse voice called out above the rest of the fray.

"Yo, sweet little mamma, you wanna fuck?"

Startled, I turned in the direction of a line of inmates being herded toward me like cattle. They were shackled together with leg irons, the chains dragging along the cold cement floor, scraping and rattling as they moved.

Many of the men were pimply faced and didn't look old enough to be out of high school; most of them weren't much older than my own two daughters. Studying the fish line, I spotted a wily smile on a fleshy black face that told me he was the offender. He blew a kiss in my direction, and his rotund frame went into motion. He sensed my panic and laughed at my fear. His small, deeply embedded eyes almost disappeared as his face contorted into a lecherous grin.

I thought of my Southern Baptist father's strong sense of proper decorum around women. He would have been incensed at this affront and told the inmate so in no uncertain terms.

The line of inmates stopped opposite me. The hall seemed to shrink as their leering eyes roamed over my body like hot sweaty hands exploring every crevice. I wanted to disappear. Finally, a deputy called out to them.

"On the wall, home boys! Don't mad dog the lady."

The inmates turned and pushed face first into the cold wall. Now they stood quietly. The deputy leading the line walked over to the deputy's booth and after a short conversation returned to the inmates.

"Okay, ladies, let's move it!" he shouted. With that command, the line continued on down the hall, the men laughing and whispering.

"Thanks," I said to the guard who had spoken up for me.

"Yeah, sure thing, babe."

Caught off-guard by the inmate's remark, I couldn't remember what the deputy that opened the gate told me to do. *What had he said? Oh yes, the key, check out the key.* Catching my breath, I walked what seemed like a hundred miles to the deputy's booth. Actually, it was only ten feet away.

"Excuse me, sir, am I in the right place?"

"Don't know, sweet cheeks, depends on what you want." Laughter followed from behind him.

My face reddened. "The office key, please." With less hassle than I had endured earlier, the deputy added my name to the roster, and I took possession of the single silver key. It lay cold on the palm of my hand—a powerful key that opened doors in a jail that housed more than six thousand inmates, and was part of the largest jail system in the world.

"Each time you leave the jail, you are to turn the key in at this booth. If you don't check it back in at the end of each workday, we will come to your house and retrieve it from you. Understood?" The deputy's voice sounded like he was reciting a mantra.

"Yes, sir." I dropped the power symbol into the side pocket of my skirt and prayed that I would remember to turn it back in when the day was over. Visions of a swat team breaking down my front door and tear gas pouring out of my broken windows flashed before me.

I reminded myself to pay close attention to what the dark shadow on the other side of the glass was saying, uncertain of what to do next.

Without acknowledging me, the deputy opened the window, leaned out of the opening, and called to a uniformed man standing a few yards to the left.

"Hey, Gonzales, take this lady up to 7100."

The deputy nodded, giving me a quick appraisal, not bothering to introduce himself.

"7100 is on the second floor." Gonzales stood five foot ten, wore a khaki uniform, had graying hair and a neatly trimmed, full beard. He was on the verge of having a beer belly, with only a couple of notches left on his belt.

He tapped my shoulder, directing me toward the elevator located about fifteen feet to the right.

Another line of shackled inmates was approaching. Walking on the solid concrete, my black patent leather pumps echoed throughout the tubular hall, attracting their attention. Already unnerved, I lifted up on tiptoe, trying to soften the sound. The inmates gawked at me as they moved past. I heard one snicker and several others laughed and let out wolf whistles. This time there were no admonitions from a deputy.

"You're going to FOP, aren't you?" the deputy asked as he pushed the elevator button.

"I, ah...I'm...is Dr. Kline in FOP?"

"Yes, ma'am, Forensic Outpatient." The elevator doors slid open and I inhaled a strong odor of urine. Hesitating, I turned to the deputy. He had a knowing smile.

"You'll get used to it in time." I wasn't sure he was right, and began to doubt the sanity of wanting this job.

When the doors opened again, I bolted, wanting to break free from the obnoxious smell.

"Hold up, babe," Gonzales grabbed my arm to keep me from falling. "We're on third, med-surg. You want the second floor."

"How's it hanging, Jose?" A tall slender deputy with movie star good looks stepped in.

"Never better than last night, Paul, and yours?" They both laughed. I looked at the floor, pretending to not understand what they were talking about.

Gonzales pushed the button, and the elevator started its descent.

"Well, babe, if you're not a cool drink of water." The deputy checked me over as if I was a new red Mustang convertible he was thinking of buying. "You a new file clerk?" he asked with a lecherous grin.

"No," I said with more emphasis than I'd planned. "I'm Dr. Pelto, clinical psychologist."

My dream to become a psychologist and have my own private practice started when I was eleven years old. My sixth-grade teacher gave me his Introduction to Psychology textbook, and although it was impossible to understand much of what I read, the subject matter fascinated me. But as often happens in life, fate stepped in and diverted me from my goal for many years.

I'm still not sure about the reasons I wanted to work in the Men's Jail—probably had to do with being a sickly kid, overly protected, and wanting to prove I could deal with any challenge. At age seven, I contracted rheumatic fever and was confined to bed for a year. When I returned to school, my activities were severely limited. I was under constant surveillance and developed a rebellious streak. At every opportunity, I broke the restrictive rules. Now, working in the jail would show I was strong and didn't need protection from anyone anymore.

"Well, hot shit! Since when did they let girls become doctors?" I looked away from the deputy.

"Hey, sweet cheeks, you gonna analyze me?" Paul reached out to touch my shoulder. I pulled away and stood against the elevator's filthy, urine-stained back wall. I wanted to say, *I only do it for money, but thought better of it.*

"I'd sure like to come over sometime and lay on your couch."

"Some inmates are scrubbing the walls downstairs. Do they get paid for it?" I asked, wanting to direct the attention away from myself.

"Nope," Paul snapped.

"Do they have other jobs to keep them busy?"

"They fix the food for the staff and inmates. You'll get a chance to evaluate their culinary skills down in the cafeteria," Gonzales answered in a more tolerant tone.

"Jose, you got some sense of humor. All these perps do is sit around on their fat asses and complain all day."

"Why not painting or repairs?"

Paul jumped back in. "Honey, the unions would go through the fucking roof. They have contracts with the county and they make a hell of a lot of money. They'd go out on strike if they lost these jobs to the inmates."

"It would save us taxpayers a lot of money if the inmates did the repairs."

"Sweet cheeks, you sure you're a psychologist? You sound more like a union buster."

"There was a great story about drugs being brought in here a while back." Gonzales sensed the growing tension between Paul and me and wanted to cool the situation down by changing the subject. I took a deep breath and exhaled slowly.

"One of the perp's mothers sewed a baggy of coke into the crotch of her kid's skivvies and left 'em with the deputies to give to him. She didn't know her boy had got kicked out in the midnight release. The kid's shorts lay around the booth for several days until a deputy decided to clean up. He picked up the shorts and noticed a lump in the crotch and cut it open and found the contraband. A few days later the ditzy broad came back to visit her other son. The deputies were waiting for her. Cuffed her on the spot and transported her over to SBI."

"SBI?" I asked.

"Sybil Bran Institute, woman's jail. Babe, you're a fish. You gotta lot to learn," Jose answered me with a softness in his voice.

"A fish?"

"Yep, someone new to the game."

"That's me," I mumbled under my breath, "but it won't take me long to catch on."

"These inmates are real creative," Paul said as he licked his lips. "They say they can get anything they want in here. Even a good piece of ass. Know what I mean, babe?"

Yes, I did, but I wasn't going to let him know he was bugging me!

I gave Paul a sweet smile—one that could probably give you a cavity.

In the '60s when I grew up, being called honey, babe, or sweetheart sounded endearing and protective. I know other women would have been offended, but I wasn't. Now, the way the deputies were using the names, I felt demeaned. This was sexual harassment. And I didn't like it. But this wasn't the time to make an issue of it. I would bide my time.

Finally, the elevator doors opened after what seemed like a hundred years, and I stepped out, followed by Gonzales. We were in a hallway that mirrored the one below, long and foreboding. It was covered with the same mustard-colored paint as the first floor. The gray cement floor glistened from polish, wires covered the overhead fluorescent lights, and an instrumental version of "Mack the Knife" spilled out of the speaker system. The air was still and dead.

Even with no windows, the overhead lights gave the appearance of bright sunlight. In this sealed environment, I couldn't tell if it was day or night, or if there was still another world existing outside the building. I was incarcerated and couldn't escape this prison any more than the inmates could.

Four coin-operated telephones hung on the wall opposite of the elevator and to the left of an office door. A wooden bench secured to the concrete floor sat beneath the phones. It was reminiscent of the pews I sat on as a kid when our family attended the Baptist Church. During the endless sermons about fire, hell, and damnation, we kids would entertain ourselves by paging through the "Broadman Hymnal", saying "between the bed sheets" after the title of each song, like "How Great Thou Art", between the bed sheets, or "Onward Christian Solders", between the bed sheets. Well, you get the idea. Anyway, back to the jail.

A man with jailhouse pallor, from lack of sunshine, stood talking on the phone. By many accounts, he could be called handsome, with good bone structure and the kind of thick, dark, wavy hair you'd like to run your fingers through. He stood with his foot propped on the bench already covered with multiple scratches, half leaning onto the doorframe of an office—an office I would be calling home for the next three years.

The opening of the elevator doors had diverted his attention from the phone call and he turned to stare at me. His green eyes sparkled as he perused my body, starting with my heels, black stockings, and up my soft black dress to my ample breasts and short red hair. He gave me a nod of approval and flashed a boyish smile.

I started to blush. It was flattering. My ego had been hurt sleeping with my first husband for over a year and not being desired by him. I craved male attention. My father was gone, working for the railroad, for long periods of time when I was little, and my brother, who was nine years older than me, left for the Navy the summer he finished high school. From then on, our house consisted of my mother and me.

The man on the phone caught my eye and we exchanged an intimate moment. I felt myself flush and my heartbeat speed up. He smiled. I smiled back.

I took a deep breath, exhaled slowly, and relaxed a little. *Why had I expected all of the inmates to look mean and surly?*

The tone of his voice was soft and caressing, and his laugh contagious as he replied to the person on the other end of the line.

He looked vaguely familiar, but I couldn't remember where I had seen him. Maybe on the nightly news?

I tapped the deputy on the shoulder as soon as we were out of earshot of the man on the phone.

"That man seems very pleasant. Who is he?"

"That's Ken Bianchi, one of the Hillside Stranglers. Would you like to hear what that 'pleasant guy' did, along with his cousin Angelo Buono?" Before I had a chance to answer, Gonzales continued. "Together, they murdered ten young women and threw their bodies out along the hillsides in L.A."

The deputy stopped abruptly and turned to face me. I stopped short to keep from bumping into him and drew in my breath.

"I remember the murder of Kristina Weckler. She lived next door to Bianchi when he had an apartment over on Garfield. Ken flirted with her, trying to get her to go out with him. She turned him down cold. Maybe she sensed something evil about him. Pissed Ken off, big time!

"One night he rang her doorbell, said her car had been hit in the parking lot. Told her he was a reserve police officer and offered to file a police report. Angelo Buono waited downstairs. When Ken arrived with Kristina, they forced her into Ken's car and drove over to Angelo's place. That's where most of the Hillside stranglings occurred. Then these two winners," the deputy said with force, "took turns raping and sodomizing her. God only knows what else they made her do, probably finished off by forcing her to give them each a blowjob."

I looked back at the man on the phone. He sounded so sincere, laughing and gesturing with his free hand. Bianchi winked at me and flashed a seductive smile. I froze.

"After Buono and Bianchi got their rocks off, they wanted to do some experimenting. Those two assholes injected Windex into Kristina's neck and elbow; she went into convulsions, but, unfortunately for her, she didn't die right then."

The deputy clenched his teeth, attempting to hold his anger intact. The veins in his neck stood out like ropes and pulsated with each heartbeat. I edged toward the wall and rubbed my hand on the cold cement in a feeble effort to calm down. *I could have been one of their victims.*

"Next, they gassed her. Bianchi connected a pipe to the gas outlet on the kitchen stove, placed the flexible end of the pipe down beside her neck, and covered her head with a plastic bag. These assholes thought it would be fun to see how she reacted when they turned on enough gas to almost send her into unconsciousness, then shut it off so she could revive, and then turned the gas on again. They repeated this process God only knows how many times. They did it for entertainment purposes. She finally did black out. When they got bored, they grabbed a cord from Buono's upholstery shop and strangled her. Later, they drove her out into the hillsides and discarded her nude body."

Leaning against the hard wall, with my heart pounding, I felt dizzy and disoriented. I thought to myself: *If I had met this man in a bar, I would have danced with him and let him buy me a drink; probably agreed to date him, if he hadn't had LACMJ* (Los Angeles County Men's Jail) *written in block letters across his back.*

Oh God, I've been so careless in dating. I can't tell the good guys from the bad ones. It may turn out that this wasn't a good choice for my first job as a psychologist.

Gonzales interrupted my thoughts.

"There's been a rumor floating around here that Bianchi persuaded one of the nurses to sneak into his cell late one night to have sex with him. I don't know exactly what happened, if the gossip is true or not, but she got fired. Too bad, 'cause she was a good nurse."

I pulled away from the wall in time to see another man wearing a blue jumpsuit approaching us. *When are we going to get away from the inmates?*

"Good morning, Deputy Gonzales," the inmate called out, cheerfully. "When you get a chance to unlock my door, I'm ready to go back into my cell."

An inmate locked out of his cell!

"Sure thing, Eli. Have a seat on the bench. I'll be right back."

When Bianchi saw Eli approaching, he hung up the phone, smiled and leaned forward. Eli sat down close to him. There was an obvious comfort between them.

"Those men seem very friendly with each other."

"Yeah. Elihua Komerchero, he's a nice guy, always very friendly."

"That's Elihua Komerchero? One of the Trash Bag Murderers? I caught a story about him on the news driving in this morning."

"That's him."

I looked back at Komerchero, talking and laughing with Bianchi. *How could they be so pleasant and yet capable of such unspeakable crimes?*

"Excuse me a minute; wanna check to see if Kline is in his office." Deputy Gonzales took a few steps to the right and looked into a corner office, an almost useless act, as two of the walls had oversized glass windows reinforced with wire mesh.

The deputy mumbled something, shook his head no, and made a left turn down the short hall, pulling out his keys as he walked.

I followed behind, looking at the steel doors on either side of the corridor.

"Where do those doors lead?"

"They're one-man cells. See that red flag with K-10 written on it?" He reached out and straightened the red kite-shaped piece of cardboard taped to the steel door. "That's notification that the inmate is high-profile, someone the public is aware of, like the

Hillside Strangler. Because of their notoriety, they are at high risk of being hurt by other inmates. They don't mix with the general population. It would be a real feather in an inmate's cap to take out one of these famous killers. Many of the high-profile inmates are housed in this area or downstairs in the main hall in 1700 or 1750. The red flag reminds us to use special handling."

"What does that mean?"

"We've got to take special precautions to keep these perps safe. 'Bout the only time they leave this floor is to go to court or the medication line. Then they have a deputy with them. They got their own visitors' room across the hall." The deputy pointed to a glassed-in booth, where a man's navy blazer, gray slacks, and a white shirt hung from the window frame inside the room.

The one-man rooms were a surprise; I expected to see the cells laid out in long rows with steel bars, like in the movies. And these killers were out walking up and down the hall without shackles or a deputy standing at the ready. *Had an inmate ever taken a staff member hostage?*

We walked a few more steps and stopped in front of a metal door with a large wire-reinforced window.

"Here you are, ma'am." The deputy unlocked the door to the Forensic Outpatient office suite and held it open for me. "Go on in; I'm sure someone can help you in there."

"Doc," Gonzales reached out and gently touched my shoulder with concern in his voice, "please be careful if you're gonna be working with these guys. Especially Bianchi; he's a real smooth talker and will try to work you. Never forget he's a killer."

The deputy turned to retrace our steps, paused, and looked back at me over his shoulder with a strange smile. "By the way, good luck," he called out as I headed forward into the FOP office suite.

I stepped through the door, feeling like it was going to take more than luck to cope in this place. I would understand that even better as time passed.

CHAPTER 2

WATCH WHAT YOU'RE EATING

Walking into the Forensic Outpatient office, I stepped into the first office on the right, relieved to be behind a locked door. It was a room devoid of windows or wall decoration. Four cluttered, wooden desks had been left unattended. Two desks butted up against the north wall and two faced south. Regulation office chairs sat at odd angles, waiting for their occupants to return. The room measured about twelve feet by eighteen feet, and reminded me of a small cement cracker box—a miniature of the jail itself.

Backing out of the room, I turned to the left into a hall that was wide, dimly lit, not inviting. Several steps later the wall to my right opened up, exposing a larger room with six desks facing toward me. Unattended electric typewriters sat humming on several of the desks. Gray file cabinets piled high with supplies lined the entire right wall. Two women stood at the open drawers, filing charts. On the far wall, directly in front of me, three large windows had been completely covered with thick plates of steel, welded in place. I realize now that I wasn't really interested in the furniture arrangements. This was my attempt to bring some normalcy into this horrible world.

"Can I help you?" A petite Mexican lady turned from her filing at the sound of my footsteps. Her thick, shoulder-length hair overwhelmed the soft round face.

"I'm Dr. Pelto, the new psychologist. This is my first day." After stating the obvious, I wished I'd kept my mouth shut. "They told me downstairs that I could find Dr…" My mind was a complete blank. Have you ever gotten so anxious you just wanted to sit down and cry? I was close to that point.

"Is the head of the department here?"

"He's in a Mental Health meeting over at the Central Office, along with most of the administrative staff. He'll be back in a little while."

"Thanks."

"I'm Lupe. Hold on, I'll be right with you. He told me to expect you this morning. Are you okay? You look a little piqued."

"No problem, but thanks for asking."

Standing in the doorway, I watched Lupe finish her task. The other women glanced at me, momentarily abandoning their filing and nodding a silent greeting, which I returned in kind.

"Come on," Lupe said, as she slammed a file drawer shut with a sigh of satisfaction. "I'll show you where you can wait for Ron."

"Ron?"

"We don't stand on ceremony around here, we gotta work too close. You ever worked in a jail before?" Lupe continued on, before I had a chance to answer no. "It's tough, being around these cons every day. The stress gets to you. You're gonna need all the support you can get. You'll see real soon." Her voice trailed out behind her as she escorted me across the hall to another room, larger than the two previous ones. Same mustard-painted walls. Same gray cement floor, but lacking the glossy polish.

Lupe showed me to an empty chair sandwiched between two desks that butted up against the wall on the left side of the room.

"Take a load off, he'll be back shortly." She departed and I gratefully settled down on the hard wooden chair, dropping my purse on the floor. From this vantage point, with my back to the wall, I could easily survey the entire room. Most of the tubes from the overhead fluorescent lights had been removed, leaving the room in semidarkness, in sharp contrast to the brightly lit halls. Small table lamps sat on the desks, trying to dispel the gloominess of the clinical office. There were no windows and no air movement. On the far wall, three posters were hung: one of Christ with his arms outstretched, as if to say, "Come unto me"; one of Robert Redford; and a smaller one of Tom Selleck. The rationale of choosing the particular combination of these three men to look up to all day escaped me.

Eight desks faced the door, four on each side of the room. A long table piled with files was situated in the middle. Three black women and one Mexican man sat at their desks, heads down, involved in paperwork. Two white women stood by the back desks, further down the same wall I was leaning against. Both women were tall, slender, and looked to be in their mid-thirties. One wore blue jeans so tight they left nothing to the imagination, and the other a skirt so short she almost needed a hairnet.

Earlier this morning I had stood in front of my bathroom mirror having just stepped out of the shower, shivering from the cold and anticipation, naked as a jaybird, trying to figure out what to wear. I had no idea what attire would be appropriate working in a facility with six thousand male inmates plus another several hundred male sheriff's deputies.

I had dressed carefully, choosing a conservative dress with long sleeves and a hemline that stopped just below the knees. I pulled on black pantyhose, walking over to the full-length mirror to inspect the stockings to make sure they didn't have any runs. I didn't want to look like a nun, but I didn't want to look like a whore, either. I was looking forward to getting to work to see what the other women wore.

I rechecked my make-up a couple more times, not wanting to look overly made up, combed out my short red hair, slipped on my new three-inch heels that raised my height to five-foot-eight, and left early for my trip to downtown Los Angeles. I was rushing because I didn't want to be late. And I do have to admit, I've developed a bad reputation. My dad always teases me, saying that I will probably be late to my own funeral. I sure hope he turns out to be right.

With some apprehension, I gathered up my purse, the written directions I had gotten from the sheriff's department a few days earlier, and my L.A. County Mental Health badge. I also made sure I had my driver's license. Thank goodness it wouldn't expire until my birthday in December. I couldn't think of any other forms of ID they might require. I pulled out the pictures of my two daughters as well as the first credit card I'd ever owned in my name, and left them on the dresser. I was fearful my purse might get stolen. You may laugh at the idea that any of your belongings could be stolen while working with all that law enforcement personnel around, but later on I learned that another worker's 240 Z was stolen out of the parking lot. And that was in broad daylight.

Now, as I sat waiting for Ron to return, I laughed to myself for worrying about being on time and how to dress. Even in my conservative dress, I was bombarded with catcalls and lewd remarks. That was probably going to be the norm. Little did I know, lewd remarks would be the least of my problems.

In an attempt to push aside my concerns, I turned my attention to the two women's conversation.

"That damn adam henry." Short Skirt was talking. "I can't believe he gave me a DUI and hauled my sweet little ass off to Sybil for the night. I'd only had a few beers down at the cop bar. Hell, I've drunk a shitload more than that and made it home just fine. Bet that asshole was there, somewhere in the back of the goddamn bar, just waiting for me to leave."

"I'm surprised he didn't get you for indecent exposure," Blue Jeans said, pointing to her friend's mini-skirt.

I wanted to laugh, then thought it wasn't a good idea.

"Very funny! When he pulled me over," Short Skirt continued, "I flashed him my CMJ badge and told him I work at Central Men's Jail. He didn't give a shit. After I shed a few crocodile tears, he hinted that if I gave him a blowjob he might be able to help me get off. You know, if I got him off first. Sonofabitch thought he was some kinda comedian."

"Man! He wanted a BJ? What an asshole." Blue Jeans showed her indignation.

"Well, I tell you, I wasn't buyin' that shit. Figured he'd haul my ass off anyway and say I was trying to bribe him with sex. I told him to stick it where the sun don't shine. That macho dude cuffed me and threw me in the back of his black and white. Sooooo, off we went. Can you imagine me, in the backseat of a chippy chariot? God, I hate those fucking highway patrol guys; they're so smug, they think their shit don't stink. And… If my husband finds out I spent the night in Sybil, he's gonna kill me.

"I called my husband from lock-up," Short Skirt continued. "You know, my one phone call. Told him I had to work late, so I spent the night with you. He didn't call you, did he?"

Blue Jeans crossed her fingers behind her back.

"Oh, God! Yeah, he did. I told him I hadn't seen you. Said you must be out hooking on Sunset Boulevard; you know, to make a little extra money."

"You didn't really, did you? Oh, man! Wait 'til I get home tonight."

Short Skirt sounded panicky.

"Relax," Blue Jeans said. "I'm jus' pullin' your leg. He didn't call me. If he does, I'll cover for you. But remember, you owe me."

"Holy Christ!" Short Skirt laughed with relief.

"Tell me how come you didn't call puddin' cheeks? He would have been more than happy to help you out."

"Hush! You bitch! Come on; let's hit the rows. I got a list of fifteen crims we've gotta interview before lunch."

Blue Jeans grabbed a clipboard and a pen from her desk and walked past me without acknowledging my presence.

I had heard all of the words before, I just wasn't accustomed to hearing women talk that way. Our family was in attendance at the Baptist Church whenever there was a service. My parents didn't cuss and didn't allow my brother or me to, either. Even darn and geez were off limits. These words were considered substitutes for damn and Jesus.

Sherry and Bobbie looked and sounded like a couple of hookers. Looking back now, I see how judgmental I was and, unfortunately, my attitude was probably apparent to them.

I sat quietly, looking around the clinical office, hoping to make eye contact with one of the clinicians. Hoping someone would give me a silent cue that I was accepted. I felt terribly alone. No one spoke to me or even nodded in my direction. This was a Mental Health Office where people are trained to be caring. These people were hard and cold.

Feeling lonely wasn't new to me. I had divorced Ernie Pelto, my first husband, eleven years earlier. I wanted the divorce. But managing my life, while going to school and raising my daughters, had been very difficult. Never having lived alone, made important decisions, or paid my own bills caused me many sleepless nights.

I felt like a tiny goldfish thrust out of my protected environment into the ocean, being tossed around by wild, unpredictable waves. There was no structure anymore. No one would be coming home at five o'clock every evening expecting dinner, and no one would be there when I woke up in the middle of the night hearing strange noises, scared someone was breaking into the house.

For a long time, I couldn't get my bearings. I was screaming inside and had to hide it from my children. They were six and nine when we separated and already upset about losing their father. My daughters were dependent on my strength. I lost weight, couldn't eat, and couldn't sleep. I had to grow up fast.

Now, I desperately needed this job. My debts left over from college were staggering. Even though I had worked full time, my meager salary barely covered our essentials. Thirteen years is a long time to struggle through school to complete a Ph.D.

Sitting and waiting for Dr. Kline to arrive, I began to worry that I might not be able to handle the job.

Finally, I couldn't sit still any longer and walked back to where Lupe continued to work on the filing. "Where's the ladies' room?" I asked.

"Come on, I'll show you," she said. "I need a little break anyhow."

She walked me to the lavatory, which was just beyond the first office in the FOP unit. There was no identifying sign on the door.

"Is this a unisex bathroom?" I didn't want to burst inside to surprise a man facing the urinal.

"No, this is for girls only. You got a problem dealing with men? Look around, this whole joint is male. We're almost invisible."

I didn't respond, just pulled open the heavy metal door and walked in.

"Red Roses for a Blue Lady" was blaring out.

I slipped into the first stall located on the right wall, opposite the other wall that had four sinks and was covered with a mirror. I sat down, propped my elbows on my knees for support, leaned forward to rest my head in my hands, and stretched my shoulders forward, trying to pull out some of the tension.

It felt good to be alone. I could finally, totally, let down. I didn't have to smile or look attentive.

I took in several deep breaths and exhaled slowly while examining the graffiti-decorated stall. Hearts, phone numbers, and who loved whom were displayed. On the right wall, an old familiar adage was printed in bright red lipstick. It read: "Here I sit, brokenhearted, come in to shit, but only farted."

I laughed out loud. Things are the same everywhere, even in a jail.

"Vonda, you okay?"

Sherry, AKA Short Skirt, had pulled the bathroom door open.

"I'm fine," I managed to choke out.

"Ron called and said for you to go to lunch with us 'cause he won't be back till later. We're out here in the hall waiting for you."

I got my pantyhose pulled up, my skirt pulled down as fast as I could, and barely got my hands dried before I pushed open the bathroom door.

"Come on. It's getting late. Let's go eat." Sherry grabbed the handle on the heavy door to exit the FOP unit.

"Wait, what do I do with my purse?"

"Oh shit, come on. You can put it in my desk." Bobbie, AKA Blue Jeans, said. I followed her back into the office and dropped it into a drawer.

"The Hawaiian Wedding Song" was playing.

"Do they play that elevator music all the time?"

"Yeah," Bobbie answered

"Why?"

"Beats me," Bobbie said, turning to look at me. "I think some do-gooder social worker or psychologist decided it would keep the inmates calm. It may calm them down, but it bugs the holy shit out of me."

"Don't worry," Sherry said. "After a while you'll tune it out."

We exited the FOP office and the heavy door banged shut behind us, echoing down the long hall.

Our heels clattered on the unyielding floor as we walked past Ron's office and the unattended telephones on the way to the elevator. Sherry pushed the down button and impatiently tapped the closed doors with her red fingernails.

"Are there any stairs around here?" I asked. "It would beat using this elevator."

"Not for our use," Sherry said. "Stairwells are all locked; deputies have the keys."

"There's no other way out of here?"

"Nope!" Bobbie added.

What would happen in case of an earthquake or fire?

"There's no other way out?" I repeated.

"Don't worry. I'm sure the deputies would be more than happy to open the door for you in case of an emergency." Bobbie's tone let me know she didn't like me.

The elevator arrived, and we stepped into an empty car with the familiar odor of urine.

"Did you notice that 02 that just got off?" Bobbie asked. "That slime pissed in here again. Every time he rides in it, he pees. Guess he's marking his territory. Must think he's some fuckin' tomcat."

"I don't know why in the hell they gave him trustee status," Sherry said.

"Yeah, he's a real adam henry," Bobbie said. "I caught him the other day and confronted him. He denied doing it."

"What's an 02?" I asked.

"02 is a black. It's the administrative code we put in the race box on the forms," Sherry said.

It's going to take me a little time to learn the codes and nomenclature.

The ride was slow as the elevator lumbered down to the first floor. Finally, we arrived with a jolt, stepped off, and turned to the right, away from the deputy's booth where I had entered a few hours—a lifetime—ago.

"What do you think you're doing, homeboy?" a deputy shouted. "I told you to stay on the wall."

A deputy was pushing a huge flashlight into an inmate's back, propelling the man face first into the ugly mustard-colored wall.

I stopped. The inmate looked like a scared kid; probably not more than eighteen or nineteen years old. The deputy didn't look much older. But the deputy had the power.

"Get a move on!" Bobbie called to me.

"What's happening with the boy?" I asked.

"Nothing. He probably just turned to watch us walk past," Sherry said.

They continued on down the hall ahead of me to the gate I'd seen earlier this morning. It butted up against another deputy's booth that housed the main electronic controls for the entire jail. Unlike the one at the entrance to the jail, it was brightly lit.

No one acknowledged our presence as we stood, waiting to be admitted. The deputies controlled the gate and opened it at their whim. We stood waiting.... And waiting.... The young boy's bruised face, barely holding back his tears, kept flashing before my eyes.

The sound of multiple footsteps distracted me, and I turned to lean against the glass wall to observe them.

Two deputies bracketing a line of twenty inmates in orange jumpsuits walked toward us. The men, outwardly compliant, marched along in silence, their heads bent downward. The procession reminded me of a scene from a movie, where the slaves, beaten into submission, meekly follow their captors to a waiting ship.

Just a few feet before they reached us, the lead deputy made a left turn. The inmates followed down a wide hall to the old portion of the jail.

Sherry and Bobbie were oblivious to the commotion. I couldn't imagine myself ever becoming as oblivious.

"Why do the inmates have different colored jumpsuits?" I asked.

"Yellow for the hospital, orange for juveniles, white for kitchen, and blue for general population. The color tells the inmate's classification and the module he is assigned to. If someone is out of his area, the deputies can spot him immediately." *One more bit of information to remember.*

Shortly, two deputies came sauntering up to us. The taller of the two stepped forward and blew a kiss to the deputy sitting in the booth. The uniform inside blew one back, got up, and released the switch that set the gate in motion. It made the familiar grinding sound as it slowly slid to the right.

"Sher, thanks for waiting for us." I recognized the gray-haired deputy as the one who had escorted me up to the FOP unit earlier this morning. He recognized me and smiled with his dark, kind eyes.

Our small group stepped into the sally port and waited as the grinding noise of the gate closed slowly behind us. It would take me a long time to get accustomed to the slamming doors and crashing gates.

Through the opposite gate, I could see the hall that led to the administration offices as well as the visitors' rooms and the deputies' gym. To the left, in front of the deputy's booth, a staircase led down two flights to the Officers' Dining Room.

We moved forward to begin the downward journey. The overhead lighting on the concrete stairwell was minimal. I felt uneasy and reached out to slide my hand along the hard metal railing for support. A hot draft, filled with a mixture of unpleasant food odors, floated from the lower level and billowed up my skirt.

It felt as if I were descending into hell.

"Vonda, don't eat anything you can't identify," Sherry warned as we walked down the long, steep stairway.

"Why not?"

She whispered to me as we joined the already long cafeteria line. "You have to watch what you eat. The inmates make the food. Sometimes they spit or shoot their wads into it. They may even drop in stuff like cockroaches. One guard found a turd in his stew. There it was, a big chunk of shit floating in the sauce. He almost ate it. Said it looked like a piece of beef. You can't trust these crims." I didn't know if she was kidding me or not.

"A lot of the old-timers working here bring their own food in."

The images hit me at the same time a mixture of cooking smells and male sweat did. When I arrived at the front of the cafeteria line, I was taking an internal vote on whether to eat or not.

"What would you like, ma'am?" a man in white pants and matching shirt behind the serving line asked.

My stomach sent up growling noises. I'd been too excited to eat before leaving home this morning. If I didn't eat now, I'd have an attack of hypoglycemia before the afternoon was over.

The good news: The food was free! The bad news—well, you already know the bad.

Steam poured out of the huge pans in the hot-table, partially obscuring the food. The first entrée looked like stew in some kind of grayish gravy; dead fish with their heads still on, staring out blindly, were laying in the second; followed by containers of green beans that looked overcooked, and mashed potatoes. The last container held slices of roast beef in brown juice.

I passed over the stew, the potatoes and the gravy, the fish, and finally decided on a slice of roast beef without the juice and some vegetables from the salad bar, which I served myself.

Standing beside the salad bar reminded me of a waitress job I had while going to college. One night I went out with one of the regular customers and got drunk on gin martinis. The next morning I had such a terrible hangover that I couldn't make it in to work and was fired. Luckily, restaurant jobs weren't difficult to find, and I found another one the next day. The pay wasn't great, but the hours were flexible.

But none of the cafes I had ever worked in were even close to the size of this ODR in the jail. It was a large, rectangular space, deeply underground, with dung-yellow walls and semi-polished floors. There were no windows or wall decorations and no tablecloths or even plastic flowers to adorn the tables. It was a stark room filled with long, metal tables just like the dining rooms in which the inmates ate.

Toward the back of the room, I spotted Bobbie and Sherry, along with the two deputies we had met at the sally port. Sherry caught my eye and waved me over. She was finishing the story about the Highway Patrol officer arresting her on the drunk driving charge.

Quick introductions went around the table. I knew Gonzales; the other deputy's name was Johnson. He looked at me through pale blue eyes and red hair that had faded with the intrusion of gray. He reminded me of my brother. At six-foot, Johnson could be called lanky. I guessed that if he spent any time in the sun he would probably freckle.

"Those guys really can be muthers," Johnson said around a mouthful of food. "If I'd had the duty that night, I could've helped you out."

Gonzales nodded vehemently as if he would have been more than happy to help Sherry out of her predicament. He winked at her and she reddened slightly before she winked back.

I turned my attention to the small bits of gravy that clung to the meat the trustee had shoveled onto my plate. I smelled it. Smelled okay, so I crossed my mental fingers and took a bite. Not bad!

"Hey, guys." Bobbie wanted the floor. "You'll never believe what fell out of an inmate's pocket this morning. It's really hot!" She wore a Cheshire cat grin.

"But, I don't know if I should really say anything about it or not. Oh, never mind, I shouldn't have brought it up." She sat quietly, waiting for someone to take the bait.

Her expression revealed that she was dying to tell us her secret.

"Aw, come on," Gonzales said. "Spill it, sweet cheeks."

"Yeah, don't hold out on your friends," Johnson chorused.

Bobbie finished her last bite of meat and waved a trustee over. They all ordered john waynes and dessert as the inmate cleared the dishes away. I followed suit, ordering dessert and a john wayne, too, hoping I'd like it.

"You gonna tell us what happened, or not?" Sherry said with slight irritation.

Finally, Bobbie leaned forward, lit a cigarette, and took a long, leisurely draw before continuing.

"Pictures fell out of Bruce's pocket—you know, the trustee that's light in his loafers."

"What's the big deal about that?" Sherry asked.

"They were nude pictures of someone we all know."

"Nude pictures? Male or female?" Gonzales asked.

Bobbie leaned back in her chair, puffing her cigarette, her eyes filled with mischief as she prolonged the moment. She waited until the trustee arrived with our dessert: ice cream sundaes, sealed in individual cardboard containers with strawberry, caramel, or chocolate toppings from which to choose. A john wayne? Black coffee!

"Come on, Bobbie, give it up," Johnson said, winking.

"Shit! I think you're making this all up," Sherry said between bites of ice cream.

"Uh-uh. Not on your life." Bobbie grinned. "I'll give you a hint. It's someone who works in FOP."

"Is it an 01?" Johnson asked.

"An 02?" Gonzales wanted to know.

"It's an 01 who dates an 02," Bobbie replied. "Pat?" Gonzales guessed.

"Judy?" Johnson guessed.

"I bet I know who it is." Sherry rolled her eyes. "It's Felicia, isn't it?"

"Bingo!" Bobbie confirmed. "Bruce got 'hold of some nude shots she gave an 02 deputy she's sleeping with. He sent them out with a friend and had them duplicated. Now he's selling those suckers all over the jail. Makin' big bucks on 'em, too."

"Hey, girlfriend," Sherry said, "this sounds like a new career. We'll get some prints and set up Bruce to sell them for us. We'll even cut him a percentage."

"Good idea," Gonzales said. "With a few snapshots, you three lookers could make some serious bucks!"

"You wish!" Sherry said, laughing.

"By the way, have you guys met the new social worker, Mitzi?" Bobbie asked.

"No," Johnson said. "Is she as good looking as you three babes?"

"Well, I do have to give the devil her due, and I do mean devil. She has a great rack, bought and paid for. You know, after market, probably cost a few grand," Bobbie answered with a smirk.

My first degree was in Social Work, and it wasn't a good fit. I felt like a duck waddling around with a bunch of pecking chickens. Social workers want to direct peoples' lives; psychologists want people to direct their own lives.

I sat listening to this friendly banter as the trustees refilled our cups. They moved around the room like ghosts, clad in white shirts and matching pants. When not engaged in service, they stood along the walls quietly, waiting to be summoned like waiters in a four-star restaurant.

"Excuse me, but are the waiters dangerous?" I asked.

"They're mostly paper hangers, bad checks," Gonzales answered. "They're trustees, which gets them extra perks, more roof time, more food, and lighter duties. They're looked up to by the other inmates, too."

"Hey, Vonda, did you hear about that inmate housed just outside our clinical office, Douglas Clark? He's been all over *The Los Angeles Times* for months." Sherry had the floor.

"Not yet."

"Cops found a woman's head in his fridge," Sherry continued.

"What?" Reading the newspaper hadn't been a priority. I could barely keep up with school, work, grocery shopping, and the kids' problems.

"Clark's one sick bastard," Gonzales said. "One night he placed the head on the kitchen sink and told his girlfriend to make it up. She got her cosmetics out and put blush, lipstick—everything on it. They kept the head in the refrigerator for a few days and then wrapped it in women's clothing and dropped it in a nice wooden box. Some poor schmuck on his way home from work saw the box and thought it might contain some type of treasure. He opened it and found the severed head."

"They say he used the head for some strange stuff. He also used some of the other body parts for fun and games," Sherry added.

"I heard a rumor that he mounted a vibrator in the severed head's mouth," Gonzales said.

I studied Gonzales' face to see if he was kidding; he didn't smile.

"You got to be kidding," Sherry said. "You're pulling my leg."

"Hey, baby, I wouldn't mind pulling your leg if you'd let me. Meet me in Manson's old cell later and we'll have a go at it," Gonzales quickly shot back at her.

Sherry raised her middle finger and pointed it toward him.

Trying to appear to enjoy their conversation, I smiled, then swallowed hard.

"Well, if you ask me," Bobbie chimed in, "I've never found any man worth losing my head over."

Gonzales and Johnson laughed. I laughed, too, wanting to be accepted. But laughing about a woman's death, and the desecration of her body, was very uncomfortable.

Sherry turned to her girlfriend. "Hey, little buckaroo, I heard you give the best head in town, but apparently you're not as good as Clark's women. You don't give your all."

"Come on, you're not supposed to tell our secrets," Bobbie said.

"Clark's one sick sonofabitch," Johnson said. "But Manson! Now, he ranks number one; the coldest fucker I ever worked with. I spent time with him—got the detail that helped keep him alive during his trial."

I leaned forward, curious about the Manson Family's killing spree.

"The press thought Charlie stayed in jail the whole time he was on trial, but he didn't. The D.A. had him moved every two days. Two unarmed deputies stayed with him in his room and two armed deputies stayed right outside his door. I got assigned to the periphery, checking out the parking lots and outside doors. I hated being any closer to that fucker. You ever see his eyes? Shit, he could freeze water just by looking at it."

I remembered seeing pictures of Manson on TV and knew the deputy didn't exaggerate.

"They brought in all his food. His favorite was chicken, and he hated onions. A deputy had to check his food every meal. Lots of people would have paid big bucks to get to him.

"The LAPD were always bringing in donuts 'cause they wanted to meet Charlie. Asked him about all kind of things. For instance, did you know his favorite TV show was Hee Haw? Guess that ties in with him wanting to live out in the boonies."

"Why did he ask his followers to kill all of those people?" I asked.

"Who knows? Manson was an abused child, maybe that caused it," Johnson said. "I pulled inside duty one day and he got to talking about how rough he had it as a kid. Never happy. Never felt loved and never learned to love anybody else. Did you know that when he lived up in Haight-Ashbury in Frisco, he told people he was The Gardener? 'I tend to the flower children,' he would say.

He didn't love his followers; just needed them to love him. Made him feel important.

"Told me he was fascinated with how much he could get his 'family' to do. Just a game to him. He'd have the girls perform all kinds of weird sex acts. Bragged he couldn't believe how far they'd go to please him."

I bit my lower lip.

"Tex Watson told the court that Manson ordered him to take a knife and a gun up to where Terry Melcher used to live. 'Kill everyone in the house in as gruesome a manner as possible.' They stabbed and mutilated Sharon Tate and her four friends. They kept stabbing them even after they were dead. Sharon Tate was eight months pregnant.

"After the murders, they wrote 'die piggy, piggy' on the walls with the victims' blood. An investigator said the place was a bloody mess. One of the deputies had to beat cheeks outside to throw up."

"Manson go to Sharon Tate's?" I asked.

"No. But a few days later, he went to the LaBiancas' home and stayed around while they were being killed. Told them they wouldn't be hurt if they cooperated. Probably just thought he wanted to rob them.

"Manson's a wiry little fucker, didn't look very threatening. After he tied them up, he let five of his followers in."

Unlike the Tate home, the LaBianca location seemed to be chosen at random. There's some speculation that the home Tate rented at 10050 Cielo Drive was picked as a revenge target because Manson kept calling it the Melcher place.

A year before the killings, Manson lived high on the hog. He and some of his followers rented a home owned by one of the Beach Boys, and hung with the fast Hollywood crowd. Manson had dreams of becoming a rock star and believed that producer Terry Melcher, the son of the actress Doris Day, would jumpstart his career. That didn't happen and Manson, along with his group, landed on the street, broke and homeless. They were mad as hell.

"Can I get anything else for you?" The trustee had returned.

Bobbie and Sherry ordered coffee refills. I didn't order anything; my stomach was churning.

"You want some, Jose?" Sherry asked as she leaned over and touched his hand.

"Baby, I want anything you got ta give me." He winked at Sherry. She grinned and blew him back a kiss.

The trustee took our orders and departed quietly as Johnson continued with his story.

"Sharon Tate and her husband, Roman Polanski, had the misfortune of renting the house from Melcher. They became Manson's targets. God only knows what else the animals did to those poor people."

I'd heard about the killings on TV but that didn't have the immediacy—or chilling intimacy—of the deputy's retelling.

"One day," Johnson said, "I asked Charlie if he felt guilty about what had happened. He said, 'Hell no, why should I feel guilty? I didn't kill nobody."

Manson was caught and jailed back in '69, convicted, and sent to Folsom State Prison.

The hour was over; time to head back upstairs, wait for the deputies to open the gate, walk the long hall, and take the elevator back to the second floor. It was barely past one o'clock, already a long day.

"You gonna be all right?" Sherry asked as she unlocked the door to the FOP offices.

"Sure. I'm fine."

"You look kinda pale," Sherry continued.

I offered her half a smile.

Sherry pulled out her hand mirror and put on fresh lipstick before exiting the unit along with Bobbie to return to module 4500 and finish their interviews with the mentally ill inmates.

They invited me to go along with them, but I declined, needing some time to process this new world.

The entire FOP suite was deserted. The stillness in the air was deafening!

Agitated, I walked over to the clerical office. Looking at the wall lined with file cabinets, I thought of the thousands of men's lives documented in the drawers. Their lives, past and future, were caught on a few pieces of paper.

Checking the drawers, I found the files arranged numerically.

Government bureaucracy. The inmates were only numbers on a file.

I moved around the office, looking on various desks for some clue to the filing system.

"Dr. Pelto, is there something I can help you find?" I turned to see Lupe entering the room, the other secretaries following closely behind.

Inexplicably, I felt guilty for snooping around the desks, and figured the secretaries resented my intrusion.

I tried to sound casual. "I was looking for Kenneth Bianchi's file." Out of the corner of my eye, I noticed a strange glance exchanged between the women.

"He's the Hillside Strangler!" The statement hung in the air.

"I know."

"You need to speak with Ron before pulling any high profile inmate files," one woman offered.

"From now on, if you want a file, ask us," another added.

I left the office quickly, returned to the deserted clinical office, settled down on a chair, and leaned my head against the wall, closed my eyes and thought back to how and why I had wanted this job.

CHAPTER 3

BE CAREFUL
WHAT YOU ASK FOR

It was in the spring of 1980: You talk about the constellations being out of alignment, that's what happened to mine. The stars dropped a real whammy on me. My life felt like it was on a roller coaster. Maybe it was a punishment for past karmic mistakes. Who knows? I sure didn't. At any rate, my life turned from elation when I walked down the aisle to be awarded the Ph.D. degree on Friday night, to total dejection on Monday morning when I found myself needing another job.

On that fateful day, my supervisor informed me that they were not going to allow a psychologist to supervise the fifteen hundred internship hours I needed to be eligible to sit for the California State Boards. "You're an excellent therapist," she said, "but it's Orange County Mental Health's departmental policy, not mine."

After attending college for the past thirteen years, working as a waitress, then a Mental Health worker at Orange County, I thought that the last obstacle to getting my license and opening a private practice was in sight.

After licking my wounds for a week, I hit the bricks running, looking for another job: a job where a psychologist would be willing to give me the necessary supervision. Luckily, the summer heat had not settled in yet.

With my ex-husband out of work, and my children in school, well, you know how many extras they need. My check barely covered food—forget fancy dresses and graduation parties.

After interviewing at numerous private agencies without being hired, I turned to Los Angeles County Mental Health, where I told the personnel interviewer that I'd be willing to work in the Men's Jail. She raised her eyebrows and flashed me a look of disbelief, thinking I was either crazy or pulling her leg. But after she studied my face, she could tell I wasn't.

After working with sexually molested victims and their perpetrators for the past seven years at Orange County Mental Health, it seemed that felons in the jail couldn't be much worse.

My third and final interview was held at the county personnel offices on the fourth floor, in a stuffy, windowless room. Dr. Kline, the head of the Forensic Outpatient unit in the jail, invited me to take a seat. With a warm handshake, a pleasant smile, and an air of informality, he sat down on a cushioned chair close to mine.

"We've had a wave of horrifying crimes here in the Los Angeles area in the last few years. Began back about ten years ago when Charles Manson's Family committed those seven gruesome murders. Since then, we've had five additional killing sprees. It's like a door to hell opened up, and the Hillside Stranglers, the Freeway Killers, the Sunset Strip Killers, Arthur Jackson, and John Holmes all slithered out. Collectively, these men have killed more than one hundred people."

I shifted in my chair, wondering what these killers had to do with me.

"Now, most of these killers have been arrested. And they are housed in the Central Men's Jail awaiting their due process. Thank God, there haven't been any more killing sprees, and we hope it stays that way."

Dr. Kline walked over to a long counter on the left side of the room and reached for a coffeepot sitting on a hotplate. "You want a cup?"

"Sounds good. Cream and sugar, please."

"Cadillac, huh? No problem." He stirred the additives into my cup and returned to set the coffees on the table situated between our chairs.

He smiled and continued talking.

"In the late part of 1980, Vernon Butts, one of the Freeway Killers, was arrested and confessed that he and William Bonin had used various knives, ice picks, acid, and chloralhydrate in the commission of six murders. Butts admitted he was there, but contended that Bonin actually committed the crimes. Bonin got off on hearing the boys scream, got him real excited."

What a terrible person!

"The State was already after Bonin; he had a long history of sexual offenses and had been in and out of jail numerous times for raping and molesting boys."

"Why on earth did they release him?"

"Unfortunately," Ron sighed heavily, "that's the way the system works."

I had a lot of "yes buts," but decided to stifle them.

"Butts' testimony could have gone a long way to shore up the legal system's case against Bonin. District Attorney John Van de Kamp offered Butts a plea bargain: Plead guilty to taking part in six of the twenty-one murders they were suspected of, and the State of California would offer him a life sentence instead of seeking the death penalty. All he had to do was agree to testify against Bonin."

"Did he agree to the plea bargain?" I took a sip of coffee, trying to look blasé.

"Said he'd consider it."

Dr. Kline leaned back in his chair and I moved forward on mine. Attempting to calm myself, I scrunched up my toes in my black pumps, hoping he wouldn't notice my uneasiness.

"Butts was poised to testify against his friend, when he became despondent and tired of incarceration. He made the choice to end his life. Hanged himself! No one knows if he would have testified or not.

"Unfortunately, the Mental Health team was not apprised of his growing depression. One early morning, a deputy making his usual rounds found Butts dead in his cell."

"How could Butts hang himself?"

"He knotted one end of a towel to the disability bar next to his toilet, and then assumed a kneeling position with his back to the wall. With his left hand, he reached around and attached the other end of the towel to the bar. It formed a crude noose across the front of his throat. He lunged forward, fast and hard against the towel. His air supply was cut off immediately, and he lost consciousness. It only took a few seconds. The weight of his body leaning against the towel caused death by strangulation. It was an eerie reminiscence of how his victims died."

Kline offered me a cigarette. I declined. He lit his and took a long drag before he continued. Right now, I was tempted to take up the habit.

"The key witness against William Bonin died with Vernon Butts."

I felt edgy and walked over to pour another cup of coffee.

"If we had suspected Butts was suicidal, we would have moved him into the hospital unit and placed him on suicide watch. By the time the deputy found Butts, he had already turned blue and his eyes were bulging. Not a pretty sight."

Why are you telling me all of this?

"The D.A. was mad as hell at us, the press had a field day, and we got a lot of heat over it. Believe me, we can't ever let that happen again."

The overhead fluorescent light flickered and struggled to maintain its illumination. I was fearful we would be plunged into total darkness.

"Are we okay in here?"

"Oh, that? No problem; happens all the time." Dr. Kline took a drag on his cigarette.

Momentarily, it felt like he was telling me ghost stories as we sat around the fire at a Girl Scout campout.

I leaned over, picked up my coffee gingerly as if it were still hot, and took a small sip, wondering what he was leading up to.

"Dr. Pelto, after Butts' suicide, we decided to create a new position in the jail's forensic team. We want someone to see the high-profile inmates, the men whose names and faces are featured prominently in the news media. That's the job we're offering you."

There it was! My stomach tightened. I sat silently, remembering I had agreed to interview for this job.

"Your office will be located inside the jail."

My breathing became shallow. I rose, walked to the coffeepot, and poured another cup, even though I didn't want one. These weren't the kind of job duties I had expected. Psychological testing, talking with depressed inmates, and dealing with their loved ones—that's what I expected. It didn't occur to me that I would be talking with serial killers.

Even though he explained the job duties to me, there wasn't any way I could fully appreciate what I would be asked to do. At that point, it didn't matter. I needed a job!

My body reacted with the same uncomfortable feeling that I had had just before walking down the aisle to marry Bob Fife, my second husband. Standing in the vestibule, I had turned to my father and said, "This may be a big mistake."

"The main thing is we have to keep these guys alive during their incarcerations." Dr. Kline's lips parted in a half smile as he continued in an almost inaudible voice. "The State wants the opportunity to extract its own revenge.

"Do you think you can handle the job?" Kline eyed me carefully.

"Yes. No problem." I hoped!

CHAPTER 4

FROM YOUR LIPS TO GOD'S EAR!

"Dr. Pelto," Dr. Kline said as he walked into the clinical office, bringing me back to the present.

My first impulse was to giggle when he called me Doctor, but I loved it. I felt like a fraud! I couldn't believe that I had actually gotten my degree. I figured any day now someone would expose me and prove that I was masquerading as a psychologist—kinda like dressing up in your mother's clothes. Luckily, he couldn't read my mind.

"Sorry about being held up in the meeting for so long. Did Lupe show you around the unit?"

"I looked around on my own."

"I was afraid you might chicken out after you had time to think about what the job entails," Kline said, grinning sheepishly. He was in the process of removing his tie as he walked toward me.

"You did seem nervous during our last meeting at the personnel offices." He looked tired, with dark circles under his eyes and a sallow complexion.

There were warring factions going on inside me, both excited and scared at the same time. Part of my brain said, "Run like hell! You can't handle this job!" Yet, the other part of my brain said, "Oh, yes you can!" This was bizarre—bizarre to want to talk to these killers, these powerful celebrities, who lived by their own horrible rules.

"Dr. Pelto, you seem faraway."

I know.

"So much hot air at these meetings, and nothing ever seems to get accomplished. I swear, we could cut the county taxes in half if we didn't sit around and haggle over trivia. So much bullshit! And speaking of bullshit," he laughed at himself, "come on, we'll go to my office and talk."

I followed him out of the Forensic unit and stopped, transfixed, staring at Ken Bianchi, who stood staring out of the small window in his cell door. His smile: so seductive, so enticing! Automatically, I smiled back, then reminded myself who he was: the Hillside Strangler!

Charming man; be careful, Vonda!

"Some Enchanted Evening" floated out from the speaker system.

Dr. Kline walked on to his glass-enclosed office and stood, holding the door open for me. His office was located at the intersection of two halls, one that ended in the Forensic Outpatient unit, the other that led to the Forensic Inpatient unit.

"Have a seat." Kline pointed to a wooden chair on the opposite side of his desk.

Before I could get settled into the chair, he sneezed and grabbed a tissue from the Kleenex box sitting on the corner of the desk.

"Bless you."

"You'd better get a flu shot and start taking vitamins. You'll be exposed to all kinds of bugs in here. If you ever need any antibiotics, go see Magic Fingers—he'll give you some."

"Magic Fingers?"

"He's a doctor who works in the medical-surgical hospital in 8100, third floor. Just don't bend over."

"Why not?"

Kline laughed. "Fingers thinks even women should have prostate exams."

What?

"I thought we'd talk a little while, give me a chance to tell you about the job we've designed for you. Don't know if you remember me telling you that we've never had anyone do what we're asking you to do."

I remembered!

"Dr. Kline, I'm concerned about my internship. I have to finish it before I can take the State Boards. When do you...?"

"Don't worry, we'll take care of it."

He cut me off so fast I was afraid he'd changed his mind. *Oh, my God, what would I do?*

"Here in 7100," Kline continued, unaware of my mounting anxiety, "the Sheriff's Department houses most of the inmates who need protection from the general population: serial killers, celebrities, attorneys, police and their families, and men who have been accused of white-collar crimes. They all have a keep-away K-10 status. You'll notice the red flag on their doors."

"A deputy pointed them out to me earlier."

"Okay to call you Vonda? Have you had the Doctor's degree long enough to go by your first name, instead of Doctor?"

"Not a problem."

"Back to your duties. The shit really hit the fan when Vernon Butts killed himself. The D.A. was afraid that Bonin might walk again; he's beaten a lot of raps in the past. They held us responsible."

"Did he seem suicidal?" I squirmed around on the hard wooden chair.

"I don't know; no one gave us a heads' up."

I felt ambivalent about Butts committing suicide and wondered if it really was self-inflicted. Later, after I read the coroner's report where he stated the death was a suicide, I still wondered. Never got an answer that satisfied me. No one likes to think of someone killing himself and, yet, maybe I could understand the demons that haunted him. If I'd been here, maybe I could have helped him.

"Your primary job will be to see the high-profile inmates. I'd also like for you to serve as my assistant. It wouldn't mean extra pay, but it would be a good career move. And it would put you in line for my job if I ever decide to transfer out. Working with the dregs of society for the last ten years has taken a lot out of me. Would you be interested?"

Never having been political, I was hesitant about accepting the position. I think it's fun going against the establishment and breaking rules, but sitting through boring meetings is the worst. On the other hand, I knew it would look good on my resume.

"It would be a smart thing to do. I'll take it." As soon as the words came out of my mouth, I was sorry. But Ron would be in the jail long after I became licensed and quit to open my own private practice. Anyway, that's what I told myself.

"We'll make up a flow chart and hand it out at the morning staff meeting. I've never had an assistant before, but I've needed one. Vonda, it's good to have another psychologist to work with.

"There's a filing mess that needs to be cleaned up. I'd like you to oversee it. We have about ten boxes filled with charts that have to be reviewed and made ready for storage. Unfortunately, the clinicians have to read through them and decide what can be culled. I'm not here enough to get it done. Guess I should warn you: The staff won't be happy about working on them. But it is necessary.

"As for your caseload, it's all high profiles."

"Who do I start with?"

"You can start with any of the high profiles you want."

I didn't want to look stupid, so I just said, "Okay," and hoped he would give me enough information to be able to choose.

As he rubbed his eyes with his middle and index fingers, Kline continued. "Jim Munro has been asking to see someone. He's one of the Freeway Killers, housed down the hall and around the corner. See him first and then set up your own schedule."

Without warning, Ron jumped up and raced out the door. I jumped, too, fearful one of the killers had gotten loose. I watched through the glass wall as he intercepted the two women—Sherry and Bobbie—I'd overheard talking about last night's adventures earlier today.

Safe, so far! I took a deep breath, relieved, and leaned heavily against his desk. After a short conversation, they walked back into the office. I stood up quickly, not wanting to look weak.

"Vonda has agreed to be my assistant," Ron said. "She will be in charge of cleaning up that filing mess. She'll set up a schedule for everyone to work on it. Hopefully, we can get it done before the end of the year."

"Vonda, are you going to be walking the rows in the Ding Tanks with us?" Bobbie wanted to know.

"No," Ron quickly cut in before I had a chance to ask Bobbie what she meant. "Vonda will be seeing the high-profile killers only." And he emphasized 'only.' "She won't be interviewing the mental patients on 4500."

Short Skirt and Blue Jeans exchanged a quick glance that didn't look friendly, then left the office and walked back toward the FOP unit.

"Sorry, I've got to get back to Central Office for another meeting." Ron turned, walked to the elevator, and pushed the down button.

"Ron, wait! Will I be in any danger working with these killers?"

"You're probably safer in here than you are out on the street."

Ron caught my look.

"Don't worry," he said lightly.

He stepped into the elevator, leaving me standing in front of the Hillside Strangler's cell.

"You'll be just fine!" he called out as the doors closed.

From your lips to God's ear!

CHAPTER 5

SHOW ME THE WAY TO GO HOME

When four-thirty rolled around, I was agitated, having difficulty breathing. The jail wasn't what I had expected. How naive I was! It was much worse! The cellblocks were filthy, with rats and cockroaches scurrying around them freely. The clinical offices weren't much better, and the job duties were overwhelming. Frazzled and demeaned, I just wanted to get home.

With a sick feeling in my gut, I thought about the year that lay ahead of me. I had to complete my internship before taking the State License Boards to become licensed. A lot of friends had taken and failed them several times. Then there were the two additional years it would take to become vested in the county retirement plan. *It might not be worth that additional pain.*

The sun had already dipped behind the jail when I walked out into the afternoon light. The birds, oblivious to their surroundings, were chirping gaily, reveling in their freedom. I'd never given any thought to how it would feel to be incarcerated. That's how I felt today, incarcerated—as caged as any inmate.

Dark clouds were pulling together in the east, and it looked like there might be rain for the week ahead. The air felt cool and clean.

Maybe it was the presence of the rare rain clouds in the dry Los Angeles basin, but the world outside the huge concrete monolith looked completely different to me.

It felt like I'd spent the day on a spaceship. This was an alien world, a world where I rubbed elbows with men who tortured and killed for no reason, and felt no guilt. On the other hand, it was a world where young men caught in a cold, cruel system came out scarred for life. Some of them looked barely old enough to be weaned from their mothers.

My Audi Fox sat patiently waiting, welcoming me back into my familiar world. In celebration of landing a well-paying job, I put a down payment on the car. Even though it wasn't new, it was mine; anyway, it would be after thirty-six payments. Settling into the smooth leather seat, I locked the doors and wiped nonexistent dust from the dashboard. The touch and smell of the car were a welcome relief from the rank odor of the jail.

The engine started easily. I wormed my way out from under the shadowy parking structure, feeling relief at putting distance between me and the gray fortress. Driving out into the vanishing sunlight, I watched slivers of light glint off the Audi's silver-blue fender, hoping to lighten my spirits.

After safely maneuvering the car onto the freeway, I reached down and switched on the radio. My mind was whirling. It would be difficult to sleep tonight.

My parents didn't know that I had taken this job. They wouldn't think it a wise choice. The expressions on their faces when I was growing up often relayed a message that I was out of step with the rest of the family. Sometimes over the dinner table they would joke and say I was adopted. That wasn't true. Born in Phoenix, Arizona, at a time when newborns were being sent home with the wrong parents, my mother demanded to see me before leaving the delivery room. The doctor said, "Mrs. Brock, no mistake, you have the only redhead in the nursery."

For some reason, and I don't know what it is, I've always been fascinated with the dark side of life. That in itself is not so unusual. There is something in our emotional make-up that makes us curious and excited about terrible and forbidden events. We are voyeurs. We like to see into the world of the unknown.

From a young age, I was out of step with my classmates. My interests were different. I didn't like babies, the latest fashions, or homemaking skills.

In the eleventh grade, our social studies teacher assigned us to investigate various professions that we might want to pursue. When I decided to interview the local funeral home director for the school project, that validated my strangeness. Although I had already decided to become a psychologist, I was intrigued with the funeral business. Most certainly, had the profession of forensic psychologist been popular back then, it would have been my choice of vocation.

Chuck Newbrey owned and operated the funeral parlor in our small town. When I arrived that morning for the interview, Mr. Newbrey was busy and asked his apprentice to meet with me.

Fate again stepped into my life.

Jay was twenty-four, single, and more than willing to answer all my questions. He explained the embalming procedures, showed me around the mortuary, and asked me out on a date.

We became a regular item. Much to my chagrin, he would come to the school driving the big black hearse to take me to lunch. He loved watching my classmates' expressions better than I did.

One evening when I was fussing about my hair, he offered to give me a perm and do my make-up if I would lie down on the slab in the embalming room. I said, "I don't think so!"

In spite of everything, I let him put a ring on my finger a few months later. I liked the idea of being married to a professional man and working in the business with him. I could do the hair and make-up, and he would do the embalming. But he still wasn't going to do my hair.

Late one Saturday afternoon, Jay called me to come down to the mortuary for my first lesson. He had to prepare a man's body for viewing early the next morning.

I was so excited. What an adventure, and a perfect start to our eventual life together.

I arrived at the mortuary and found Jay waiting for me to help him move the body into the embalming room.

The tall eucalyptus trees outside the funeral home fractured the lowering desert light, casting eerie shadows on the patio as we went out to the old metal refrigeration unit. The mortuary was too small to have this large equipment inside. The patio, located just outside the embalming room door, was a perfect place.

The refrigerator looked like a large metal tic-tac-toe board, with nine doors sporting sturdy handles that opened into the storage compartments. Each cubicle housed a single corpse laid out on a sliding metal slab.

"I'm not sure which berth our guy is in," Jay said in a matter-of-fact voice.

He stepped forward, opened the first metal door, swung it wide open, and exposed the interior of the chilled vault. He grabbed the metal crossbar and gave it a tug. The tray didn't budge.

"Stuck. Sometimes it gets so cold in there that the bearings freeze up," he said and gave it a harder yank.

This time the tray broke loose and the momentum carried it out into full view.

I could tell from the contours of the smooth sheet that the corpse's hands were folded over his private parts and the legs angled out so that the feet touched the sides of the tray. The body looked enormous under its white shroud.

Suddenly, there was a loud cracking noise and the tray began to list to the left, away from where Jay stood. He grabbed at it, trying to bring it level again.

Just then the other portion of the metal support gave way with a loud noise. The tray, with the body riding on top, began moving toward me in slow motion.

I yelled, "Oh, my goodness! Jay...it's...it's...." Before I could finish the sentence, the back portion of the tray caught on the support and stopped abruptly. The front supports gave way completely and the tray slanted downward at a forty-five-degree angle.

I stood at the end of the tray, and before I could get out of the way, the body came at me like a toboggan on a downward slope. Helpless, I held up my hands as if I could stop the rushing onslaught of the shroud-covered corpse, but it outweighed me by at least a hundred pounds and wouldn't be stopped. As the body slid forward, the sheet caught on the back handle and pulled off, exposing a naked Indian man.

Propelled backward into the bushes, I landed on my back with the cold, nude corpse riding on top of me.

What does a girl do when she finds herself in such a compromising position?

I wet my pants and started to scream and cry; that's what I did. I wasn't hurt physically, just scared witless.

Jay rushed over and pulled the pale cadaver off me.

In a flash, I was up and heading straight for the door.

"Vonda! Sweetheart! Wait! Where are you going?"

"Home."

"No! Don't go. Come back. We'll talk."

"I'll call you later." That's all I could whimper out. Tears were flowing and I was shaking like a willow in a windstorm.

My career as a mortuary make-up artist had come to an abrupt end. I cried for days after breaking up with Jay. Nightmares plagued me for the next few weeks and actually lasted longer than my engagement had.

Now, I had to laugh at myself. Working with the dead would have been much less frightening and stressful than working with live serial killers.

The car's radio crackled, drawing my attention back to the present. It was in mid-broadcast, updating the latest developments in the Trash Bag Murder case.

District Attorney John Van de Kamp announced today that separate juries will decide the murder cases against Joseph Zakaria and Yehuda Avital. Komerchero claims that suspects, Yehuda Avital, an accused cocaine dealer, and Joseph Zakaria persuaded him to bring Eli Ruven and his wife, Ester, to the Bonaventure Hotel on October 7, 1979, to discuss a botched cocaine deal.

Komerchero was present in the luxurious hotel room when Avital dismembered the bodies with a meat cleaver. In exchange for his testimony against the other two, Komerchero will be allowed to plead guilty to manslaughter charges and avoid the death penalty. The three defendants stand accused of the grisly murders of a man and his wife. They disposed of the body parts in various trash receptacles around Los Angeles.

I broke into a cold sweat, realizing the type of people with whom I would be dealing. I had entered into a world that was far beyond my comprehension.

To erase the image of a blood-spattered hotel room, I pushed a cassette into the tape player and surrounded myself with the soothing voice of Carol King singing from her album "Tapestry". I eased into the slow lane of the crowded freeway and stayed there until I reached my exit, barely aware of Carol King's mellow voice filling the car.

My head ached from all the information I had been given during the day. Jose had warned me, "Never get on an elevator alone with an inmate; he could take you hostage, get an escort when you go to the old section of the jail; all doors and fire escapes are locked." *Get used to it: There is no escape.*

Jose also said on the elevator ride up to FOP this morning, that "the cops use this elevator to take guys high on LSD or PCP or coked up, up to the FIP unit to sober up, and anything can set these druggies off. They can get out of control and become as wild and as strong as King Kong with jock itch. Be careful around them."

The stench of the jail was still in my nose, and I could visualize the inmates moving along the walls, shackled with leg irons, dragging along the cement floor as they were herded from one module to another.

Turning southward onto the San Gabriel Freeway, I suddenly remembered the key. Had I turned it in? I clutched the steering wheel with one hand and reached into my pocket with the other. Thank goodness! My pocket was empty.

After turning off the freeway, I drove through my familiar neighborhood. Ernie, my first husband, and I bought the four-bedroom tract house twenty-one years earlier. While it was still under construction. I was so excited about having the home that I took the girls and drove down the dirt road every day to watch the house being built. Luckily, I won the house in the divorce settlement and had been able to keep up with the payments.

The house was quiet when I arrived. On the dining room table lay a note from my daughters saying they had gone to dinner with their father.

In three days, we would be divorced eleven years. Deanne and Tera loved their father and missed him when he left. Gratefully, Ernie understood that and took them to dinner a couple times a week and kept them over the weekend two or three times a month. I adored my children, but was relieved that they were gone this evening.

Deanne is my oldest child and although she wasn't planned, she was adored from the moment I saw her. At the time of my pregnancy, I was working at the Long Beach Shipyard, putting Ernie through college. Money was very tight. But she was a beautiful baby and enriched our lives more than I could have ever imagined. Now, she was engaged to marry the boy down the street. It was difficult to realize she was old enough to leave me. She has brown hair and eyes to match, bright and energetic, and slow to anger.

Tera, my youngest, was planned for more than a year. I spent most of my pregnancy planning for a girl and picking out names. It's a good thing that it worked out so well. I never even considered boys' names. Tera can be quick-tempered, but she cools down quickly. She has blue eyes and blond hair.

Both of my girls are long legged, towering over my five-foot-five frame by several inches, and neither of them inherited my red hair. They are so much pleasure.

When Ernie and I separated half way through my second year at Long Beach City College, I had to get a job; waitressing was the only thing I knew. There was little time left for my children. Their time with their father gave me an opportunity to study and date, guilt free.

I stopped by the kitchen, poured a glass of white wine, popped a frozen Mexican dinner into the microwave, and then ambled into the bedroom to change into my flannel nightgown and pink fuzzy slippers. I washed off my make-up and gulped down the wine.

More on edge than I realized, I headed back to the kitchen, poured another glass of wine, and went into the living room. Putting on the cassette tape of Tchaikovsky's "Sleeping Beauty Ballet", I turned up the volume and settled down on the couch with my feet on the coffee table, trying to rub out the events of the day. When I closed my eyes, pictures of the young woman tortured and killed by Bianchi played through my mind. Thankfully, my daughters were safe with him locked behind bars. In spite of my efforts, it was hopeless—there was no escape.

The ringing of the oven's bell signaled that my dinner was ready. I pulled myself up off the couch and went into the kitchen to retrieve it. After picking at the beans, rice, and tacos with little interest, I tossed the remaining food in the trash.

Going into the bedroom, I turned on the television and collapsed into bed. It was tuned to a news station, and before I could engage the VCR to watch the recorded soapbox operas, the phone rang. I caught it on the second ring. Edith's familiar voice was on the other end of the line, a friend I had known for over twenty years. We met while singing in the choir at a Baptist Church in Long Beach. When she divorced, I stood by her and she did the same for me when I separated a few years later.

"How's the new job?" Edith asked.

Unexpectedly, I was distracted. Kenneth Bianchi appeared on the television screen, wearing the navy blue blazer, the white shirt, the tie with red and blue designs on it, and the gray flannel slacks I had seen hanging in the deputy's booth this morning. He looked like an executive for IBM. "In the case of the Hillside Strangler...." I watched Bianchi, smiling at the camera, exuding charm, and remembered standing an arm's length away from him. A killer I would be meeting with whenever he chose. Seeing Bianchi on television, being called the Hillside Strangler, hit me in the face. This was the reality of my job!

"Vonda? Vonda? How's it going? Are you there?" Edi asked, unaware that I was lost in this frightening new world.

"What?"

"What's wrong with you? You okay?"

"I'm sorry. My mind just wandered.

"Oh, Edi, I don't know if I'm going to be able to work there long enough to complete my internship and my retirement."

"Then quit! Get something else."

"I don't have a license. All the other jobs I looked into either required a license or they didn't pay as much.

"The jail is so depressing. Killers roam up and down the halls. They stink! They're crude! They call me foul names! The deputies flirt and call me babe and honey in front of the inmates. They're disrespectful." *I'm rambling.*

"Except for the killers being loose, the jail doesn't sound much different from where I work," she said.

"You don't realize. It's...." She interrupted me before I had a chance to explain.

"Vonda, relax. You'll get used to it. You haven't had to work a regular job for years."

"Edith, it's not only that, but..."

"Well, now you have to get up every day just like the rest of us. Even when you worked at Orange County, you got to leave early every Friday to go to school. You're used to having lots of free time."

She wasn't listening, and I needed my friend to understand. Finally, it dawned on me; there were no sufficient words to help her understand what I was feeling.

"Today this 02 hit on me, then he got me a cadillac."

"What on earth are you talking about?"

I'm talking the lingo. The jail was already infiltrating my vocabulary!

"He got you a cadillac?"

"Coffee with cream and sugar. That's jail shorthand," I explained. "My boss asked a black deputy to take me on a tour and introduce me to some of the deputies I'll be working with."

"Great! You and all those men?" Her voice had an excited tone.

"Edi, I'm trying to tell you what happened. He escorted me to the old part of the jail. We stopped for coffee, he put his arm around my shoulder, and then squeezed me up to him real hard. I didn't like it. The expressions on the other deputies' faces told me they think I'm going to be an easy mark. I got away from the deputy's grip. He wasn't deterred. Walking back to my office, he asked for my phone number."

"Is he good looking?"

"Well, yes, but that's not the point; I don't know how to handle these men. My safety depends on them. Ron warned me that most of them are married but don't act like it."

"Vonda," she sounded irritated, "for God's sake, nothing is going to happen to you. It's just another job."

"Well, anyway, later we were sitting in a meeting and I mentioned the deputy hitting on me to Sherry. She started kicking me under the table. I didn't understand why, but I shut up. Later, she explained that Felicia, who was sitting across from us, is dating him."

"Do you think she heard you?"

"I think so, because she wasn't friendly to me."

"Vonda, you sound paranoid."

"Every time I heard a noise, I jumped."

"The deputies aren't going to let anything happen to you. If you don't like the job, transfer out, find something else, or adjust."

In my frustration, I raised my hand to the phone to try to explain the Men's Jail to her; then I gave up. I didn't have adequate words.

"Ibsen's "Doll House" is playing at the Music Center next month; you want to go?" Edi changed the subject.

"Sounds great. Drive into town and meet me at the jail. There's a lower-level parking area where you can leave your car. I'll treat you to dinner in the ODR, show you around, and then we can take my car to the play."

"I'll pick up the tickets," she said.

I did feel a little ornery telling her where to park and where we would be dining. But I knew my friend would have a different view of the jail after her visit.

We said our goodnights and hung up. I switched off the TV, pulled the covers up over my head, curled into a ball, and embarked on a restless night full of nightmares.

I didn't hear my girls come in.

CHAPTER 6

THE NIGHTMARES BEGIN

My sleep was fitful. My dreams weren't sweet. They involved killers chasing me, cornering me, trying to strangle me. Repeatedly, I tried to scream for help but nothing would come out. A metal gate slammed shut and I was trapped in the sally port with the Hillside Strangler. His hands were around my throat, choking the life out of me. I grasped for air. I was suffocating to death. Looking around, I saw the staff members pointing at me, laughing. No one came to my rescue.

Gratefully, I woke up from the nightmare, at first disoriented, unaware of being in my own bed. I reached up and discovered Pywacket, my Siamese cat, curled around my throat. She was lying halfway across my mouth.

I opened my eyes and looked around the darkened bedroom, realizing I was safe. The clock chimed three. I curled up in a fetal position and pulled the covers up well over my head and struggled to go back to sleep, hoping not to have anymore bad dreams.

It seemed like I had just fallen back asleep when "Jeremiah Was A Bull Frog" blared out from the clock radio. Six a.m—time to get up. I walked to the shower in slow motion and stayed under the hot water until I looked like a prune.

Wanting to move silently down the long concrete corridors, unnoticed by the inmates, I decided to wear clothes that would match rubber-soled shoes. Standing in front of the mirror, I laughed at myself. Here I am, Dr. Pelto, building my wardrobe around quiet shoes, so I can vanish into the mustard-colored walls.

I ambled into the kitchen to the smell of fresh-brewing coffee and to find Deanne cooking eggs at the stove. Bless her heart!

"Mom, how's it going at the jail?" She asked, stirring the eggs.

"Not sure I can handle it."

I poured each of us a cup of coffee, went to the breakfast table, and using a hand mirror, started putting on my makeup. This was a chance for us girls to catch up with each other's news. From the time my daughters started wearing make-up, we had performed this family ritual each morning.

As Tera entered the kitchen, I thought about how much I loved this time with them.

"Dr. Kline, my boss, introduced me to Lieutenant Chandler," I said to Deanne as she set plates of scrambled eggs and toast on the table. "He's the head sheriff who runs the jail and has his offices on the first floor, close to the gate where I walk in each day. You wouldn't believe his office décor: brown and yellow plaid wallpaper. Strictly the fifties look. Bizarre! The deputies hang around in there and use a couple of old banged up wooden desks to do their paperwork.

"Do you have your own office?" Deanne asked.

"Not yet. Sure hope I get one today, though. It's uncomfortable sitting in the clinical office and being ignored by the staff. Ron has asked me to organize them to clean up this big filing mess, and they aren't happy about it."

"Are you scared of the inmates?" Deanne then asked.

"Sure, a little. But there are always a lot of deputies around and they aren't going to let anything happen to me." I hoped.

"How are you going to stand working with those slime balls?" Tera wanted to know.

"I don't know yet. For now, I just can't let myself think about what they have done."

I finished my make-up, picked at my breakfast with little appetite, shoved the dishes into the dishwasher, and turned off the coffeepot. After kissing the girls goodbye, I drove back to the Men's Central Jail, hoping Ron would make plans for my supervision.

It was drizzling rain and at times the traffic came to a complete stop. The slow pace was okay; in fact, I appreciated the forty-five minutes it took me to get downtown.

I would be meeting with Jim Munro, one of the Freeway Killers. This didn't seem real. But then, working in the Men's Jail didn't seem real, either.

CHAPTER 7

MY VERY OWN CELL

As quickly as the traffic had slowed, it opened up again and I resumed my previous speed. A cop was giving a fellow motorist a ticket and we, other commuters, drifted by slowly, in sympathy and appreciation that we had not been caught.

The sun was casting a soft glow, reminiscent of the sunrise in the desert where I grew up. Suddenly I wanted to be a kid again, wanting my parents to take care of me. I didn't want to face a new challenge. I was tired. Along with working and raising my two children, school had been a long and difficult process. And taking a new job has always been stressful for me, but then I guess it is for many of us. It's hard not knowing where to eat, or where to pee.

I drove the ramp to the upper portion of a concrete parking structure I hadn't noticed the day before. Just as I neared the top, a sheriff's deputy stepped out in front of the car, causing me to step on the brakes abruptly. He walked over to the driver's side and leaned into the window I had quickly rolled down.

"Excuse me, ma'am, but you can't park here. This lot requires a special parking pass."

"But I'm a psychologist. I'm Dr. Pelto. Don't I park up here?"

"No, babe, you don't. You have to have a pass."

"How do I get a pass?"

"Not going to happen; only the administrative staff is allowed up here. You park in the lower level." The lower level was dark and frightening, and I didn't want to park down there. Well, I'd ask Dr. Kline about it.

As I started to roll up the window, I said, "Well, sir, do you care if I just turn around up here?" My voice sounded huffy! Not a good idea! I rolled the window back down and called out to the officer. "I'm sorry, sir. I'm just a little tense." He didn't respond, but just waved me on.

I made a U-turn and drove down the ramp to the darkened portion of the garage, searched for an area that allowed a tiny sliver of light to shine in, grabbed my purse, locked the car door, and hurried up the stairs toward the Men's Jail.

The overpowering gray concrete monolith loomed up in front of me as I walked the dusty concrete sidewalk. Dry spiky scrub and two straggly trees trying to exist in the lifeless soil lined the path. Birds chirped gaily in the trees, unaware of the desolate world that surrounded them.

As I neared the end of the walk, the windowless building seemed to grow even larger, towering above me. I hesitated momentarily, then took a deep breath and strode forward.

A high security facility, the Central Men's Jail brimmed with men convicted of misdemeanors, serving sentences of up to a one-year maximum, and men who are awaiting trial or involved in criminal prosecution, located in downtown Los Angeles, California.

The wall opposite the doors I'd passed through had a steel-bar gate on the left side and a wall of heavy plate glass that went to the ceiling on the right. A waist-high, wooden counter was anchored to it. I dropped my purse on the shelf and squinted into the poorly illuminated room on the other side of the glass. The only light in the room came from the phosphorescent glow of computer screens, and I figured the deputies kept it deliberately dark.

"Hello, hello," I spoke into the small hole cut in the glass wall. No one replied. I could see faceless shapes moving around and hear men's voices laughing. They were rehashing a raucous party they had had the previous weekend.

I checked my watch—almost four minutes had elapsed. It was

taking longer today than it had on my first day. I tapped on the glass with my car keys.

"Excuse me, can someone help me?" I said, leaning close to the small opening.

"Yeah, ma'am, what can I do for you?" His voice sounded as irritated as I felt.

I couldn't make out the features that accompanied the husky voice, even though the deputy stood facing me.

"I'm Dr. Pelto."

"Congratulations," he spat out at me with unabashed sarcasm. The deputy's tone let me know how unimpressed he was.

It felt like I had been slapped in the face.

"Give me your ID," he said, pointing to the small opening.

I stood motionless.

"Lady, your ID, will yaw? Drop it in the tray." He upped his volume.

"What?" I was holding my breath.

"Your driver's license and Mental Health badge." The deputy's voice was elevated and slow, as if he were speaking to someone hard of hearing, stupid, or mentally retarded.

It took a little while for my brain to engage. Finally, I processed what he had demanded and began rummaging frantically around in my purse. Thank goodness! I thought, as my fingers caught the hard edge of the badge. I retrieved it quickly, along with the license from my wallet, and released my breath.

"Here you are, sir." I dropped the items into the pass-through at the bottom of the glass. I wasn't surprised my hands were trembling.

The deputy made short grunting noises as he checked his roster, found my name, and seemed satisfied with my credentials. After he put them aside, he slipped a jail ID badge back through the slot that read VISITOR in large black letters.

"Sir, I'm an employee now, not a visitor," I said with some emphasis.

"You'll get a permanent ID later, ma'am. For now, you're a

visitor. After you step inside, come over to the window and I'll sign you out a key." The dark shadow walked away from the glass.

"Excuse me, officer, but I thought I would get my badge today."

"Yo, babe, don't sweat it; you'll get it in a week or so."

"Shit, looks like we got us a fish," a husky voice said. Loud laughter followed.

"What?" I said, thinking he was addressing me.

No one responded. I got the picture, one of many lessons about the position a civilian, especially a female civilian, holds in relationship to the male uniformed staff in this environment.

I walked to the gate, adjusted my purse on my shoulder, and waited for it to open. Time passed. I paced back and forth. The deputies continued to talk and laugh. Finally, after what seemed like an eternity, a loud click sounded and an involuntary shudder ran through me. The electronic lock disengaged with a discordant grinding sound, and the heavy metal gate began to slowly open, sliding to the right.

I crossed over the threshold into a smaller darkened room. It was like being swallowed up whole as the gate reversed its direction and began to grind back to its closed position. Before I had a chance to orient myself, the door slammed shut, locking behind me with a loud clanging noise. I was caught in limbo, bracketed between a gate of bars that led to the outside world and a solid steel door that opened into the Los Angeles County Men's Jail, part of the largest jail system in the United States.

The sally port was dimly lit and claustrophobic.

I felt vulnerable and strained to see through the thick glass plate window where barely detectable, silhouetted figures occupied two desks.

I paced around the small room, working on my patience.

"Excuse me," I said, leaning close to the glass wall.

"Yeah, lady, what can I do for you now?"

"Is this where I get the key?" As soon as I asked, I remembered they would give it to me inside. My first day had been so confusing that I couldn't remember much of anything.

"No, lady, we'll assign it to you when you get inside the jail."

Another endless amount of time passed with no further instructions or movement from the darkened deputy's booth. I shifted my weight back and forth.

"Excuse me."

"Hang on, lady; don't get your knickers in a twist."

Evidently, I had interrupted the deputies recounting their party exploits again.

I reminded myself that the Central Men's Jail is a bastion of male supremacy where female civilian employees are at best tolerated, not welcomed, and I'd better get used to that fact real quick.

Finally, the electronic lock disengaged. With a loud grinding sound, the heavy metal door began to slowly open by sliding to the right, exposing the interior of the jail. That frightening sound would haunt my sleep.

I hadn't lost my temper, but was on the verge. As a kid, I was dubbed a spitfire. It came from having red hair and a fiery temper. Now, if I didn't keep my temper in check, I would get thrown out on my backside.

After picking up my key, I walked to the elevator and waited for a deputy who was going upstairs.

Stepping from the elevator, I turned to the left and walked past now quiet telephones and Ron's office, making another left down the short hall to unlock the door leading into the FOP offices.

"Vonda! Hey, Vonda!"

I turned to see Ron striding toward me.

"Good morning," he said with a cheery voice and motioned me to follow him into the FOP unit. I fell in step with him as he held the door open. "After the staff meeting, I'll show you to your new office."

Ron announced my position as his assistant, handed out a new flow chart, and gave me time to talk with the staff about the necessity of getting the filing done. Outlining my plans, I suggested we work in shifts. At the conclusion of my discourse, the group didn't give me a standing ovation. Instead, their mumbling was just loud enough to let me know they weren't happy about my new position or my plans for cleaning up the filing. Neither their attitudes nor their words sounded friendly.

After an hour, the meeting was over. I felt relieved to get out of the hostile room.

"Give me a couple of minutes," Ron said as we exited the FOP unit, "and then we'll talk about your interview with James Munro. Wait here. I'll only be a minute." He left me standing in front of the Sunset Killer's cell.

Ron grabbed a fistful of forms from his overloaded desk and then returned to lead me a few yards down the hall to my office. As it turned out, my office was directly across from the elevators and to the right of the telephones, where Ken Bianchi stood dialing the phone. He smiled as we walked around him to gain entrance.

"Moon River" was playing, but this world was certainly no "Breakfast at Tiffany's."

I inserted my key and struggled to disengage the lock.

"When I used this office, I always fought with it, too," Ron said. "Maybe we can get the lock fixed."

I finally got the unyielding lock to cooperate.

"This room is tiny. Was it a…?"

"Yep, it was a cell—the big change is the Dutch door."

My very own cell!

Ron unbolted the top portion of the door from the bottom half and pushed both pieces fully open. The room was no bigger than eight by ten feet.

"You'll appreciate it more than you know. It's nice to be able to lock the bottom half to keep the inmates from walking in uninvited, and leave the top open for some air."

My office was in the main hall, totally vulnerable to anyone that walked by. *An inmate could walk in at anytime?* That had never occurred to me. I had no protection; I wasn't going to want the door unlocked and open.

A scarred desk, with a few supplies thrown on it, two wooden chairs, a beat-up four-drawer metal file cabinet, and fluorescent tubes that cast ugly shadows on the mustard-colored walls, all welcomed me to this world.

I squeezed between the desk and the wooden desk chair so I could sit down, and then touched the ugly piece of furniture in front of me. My desk, my job, my own office, and a boss who said he would be willing to supervise my internship.

Sometimes life is good! It was a relief to be moved out of the bullpen, away from the rest of staff. Ron sat in the chair opposite me, positioned with his back to the hallway.

"Vonda, remember you're not here to do therapy. You assess for any suicidal ideation and move the inmate into the Forensic Inpatient hospital unit down the corridor if you detect any. Also, before I forget, there will be no confidentiality. Leave your door open when you do an interview. Deputies will be stopping by from time to time to eavesdrop.

"Jim Munro, one of the Freeway Killers, has been asking to see someone. Get to know him, gain his confidence, and talk about anything he wants to. These killers need to feel comfortable and supported by you. Just remember, we can't have anymore of them killing themselves."

"How do I handle the interview? Are there things I shouldn't...?"

The phone rang, interrupting my question. The caller asked for Ron and I handed the receiver across the desk to him.

"Yeah, I understand. Of course, I'll be right there." He handed the phone back to me and stood abruptly to leave. "Sorry, have to go. Forgot about this budget meeting we scheduled this morning over at the Central office. It involves funding for our unit."

I looked at his backside in a daze as he walked out, pulling the bottom half of the door shut. I was all alone. Stunned, I sat quietly, staring down at the little pile of supplies left by the secretaries.

"Vonda." Ron had returned and was leaning on the bottom half of the door. "You won't be seeing Munro after all today. He has the flu." *Great!* I took a deep breath.

"Komerchero is down at the medication line right now. Should be back about ten o'clock. I'll have the deputy let you know when he's available." The news broadcast flashed back and I saw the dismembered bodies again. My blood pressure shot up, and my pulse pounded in my ears.

"See you later this afternoon," Ron called out causally as he disappeared into the empty elevator car.

I turned back to my desk. *What do I say to this killer? Ask him about his childhood? Ask if he was abused? Ask about his crimes? Shit! Why not just ask him why in the hell he did it?*

More important to me, will I be safe in here with the Trash Bag Murderer?

Since I had a Ph.D., Ron seemed to think I didn't need any help. Not true! That piece of paper just attested to my knowledge of a bunch of useless information: such as how the eye cones work or how your tongue differentiates between sweet and sour.

There was some comfort knowing that the deputies would stop by and listen in on our conversations, but that wasn't much.

Leaning back in the swivel chair, I looked over the Intake Form, which didn't take long. It was comprised of a single page, and many of the questions were routine data that could be obtained from the computer.

Restless and unable to sit still, I walked out into the hall and looked down the long corridor. It was deserted.

In the midst of more than six thousand people, I felt terribly alone.

I walked back into the office, sat down, and looked around the bleak walls, trying to remember what pictures I had at home to bring in; maybe a green plant or a rug would help cheer up my cell.

I investigated the drawers, hoping that the previous occupant had left some treasures behind. Nothing of interest. I put the meager supplies away: a couple of pencils, three black pens, a legal- sized white tablet, and an unopened box of paper clips. Didn't take much time to drop them into the empty drawers. Then I looked down at the Intake Form again, staring through it while supporting my head in my hands.

"Dr. Pelto? Hello.... Am I disturbing you?"

I jumped. A handsome man was leaning into my office, his elbows resting on the bottom portion of the door. His blue jumpsuit alerted me that he was an inmate. Although I couldn't place the face, I was positive that I had seen it before.

"How're you doing today?" his smile grew into a charming, boyish grin. "I was wondering if I could come in and talk with you later, when you have time?"

"I'm sure I can arrange that."

"Right now, I'm on my way to see my attorney, but I'll be free later." He paused. "You look puzzled. I'm Ken Bianchi. I saw you when I was talking on the telephone. You and Deputy Gonzales walked past me."

Now I remembered. One of the Hillside Stranglers! *Vonda, you've got to get your bearings...and fast!*

"Tell the deputy and he'll call me out of my cell when you're ready to see me," Bianchi said as he stood erect.

"Sure, no problem. I'll probably have some time a little later, after I get settled." I didn't know what I had to do to get settled but I didn't feel ready to talk with him, and I was surprised he was so eager to talk with me.

"See ya." Bianchi waved and slipped across the hall to the attorneys' room.

How could such a nice looking, pleasant man be capable of committing such terrible crimes? Could he be innocent?

I picked the Intake Form up again, pretty routine stuff, name, AKA (also known as),   address, date of birth, marital status, occupation, charge, case number, prior arrests, history of mental illness, reason for referral, and some other miscellaneous requests for information.

I glanced back up at the section that asked for occupation and started to laugh. *What do you put down: Serial Killer?* I shook my head at my warped sense of humor. My mind was preparing its automatic defense mechanisms against the horrors to which I would soon be exposed.

The psychologist in me was curious and excited about meeting Komerchero, a Trash Bag Murderer, trying to understand his motivation for participating in the murders. The female portion of me was scared. I tried to reassure myself that the deputies will certainly cuff and shackle him with leg irons.

"Dr. Pelto?" A ruddy-faced deputy stood at my half-open Dutch door with an inmate in tow.

"I've got Mr. Komerchero here. You ready for him?"

"Please bring him in." I ran my fingers across the rough underside of the desk drawer to steady my nerves, then stood up as they walked forward.

CHAPTER 8

KOMERCHERO:
THE MAN WHO TRIED TO STAY
INVISIBLE

A rugged, swarthy Elihua Komerchero stepped into the doorway. His dark piercing eyes lingered on my exposed cleavage with little subtlety. I felt myself flush. Without invitation, he walked the short distance across the office and settled down onto the hard wooden chair. His shoulders were square and he held his head in a self-assured manner.

I'd placed the chair on the far side of my desk to put the maximum distance between us, feeling uncomfortable at the thought of having a killer sit any closer—although in my office, it didn't make much difference.

"Do you want me to cuff him?" the deputy asked.

"Yes, I think that's a good idea." I said as calmly as possible. *Was he kidding? Of course I wanted him cuffed.* Put him in a straightjacket, too, I wanted to add, as I sat back down working to look more in control than I felt.

The deputy turned to Komerchero and, with a stern voice, said, "Okay, homeboy, you know the drill."

Komerchero raised his arms and rested them on the sides of the chair. I could see the smirk on his lowered face as the deputy anchored his right wrist to the chair with handcuffs and then exited the room.

Was that it? Handcuff one arm to a wooden chair? Big deal! I wondered if I could rearrange my office so that I was closer to the door, in case I needed to escape.

"I'll be back shortly." The deputy's voice trailed out behind him, and he was gone before I could ask him if he would be close by.

I was mentally rehearsing how to begin the interview when Komerchero began to speak. I looked up at him, startled.

"I gave myself up," he said.

"What?"

"I turned myself in." He smiled slightly.

"I didn't know that. Mr. Komerchero, before you go on, I have to tell you that we won't be engaging in traditional psychotherapy. My job is to assess whether you should be sent to the psychiatrist for medication, if you are severely depressed and need to be moved to the hospital area, or if you're suicidal. What I'm trying to say is," I was stammering all over the place, "you won't have the protection of confidentiality, the door must remain open, a deputy will stand outside listening and may come in at any time. Don't tell me anything you need to be held in confidence because that won't be possible." Thank goodness my canned spiel got better with practice.

"It don't matter, Dr. Pelto, I already confessed to the D.A., and pled guilty to the charges.

"I jus' need someone to talk to, someone that won't lie and say I tole them stuff I didn't. It's lonely in here and those snitch bastards get you to talk about your case. They make up shit about you and tell it to the D.A. to cut a better deal for themselves."

"I didn't know you confessed. I just wanted to make sure you knew the limitations before talking with me," I said.

"Thanks for lettin' me know, but it don't matter who you talk to about me."

The interview went smoothly. Komerchero was pleasant, answered my questions easily, and denied any type of current or past suicidal ideation. Having completed the Intake Form, and feeling more confident, I put it aside and turned my attention back to the inmate sitting three feet away from me across the desk. I was about to call a deputy to return him to the cell, when I changed my mind.

"Mr. Komerchero, we're through with the intake now. Is there anything you would like to talk about?"

A deputy walked by a couple of times and paused outside my door but didn't say anything. I waved him off.

"I need to get this stuff off my chest; but first, please call me Elihua."

I nodded, surprised the Trash Bag Murderer wanted me to call him by his first name.

"Did you know that after the killings I took off?"

"I wasn't aware."

"I moved to Brooklyn, New York, scared of getting caught for those murders. I was so broke, I worked in the produce section of a couple of supermarkets to make ends meet. I gave up everything that was familiar to me or had any meaning for me, even my name. I started losing my identity, didn't know who I was anymore. Half the time, when someone called me, I didn't answer 'cause I didn't know they were talking to me. It was a terrible feeling, I felt lost, with no roots. Finally, I couldn't stand it anymore.

"After I did a lot of thinking, I decided to come back here to California, surrender, and face the consequences. I couldn't handle living with a made-up identity. You can't know what it's like to be scared you're gonna get caught all the time and not to have nobody to trust."

He reached up with his free hand and rubbed his eyes, then brushed back his hair and frowned, pulling his bushy eyebrows together.

"I got back here and took an apartment over in Reseda, you know out in the Valley. After I got settled in, I called a reporter at the Daily News of Los Angeles and told him I wanted to turn myself in. He was a good guy and arranged it all for me. He picked me up to drive to the police station."

"What happened when you turned yourself in?" I felt my stomach relax a notch. This was like many of the other interviews I had performed. *No big deal! Why had I been so skittish?*

"They arrested me and brought me over here to go through central booking. I've been here ever since."

"Weren't you given a chance to get bail?" I asked.

"No, this is a capital case." He gave me a funny look and I realized that I'd asked a naive question.

"When they interviewed me, I copped to being at the hotel but tole them I didn't kill nobody. I swear I didn't hurt nobody." Komerchero crossed his heart with his free hand.

"Avital did it all, he killed 'em both. I made a plea bargain with the prosecutors. I pled guilty to a reduced charge of voluntary manslaughter in exchange for my testimony against Yehuda Avital and Joseph Zakaria."

"You saw the murders?"

"Uh-huh. But I didn't know that Yehuda had planned to kill them. I thought he was just going to scare them. See, I knew Yehuda had been having an affair with Eli Ruven's wife, Ester. I think maybe he thought Ruven had found out about it and was going to retaliate against him, so he decided to kill him first.

"Yehuda thought they were stealing money from him, too. He'd been doing some big drug deals with them and thought they were cheating him, holding out. He was furious about that."

"Why were you all in the Bonaventure Hotel?" I guess that was a naive question, too, but Komerchero didn't seem to mind.

"Yehuda told me to get the Ruvens over there for a meeting, thought it would be more secret. He said he just wanted to discuss business with them, so I called them and told them to meet us at the Bonaventure in Room 2419. Zakaria had already made the hotel reservations. I don't know if he knew what was going to happen, either.

"When I got there, to the hotel room, I mean, Yehuda was freebasing, getting real crazy. He started walking around the room, ranting and raving about the Ruvens and how they cheated him, and that nobody fucked with him, and some other stuff I couldn't understand. Most of the time he didn't make much sense to me.

"I heard the knock, and Yehuda tole me to open the door. I looked through the peephole to make sure it was the Ruvens, then swung the door open.

"As soon as they walked through the door, Yehuda pulled a gun, aimed at them, and fired. Everything happened real fast; I barely got out of his way before he started shooting. I didn't believe it. I stood there in shock. I hadn't even seen the gun before." Komerchero shook his head. "I can't tell you how many shots he got off."

Komerchero began to hyperventilate.

"Elihua, take some deep breaths and try to relax."

"I'll try. But I got to get this all out. I feel terrible, but I couldn't have stopped him. I'm having nightmares about what happened that night. Most every night, I wake up in a cold sweat."

Something in his voice touched me and I felt compassion for him. Maybe he was just a victim too, wrong place, wrong time.

"I think he hit Eli first—he fell forward hard, on his face. The blood started seeping out from under him all over the carpet. I wasn't sure if he was dead or not. But he lay there real quiet. He wasn't moving."

Komerchero was sweating.

"He had hit Ester, too. She started moaning, so I knew she wasn't dead. She fell on her side facing me, right against her husband. The blood came trickling out of her chest like a little river and ran down to puddle on the floor. I couldn't tell exactly where she had got hit, but it had to be bad. There was so much blood all over her front.

"Yehuda walked over to Ester, reached down, and tugged at her blouse to turn her over onto her back. Her eyes opened wide when she looked up at me. I can still see her face. When I close my eyes at night, I see her staring up at me, pleading. Oh God! Please let me get that image out of my mind."

Komerchero's hands were trembling.

"Then Yehuda ripped Ester's pants down and settled down on top of her. He pushed himself hard into her body. She let out a painful cry. God! I felt so bad, standing there watching; she was suffering and I could tell she was dying. But I couldn't do nothin' for her. She kept whimpering and begging him not to kill her. 'My babies, my babies, what will happen to my babies? There is no one to care for them.' She kept saying that over and over. I don't wanna say what he said back to her. Oh God, when Yehuda got up, he had blood all over the front of him."

Tears welled up in my eyes, and I felt embarrassed. All I could think of was my own two daughters, and wondered what would become of Ester's children.

"Elihua, excuse me a moment. I'm going to step out into the hall and call a trustee to bring us down some coffee." I brushed by his chair and barely made it out of the office before the tears streamed down my face. I took several deep breaths and called to a trustee who was about to get on the elevator, and ordered the drinks. Then I walked slowly back into my office and resumed my seat.

"Are you sure it's alright for you to be telling me about your case?" I didn't want to hear anymore about the murders.

"Yeah, don't worry, Doc. It's okay. I've already confessed all this stuff to the cops, so it don't matter what I say now. I just gotta talk about it. I feel guilty about not trying to stop him.

"After Avital finished raping Ester, he dragged Eli's body into the bathroom and started chopping it up with a meat cleaver. I can still hear the noise the bones made when they were breaking. I won't ever forget the sounds or the smell of the blood, and the shit and the piss."

I can't handle this!

"What were you doing all of the time?"

"I was scared, so scared, I could hardly breathe. I was afraid to do anything. Scared to death that I might make Avital mad at me, have him turn on me, and kill me. I stayed quiet, stone dead quiet, out of his way."

Komerchero's breathing came in short gulps. He was back in the hotel room, reliving the horror. The defiance had left his eyes, and had been replaced by what I could only read as fear.

"After a while, Yehuda came out of the bathroom carrying a bloody arm with him". *I swallowed hard to keep from throwing up.* "Blood dripped down off the arm onto the floor. He was mumbling, I couldn't understand him, but I tried to smile and agree with whatever he said. My mind was trying to figure how to stay alive."

"Where was Zakaria?" I sat very still, breathing shallowly, feeling like I was in the Bonaventure Hotel along with Komerchero.

"He was there, but I don't know what he was doin'. I guess he tried to stay invisible just like me.

"After Avital finished chopping up Eli, he tugged Ester's body into the bathroom. I didn't know if she was dead yet, and I didn't want to go in there to find out.

"Yehuda was hyper...talking...talking...talking.... I could hear him in the bathroom, cussing and chopping and chewing-out Ester as if she could still hear what he said. I didn't understand half of what he was saying, but I said sure whenever he asked me anything. I would have agreed to anything he said right then."

I could see it in my mind's eye: the bloody smears on the bathroom walls; gore dripping from the body parts; chunks of skin and slivers of bones scattered around the room. I tried desperately to block the images out but couldn't.

"Excuse me, I'll be right back." I barely got into FOP, through the bathroom door and into the stall before I threw up. After rinsing my mouth and wiping my forehead with a wet paper towel, I reluctantly walked back to my office.

"Sorry, I had to take care of something."

I slipped off my right shoe and started tapping the heel of my foot nervously on the cold, cement floor, my heart pounding. I wasn't prepared to hear a confession. But then, how could anyone prepare to hear of such carnage?

"After he got the bodies all chopped up, he sent me out to get some trash bags and suitcases so we could get the bloody pieces out of the hotel."

"Why didn't you run?" Komerchero reached up and wiped sweat off his forehead.

"Where would I go? He would hunt me down. I'd end up like the Ruvens. I had to go along with him if I wanted to live.

"He made us help him get the parts stuffed into those bags. Oh God, there was blood all over the bathroom. On the walls. On the floors. Even some splatters on the ceiling. It was terrible. I just wanted to get those body parts in the bags and get the hell out of there."

I could understand his feeling; I wanted to get out of here, too.

"I swear I didn't know he was going to kill them."

I was surprised by this unsolicited flow of information. He was so anxious to talk about the murders. Komerchero wasn't just being forthcoming; he wanted to plead his case for me, telling me that he was a victim of circumstance. He wanted me to hear his side of the story before I got a different version from someone else. It seemed important to him that I like him.

Komerchero dropped his head down to rest in his free hand. I thought he was crying. He seemed truly sorry for the carnage that had taken place; I had an overwhelming desire to comfort him. Just then I looked up to see Deputy Gonzales standing at my door. I had forgotten about the deputy and wondered how long he'd been standing outside, listening. I was amazed at myself—I had forgotten my fear.

"Thanks for checking. I'm about through with Mr. Komerchero. Just give me a couple minutes."

The deputy waved and walked out of sight.

"Elihua, anytime you need to talk with me, let the deputy know. I'm here to give you emotional support. If you become depressed and feel you need some medication, I can arrange for you to see the psychiatrist."

"I'll be okay. Thanks for listening to me, Dr. Pelto."

Gonzales returned shortly, uncuffed Komerchero, and led him out of the office.

I felt emotionally exhausted, hot, and had to get out of the stuffy cell, while swallowing hard to keep from throwing up again.

I ran into Sherry and Bobbie walking out of FOP.

"Hey, Vonda, we're going down to have an early lunch. Want to go with us?"

"Down to the ODR?" I asked, recalling the huge cafeteria and its creative cooks with an inner shudder.

"No," Sherry said. "There's a kitchen in the psych hospital unit. Not much selection, but you don't have to worry about any extras being added to the food."

"I'll catch up with you in a minute." I had to make it to the bathroom; food was the last thing I wanted.

My mind kept flashing back to Komerchero and the dismembered bodies. He seemed so ordinary, with such normal reactions. His feelings were not any different than the ones I would have had. Maybe he had just gotten caught up in a horrible situation. He felt guilty and was scared. Maybe I should let someone know that he could be innocent.

After I washed my face, I felt a little better. Maybe something to eat would settle my stomach.

The hospital was arranged in a rectangle with one-man cells on both sides of the corridors. I glanced into a couple of the cells; they all looked the same with a metal cot anchored in the concrete and a similarly affixed stainless steel toilet and washbasin, with a one-foot square window in the cell door just like Douglas Clark's.

The kitchen was situated around the corner from the nurses' station, directly across from a deputy's booth. Long efficient counters ran the length of each side of the room, interrupted only by a commercial stove and a huge, brushed-chrome refrigerator, awash with stainless steel. I wouldn't say the place was sterile, but it was adequately clean.

"By the way, this is the area we're supposed to go to in case of fire, earthquake, or riot," Bobbie said. "We have to wait here until a deputy gets the keys from the main control booth and goes outside to unlock the fire doors. It's for the coroner's convenience. After a fire, they want all our charred remains together so they don't have to go all over the place looking for us."

Was she serious? Was she trying to scare me? If she was, she was successful. If I were trapped, I'd run to the nearest exit and not allow myself to be corralled in this enclosed space. Unfortunately, I didn't know where the exits were!

"They really would leave us here?"

"Vonda, you're just too much!" Bobby said.

They both laughed at me, and I felt embarrassed.

Sherry walked to the refrigerator and pulled out three sandwiches, handing one to me. "The inmates take these to court for lunch along with a piece of fruit and some chips or cookies. They call them court-line sandwiches."

The sandwich had a French roll, no dressing, a couple slices of American cheese, and two slices of ham. "Pretty boring stuff. Is this all they get?"

"Yeah. Same everyday," Bobbie said, noticing my inspection.

"They're as dry as a bone."

"Shit, some fools' 'fraid an inmate might get food poisoning," Sherry said.

"You want coffee?" Bobbie asked as she started to fill a Styrofoam cup drawn from a commercial-sized urn. I nodded in the affirmative and she pushed one toward me.

"Hey, Sher, grab some of those cookies and our sandwiches, and let's head back," Bobbie called out.

"Hey, wait up. Where's the cream and sugar?" I asked.

"Learn to drink it black; it's easier," Sherry called back to me.

She was right.

We walked back down the hall, and they left me in front of Ron's office.

Ron was sitting at his desk doing paperwork, so I decided to stop and talk about my concern.

"Ron, I just saw an inmate named Komerchero, and I don't think he should be held responsible for the crimes he's accused of."

"Why is that?"

"Well, he had to go along with Yehuda or be killed. He says

he didn't kill anyone, and I really believe him. When something happens like this, what is our duty?"

"Vonda, we don't get mixed up with the legalities. Let the lawyers and judges figure it out. We just see the inmates and let the attorneys do their job." Ron's attitude taught me all I needed to know. Cover my butt and stay out of the legal system.

"He says he's innocent."

Ron laughed. "They all claim that. You have to separate yourself out from these men."

Returning to my office, I closed the entire door and thought about Komerchero. In spite of my education, I couldn't tell if he was conning me or not. Did he just happen to be in the wrong place at the wrong time?

After eating my court-line, I walked down to Bianchi's cell. He lay in a fetal position with his knees pulled up to his chest, looking like a little boy, not a man who was capable of killing twelve women. I was glad he was asleep. I didn't have to talk to him. Guess this sounds selfish, but I just couldn't handle another killer baring his soul today.

CHAPTER 9

IS THAT A GUN IN YOUR POCKET, OR ARE YOU JUST HAPPY TO SEE ME?

Monday was upon me again. The alarm went off, I dragged myself out of bed, dressed as if in a trance, and drove to work, parking in the dirt lot and walking to the entrance of the jail.

I'd asked Ron about getting a special parking pass. "I'm sorry; it's not possible," he said. I wasn't happy about the situation but I didn't have any choice.

Leaning close to the glass wall, I could see the deputies moving around but couldn't tell if they were aware of my presence. Or maybe they didn't care that I was waiting to get through the gates. Ten minutes elapsed without a word from the darkened booth. I didn't tap on the window. I'd learned a long time ago that, under any circumstances, that wasn't a good idea.

"Morning," Sherry called out, as she came striding toward me, cutting through the dirt to the concrete path.

"They're slower than usual," I said.

Sherry stepped up to the glass and rapped on it, yelling out to a deputy inside, then she turned to me.

"Come on, little buckaroo, we'll go over and have some breakfast."

Seeing her friend approaching, Sherry called out, "Hey, Bobbie, good news. We're in lockdown."

"You headed to the annex?" Bobbie stood a little distance away, waiting for us to catch up to her.

"I'll drive," Sherry answered.

Sherry led the short distance to her car, which turned out to be in the highly prized, upper-level, staff parking lot, the one I'd gotten thrown out of on my second day.

"You have a priority parking pass! I thought only the supervisors and high ranking sheriff's personnel got the privilege. I'm out in the boonies."

Sherry and Bobbie gave each other a knowing look.

"Little buckaroo, you just got to know the right people." Sherry reached out and patted my head.

"Well, please introduce me."

A couple of days later a white envelope containing a special parking pass mysteriously appeared on my desk. I never did find out who the contact was. All I knew for certain was that the two by three card got me through the special parking gate, and it wasn't legitimate.

Sherry held the seat forward, allowing Bobbie to crawl into the back. I crawled into the front and we rode the mile to the annex, or as the general public calls it, Denny's Restaurant.

We arrived, parked easily, and walked into the restaurant. Most of the other staff were already drinking coffee and checking out the menu.

"Thank goodness for the lockdown, I'm not ready to face the inmates yet," I said.

"Well, you'll get used to it. We all have had to. The inmate count must be off. Deputies are doing a physical head count," Sherry said as she lit a cigarette.

"I remember the first lockdown I was in. When the gates slammed and locked, the reverberating sound scared the holy shit out of me," Sherry continued.

"Have you ever been in the jail when a fire broke out?" I asked.

"Yeah," Sherry nodded. "Right after I hired in. An inmate set one while I was walking the rows in 4500. The deputies got me out of there right away, but I still remember that feeling of being trapped. Just smelling the smoke now scares me 'cause we're so helpless."

"The dings set fires 'cause they're bored and want attention," Bobbie said. "They set their mattresses on fire, paper on fire, or whatever they can get their hands on. Accidents happen, too. These perps use matches and all kinds of contraptions to heat their coffee and tea."

After we finished eating breakfast and had our fill of coffee, Lupe went to the pay phone to call the deputy's booth. She returned shortly with the bad news. The lock down had ended, the gates were unlocked, and we were cleared to return to work.

"Some Enchanted Evening" greeted us as we walked through the sally-port back into the jail.

I left the rest of the staff at the elevator on our floor and ran to my office to catch the ringing phone.

"When can you come down?" Deputy Branson's familiar voice was on the phone. "Jackson says he's real depressed. Saw you in the module earlier this week when you talked with Bonin, wanted to know who you were. Told him you were a psychologist; said he really needs to talk with you."

I leaned back in my chair, stretching the phone cord.

"Word has spread around here that you got great legs and are good for getting them out of their cells. Helps break up their boredom."

Embarrassed about the leg comment, I could hear the uniform clear his throat. He couldn't know that I'd built up an immunity to that kind of remark.

I still didn't know if the deputies approved of a female shrink intruding on their territory. Much of the time, I figured they thought I was being taken in by the inmates' sob stories and thinking that they had been wrongfully accused. And that the perps shouldn't be held responsible for their behavior because they were abused children, didn't have a dad in the home, or have enough money to go to Boy Scout camp. If they did, they didn't know me. The more I worked with these killers the more I believed that something was different in their genetic makeup. But whatever the cause of their abhorrent behavior, society had the right to be protected.

"Now all these dudes want to see you." The deputy interrupted my reverie. "What's a good time for you?"

"Eleven?"

"See you then."

I headed down to the kitchen to get another shot of caffeine, john wayne style. Needed to up my energy level before starting the daily paperwork, phone calls, and talking with inmates.

When I walked in, Bobbie was leaning into the fridge, retrieving a carton of orange juice.

"Where's Sherry? She didn't go home sick, did she?" I asked.

Bobbie laughed.

"She's not sick, well not physically. She had to go to court on that deuce. Scared about what it's going to cost her. She's trying to fight it. Left right after we got back from breakfast. Probably be there the rest of the day."

"What did her husband say?"

"Shit, she didn't tell him. They've been having a lot of trouble and she figures this might give him an excuse to take a walk. I don't know if she still loves him, but she sure as hell doesn't want a divorce. Being single is the shits."

I know what you mean.

"Yo, Bobbie, you got to help me with this." We turned to see Deputy Gonzales running into the kitchen and at the same time unzipping the front of his uniform pants.

"What in the hell are you doing?" Bobbie snickered as she asked.

"Haven't got time to explain, I can only tell you she's been cruisin' for this brusin' for a long time." He winked at us and sported a broad toothy grin.

"Bobbie, hand me a banana out of that fruit bowl." He grabbed the fruit from her and stuffed it in his black bikini jockey shorts in an upright position and then attempted to zip the unyielding pants back up.

"Bobbie, help me. Fuck! This damn zipper won't budge and I sure as hell don't want to break it."

"Help you what?"

"I'll hold my pants together; see if you can get the zipper closed. Nurse Bigtits has just started out dispensing the meds; I gotta catch her before she finishes her rounds."

I looked on in amazement.

Bobbie rushed over and started working on the uniform.

She stopped working on the zipper, stood erect, and grabbed her mouth in an effort to regain control.

"Bobbie, you got to get it together; she's gonna be making her rounds pretty soon." Gonzales pled.

Bobbie bent again and started working on the zipper.

"Oh shit, I think the zipper is stuck on the banana peel," she said. "I can see some yellow oozing out from between the teeth. Jose, stop wiggling around. Vonda, stop giggling and get over here and hold these pants together. He's no help."

"Are you kidding me?"

"Shit no, get your butt over here."

I walked over reluctantly to lend my assistance, bent down, and tried to force the fabric together over the bulging banana. Each time Gonzales laughed I lost the hold on his pants and had to grab them again.

"You got to hold still or I'll never get you zipped up," Bobbie said.

"Okay, okay. Just hurry up," he said.

I looked up to see Jose glancing at the ceiling, trying to inhale and not laugh.

"I got it moving. Vonda, now just hold it right there," Bobbie demanded.

With all three of us working on the project, we finally got the banana concealed in its upright position and his uniform pants back intact.

"Okay, come on out and watch what happens," Gonzales said as he preceded us out of the kitchen.

I turned to see a growing parade of staff gathering in the hospital corridor. Oblivious to the crowd, Nurse Bigtits was pushing her three-tiered med cart.

Word had spread to the other deputies and staff in the area about the joke Gonzales was going to play on her. I was surprised she hadn't noticed our gathering group.

"Hi, Nan," Jose said in his most seductive voice as he came up beside her waist-high med cart.

"How are things going?" he asked.

"Well, things could be a lot better organized around here if you deputies would do your jobs right. You should not clown around so much. You should take this job seriously. I can't believe how immature and irresponsible you all act." She continued pushing her medication cart down the hall with Gonzales walking close beside it.

"This is a medical area, a hospital, and you should all show the inmates some respect. The men in these cells are suffering! You should not make fun of them!"

"Oh now, Nan, you know we give them all the respect they deserve." His voice had a condescending air. She stopped the cart and looked directly at him.

"We're always here when you call us. You've just got to loosen up a bit. Relax!" he said. "You know, I've noticed you have the prettiest hands. Do you use special lotion on them?"

With that comment, he reached over, took her hand, and squeezed it around the pretend penis in his pants.

"Oh, my God!!!" she shrieked. "What in the hell are you doing?" As she jerked her hand back from his crotch, she accidentally hit the cart and sent it wheeling down the corridor, crashing into a duster's cell. A loud bang reverberated down the hall. Metal to metal.

"My cell's on fire! They're bombing us! Get me out of here! You fuckers get me out of here! Help me! God, please, please someone help me. I'm on fire. Ahaaaaaa," the duster screamed.

His curdling screams echoed down the halls.

She ignored the pleading druggie, swirled around, and caught us laughing. The veins in her throat were pulsating; her mouth was wide open as if trying to form words strong enough to show her true contempt. Her rage was almost palpable. "You fucking assholes," she screamed as she ran past us, back to the safety of the nurse's station. Profanity trailed behind her all the way back to the intersection of her haven. She stopped abruptly, turned to face our group, and shouted, "This staff is crazier than the inmates."

Bobbie leaned over to me. "I don't think she's going to last in the jail very long. There's no place for uppity bitches in here. Shit, if you can't take a joke, you can't make it here."

Bobbie's prediction turned out to be correct. Nancy submitted her resignation a week later, which coincidentally was also the anniversary of her fourth month of employment at the jail. Only a few people, including me, attended her going-away party. I felt tremendous guilt for participating in humiliating her and wanted to let her know how I felt.

After everyone else had drifted away, I asked her to have coffee with me. She agreed and we walked down to the ODR for some privacy. I apologized for helping to embarrass her and for not being supportive when she was struggling to adjust to the jail environment.

With both of us being single women, having trouble in this testosterone hell hole, we could have developed a friendship.

I learned two things from her experience: First, my shit did indeed stink; and, second, I needed this job.

CHAPTER 10

ARTHUR JACKSON: I DIDN'T WANT TO HURT HER, I JUST WANTED TO KILL HER

After being admitted into High Power, I joined the deputies in their booth for coffee.

"Arthur Jackson is acting strange; don't know if he's suicidal. Shit, we sure as hell don't want anybody killing themselves. Too goddamn much paperwork!" Deputy Branson said.

My job was to keep these adam henrys alive.

"Just give me a few minutes to read his log, then I'll talk with him."

Jackson had been arrested for attempting to kill the actress, Theresa Gilda Saldana. After seeing her in the 1980 film "Defiance", he became obsessed with her and traveled illegally from Aberdeen, Scotland, to New York, to contact her mother, saying he was a film producer's representative who wanted Theresa for a part in a movie. Unfortunately, Saldana's mother was taken in by his lie and gave Jackson Theresa's address.

"Hey, dolly, you waitin' to see Jackson?" Deputy Geiger walked up behind me and started rubbing my shoulders. I cringed. *Get away from me, asshole!*

"The Senior asked me to talk with him."

"This guy's crazy, or he wants us to think he is. Thinks he'll get special treatment," Geiger said. "Jackson refuses to shower, and he's so damn tight he won't shell out a couple of bucks to buy a razor. His attorney got a court order to make him cut his hair and shave, wants him to look as good as possible when he gets to court."

"Does he sleep okay? Eat okay?"

"Not much appetite, don't know about his sleeping, I got better things to do at night than baby-sit these fuckers." Geiger flashed me a broad grin. "He's restless as hell, reminds me of a mad dog."

I finished the log and started to walk out of the booth when Geiger walked up behind me and patted my butt. I gave him a dirty look and raised my middle finger. Unfortunately, he'd already turned away from me, so the gesture was wasted on his backside.

Vonda, remember you're a psychologist and you're supposed to be above that kind of behavior!

I didn't like being a victim of such blatant sexual harassment, but there wasn't a damn thing I could do about it!

Shortly, Jackson came sauntering down the hall followed by the Senior. His gaunt body suggested poor health. He appraised me with a fleeting look of recognition, and then dropped his gaze to the cold concrete floor.

When Jackson arrived at the entrance to the interview room, he stopped before entering, examined it carefully, as if he expected something lethal to be inside, and then entered, walking slowly to the barber chair. I followed him into a room that had become as familiar as my office upstairs and sat down beside the battered desk. Jackson stepped up into the barber chair without being told and let out a loud fart.

Class act! I've got to get another job.

Arthur Jackson sat with his shoulders slumped forward, his head hanging down with straggly, brown hair falling into his eyes, partially obscuring his blank stare. His strong body odor quickly permeated the enclosed room. His mannerisms, as well as his dirty appearance, were suggestive of a homeless, disheveled bum. I thought about bringing in a lemon-scented spray can. Or maybe a perfumed hankie to hold to my nose like the ladies did in the olden days.

"I think I remember you." His voice had a thick Scottish brogue.

"Didn't I meet you a few days ago?"

"Yes, you did."

"What did we talk about?"

"Your attorney called you out before we had a chance."

"Things get confused in my mind."

"Do you remember me telling you not to disclose any information that you needed held in confidence? This isn't a therapy session, and we can't expect to have privacy. A deputy may be listening to us talk. Other than my warning, we didn't have time to talk before."

He nodded in the affirmative that he did remember.

"How are you getting along?"

"I didn't complete my mission."

"What mission was that, Mr. Jackson?"

"Why," he cocked his head and gave me a defiant look, "to kill Theresa Saldana."

I tried not to appear surprised by his bluntness.

"It is our destiny to be united. The gods have ordained it.

"She shouldn't be making those Hollywood films. It's not right for all of those men to be looking at her. She is so beautiful. She is an angel. She should be dwelling with the angels.

"She has to be transformed."

"Transformed?"

"By death."

He continued on with his own thoughts.

"Why didn't she die? Now I will have to try again. I was a fool not to use a gun." Jackson's voice rose and he began jerking at the handcuffs, making red marks around his wrist.

I looked toward the door and saw a deputy standing slightly inside the frame.

"I have to have her. Don't you see?"

"Do you want to talk about what happened?"

"I went over to her place one day and hid in the bushes. After a while, she came out of her flat. I watched as she walked toward her car. I had to do something before she drove away."

"Did you call out to her?"

"I wanted to. To explain my feelings. Perhaps if she knew how important she was to me, how much I loved her, it would all be different.

"She should be with the angels now. Don't you see, I didn't want to hurt her."

Jackson leaned his head down and supported it with his left hand. He licked his lips and frowned. "Why didn't she die? Then it would be finished."

He raised his head and stared toward the right corner of the room.

"She was trying to defend herself against me. I slashed her over and over again in her chest and in her arms and hands when she tried to fight me. She was bleeding so much. The blood was getting all over the walk." Jackson had inflicted ten knife wounds into Theresa Saldana's small body. Jeff Finn, a water deliveryman, heard Saldana's screams, struggled the knife away from Jackson, and held him until the authorities arrived.

Jackson looked at me, his voice pleading for understanding.

"Don't you see? I didn't want to scar her. I was careful not to cut her face; I wouldn't spoil her beauty."

Jackson's face wore a mystified look.

The room was hot and stuffy. Dust particles floated in the air.

"Are you thinking of pleading guilty?" I asked.

Jackson raised his eyebrows.

"Of course not. I'm not guilty. I am an agent of the Knights of St. Michael in the Kingdom of Heaven. I should be released." He raised his voice and slammed his fist down hard on the arm of the chair for emphasis. I jumped.

"If she does die, but you are acquitted and released, you won't be put to death. You won't be transformed. How will you be united with her?"

I believed that Jackson was mentally ill, and should plead not guilty by reason of insanity (NGI), but I wasn't going to say anything.

"I wrote a letter to the deputies and told them I shouldn't have to wear these jail clothes. I need my clothes, they'll make me feel better."

Tugging at the front of his jumpsuit, he looked at me with clouded eyes.

"I want to wear overalls, that's what I'm supposed to wear. They will make me better. I called the British Consulate; I want them to get a court order to make the jailers let me wear overalls."

"How would wearing them make you better?"

Jackson kept jerking at the handcuffs.

"You don't understand. I don't need to tell you. Why are you asking me?" He tilted his head slightly and eyed me with a suspicious gaze.

"If I understand better what your needs are, maybe I can help you."

"I gave up coffee and tea twenty years ago." His voice rose and filled with anger.

"I asked God why it couldn't have been another way."

His eyes were wild and he shook his head so hard that the dirty strands fell back into his face. "Why did it have to be like this? The blood squirted everywhere—it was ugly. The transformation was to be beautiful."

Arthur Jackson began to rock back and forth, and to emit a low mumbling sound.

"I should have used a gun! It wouldn't have hurt her as much. I didn't want to cause her pain. She is so beautiful—we are meant to be together. There's no other way! She has to be transformed! I am the benevolent Angel of Death. We will be joined in Heaven as beautiful doves and will fly away to be together for all of eternity."

He looked at me imploringly. His anger had faded and I thought he was beginning to cry.

Jackson was delusional and needed to be given psychotropic medication. I would suggest he be moved to the hospital area and put on regular observation.

A deputy entered the room and stood leaning against the inside wall.

"You ready for me to take him back to his cell?"

"Thanks."

After Jackson was led out of the room, I gathered up the Intake Forms, walked to the door, and nodded to a deputy to release me from the module.

I couldn't help but wonder if Miss Saldana would ever be safe from Arthur Jackson.

CHAPTER 11

THAT'S THE HILLSIDE STRANGLER

Time was passing more quickly than I could have ever imagined. I'd given up trying to find another job and settled into a routine, figuring that I would be getting my license soon and be able to quit and start my own practice.

Ron and I were meeting regularly for my supervision and he agreed to let me use time at work to study. I had worried for nothing.

But being Ron's assistant was taking up much more time than I'd anticipated. So far, there had been little of it left to study for the exams and, unfortunately, when I ultimately got home at night, I was too exhausted.

About six more months and my internship would be completed, and it would be my first opportunity to take the State Boards. I had to be ready for them.

Work was difficult. I was seeing the killers daily. Thank goodness none of them had attempted suicide. Getting the clinical staff to work on the filing mess was a real struggle. They were extremely resistant. So far, little had been accomplished.

Ken Bianchi had approached me on my first day at the jail, said he wanted to talk. Since then, I'd made several attempts to see him. Strange, no matter how many times I'd ask a deputy to break Bianchi out of his cell for me, he was never available. Either he was in court, talking with his lawyer, not feeling well, or he was sleeping. I caught up with him on several occasions and offered him time.

"No sweat, Doc," he said. "I'm not going anywhere." For a man not going anywhere, he didn't seem to be around very much.

Edith purchased our tickets to the play and the appointed night arrived several weeks later. Coming through the sally port that morning, I let the booth deputy know that a Ms. Edith Downey would be arriving about five o'clock to see me and asked him to call my office when she arrived.

It was almost four-thirty when I grabbed my make-up bag, planning to walk over to the FOP restroom to redo my make-up and comb out my hair.

"Hi, Doc."

The Hillside Strangler was peering in through my half-opened door.

"I heard you didn't see Komerchero yet, even though he's been needing to talk to you."

"Ken, I have talked to him."

"When I'm bothered by something, I have to take time to figure it out. And I'm not sure how I feel about you. I'm afraid to trust that you will be there for me," Ken said, his voice breaking.

"Ken, I am here for you. It's my job, to be available anytime you want to talk to me."

"I have to know I can count on you. You got to be here when I need you, or I can't start talking to you at all." He bent down, propped his elbows on the half-opened Dutch door, and leaned forward into my office.

"If you're free now, I'd like to talk with you," he said.

So much for powdering my nose!

This explained why he had been avoiding me, pretending to have a headache or be asleep. He wanted assurance that he could see me anytime he wanted to.

The Hillside Strangler had to think about whether he could trust me or not? What about all the women he had tortured and killed?

Not in the mood to argue, it seemed prudent to grit my teeth and wait for him to finish. His rampage continued for a while longer; I tuned him out. Bianchi was accustomed to controlling and intimidating women.

I remained seated, as Ken pushed the door fully open, walked into the office, and stood beside the desk. "May I sit down?"

"Sure. Have a seat."

When I didn't rise to the bait, his attitude completely changed. He sat down hard on the chair and leaned over to pull a dead leaf off the philodendron plant sitting on the edge of my desk.

"If you'll put an aspirin in this, it will green up again."

I studied him closely and he winked at me.

"What's happening, Ken?"

"I was watching TV the other night and heard that Lady Diana had a son. A new prince. The British people took it very well. By the way, did you know I have a son? Ryan Weston Bianchi. He was born in February of seventy-eight."

"I wasn't aware." He wanted to chat!

Bianchi was beaming.

"I love him, and really miss getting to watch him grow up."

He lowered his head and rested his forehead on his hand.

"I won't be there for his first day of school or see him dressed for the prom or his graduation or when he gets married. I'm missing out on his life. I wish Kelli would bring him to see me." His voice had an appropriate quiver.

"Kelli?"

"Yeah, that's his mother. I guess I can kinda understand how difficult it would be for her to come here to see me."

His words were unnerving. The Hillside Strangler was a father, with normal feelings toward his child, the same kind of feelings I would have if I were separated from my girls. He sounded so loving.

"Dr. Pelto, would you mind keeping his birth certificate and some of my other personal things in your desk drawer? The deputies come by and roust my cell whenever they're in the mood. I'm always worried they will 'accidentally' throw out some of my stuff."

"Drop your things off any time, Ken. I'll keep them for you." The request surprised me. It felt strange, thinking of having his personal items in my desk drawer.

"I didn't kill anyone." Ken said.

"What?" He changed the subject so abruptly I was caught off-guard. *Was this intentional? Or was I becoming overly suspicious?*

"Can we get some coffee first before we talk? I would like a hot cup. Mine is always cold."

Why not!

I picked up the phone and called the deputy's booth located across the hall from the hospital kitchen. "No problem," a uniform said. "I see a trustee strutting around over at the nursing station, flirting with the girls. The coffee's on its way."

"Now, what were you saying, Ken?"

"I guess you've read that I confessed to some of the Hillside Strangler murders and the two up in Bellingham, Washington."

"I read that."

"They say I killed those two girls up there, but I don't remember anything about them. It couldn't have been me that killed them, unless another part of me did it. I'm sure if I'd killed someone, I'd know it."

"But you confessed!"

"I had to 'cause they had all that evidence. They brought me down to L.A. to be a witness against Buono. I had to lie and say I was with him when he killed all those girls so the authorities would arrest him."

"What makes you think Buono is guilty?"

"He's a brutal man! I could tell from the descriptions of the murders that I read in the Washington newspapers that it was him. Now I'm worried.

"You're worried?"

"When they call me to the stand, they're going to see I'm lying as soon as they ask me for any details about the killings. All I really know about them is what I read in the newspapers. They'll figure out that I wasn't with him. I don't feel good about lying. But what else could I do? I just know my cousin did them. If he gets out, he'll hurt more girls."

I knew Ken had confessed to the Hillside killings and gave Angelo Buono up to avoid being given the death penalty in the two murders he had admitted to in Bellingham, Washington.

I pushed my knee hard against the side of the desk, out of Ken's sight. It had become bruised in the last few months, helping me keep my mouth shut.

The trustee arrived and peered in.

"Where do you want this?"

I nodded toward the desk. He sauntered in, set the tray on the desk with cream, sugar, two cups of coffee, and a few cookies on it, and left, his rubber-soled shoes squeaking on the cement floor.

Avoiding the additives, Bianchi picked up a john wayne and continued talking.

"Now I don't know what to do about my testimony! I had to say I was there to make sure Angelo didn't get away with the murders. Can't you see my problem?"

Bull pucky!

"Someone had to stop him. He can't get out 'cause I'm afraid of what he will do if he ever does.

"Dr. Pelto, please believe me, I didn't kill anyone. But I couldn't let Angelo get away with the murders. I had to lie."

Ken raised his eyebrows and watched my face, attempting to read my reaction to his denial. "Ken, how can you testify that you were with Buono, if you weren't?"

"I'll just parrot back to the court what I read in the newspapers.

"Doc, what should I do now?"

Trying to figure out an appropriate answer, I readjusted myself in the hard chair, and wondered if I could eventually manipulate him into telling the truth. *Maybe with enough time…?*

No! He's a bold-faced liar.

Thank goodness the phone rang just then and the deputy announced that Ms. Downey had entered the elevator and was on her way up. I was greatly relieved. I didn't have any answers for Ken.

I looked squarely at Bianchi and finally said, "Just tell the truth."

Talking to Ken was like trying to keep up with a roving target. He was slippery and a convoluted liar.

"Excuse me, Ken, I have a visitor on her way up." He didn't move, and I didn't have time to ask him to leave before I heard the elevator arrive. I walked to the entrance of my office in time to watch its doors open. Edith stepped out, wearing a stunned look on her face. Her body was as rigid as a statue. I called to her. She didn't see me, even though I stood just across the hall, twelve feet away from her. Her distress was mirrored in her expression, reminding me of the feelings I had the first day I walked into the jail. Her blond hair curled about her face, giving her the look of a fearful child. She stood barely five-feet-five-inches tall and wore a soft, muted lavender, paisley dress.

"Edith, this way." She squinted in my direction, trying to orient herself.

"Oh! Vonda! Am I ever glad to see you." She came up close and hugged me.

"Come on in."

She followed me back into the office where Ken was standing and smiling like a country gentleman. I realized I hadn't asked the deputy to cuff him down.

"Ms. Downey, this is Mr. Bianchi." I wasn't quite sure if she realized who was standing in front of her as she reached out to shake his hand. He continued to smile. She smiled back. *Nope! It hadn't registered yet.*

"Are you here to tour the jail, or you thinking of hiring in?" he asked.

I returned to sit behind my desk as Edith and Ken sat down opposite each other.

"No, I drove up here to meet Vonda for dinner. Then we're going to see Epson's "Doll House" at the Music Center." I was sorry she had used my first name, but then I figured he probably knew it already. He probably even knew that my middle name was Loretta.

"Well, Ken," I interrupted their conversation, "I see the trustee pushing the dinner trolley off the elevator. Time for you to return to your cell."

"Nice to meet you, Ms. Downey. Hope to see you again sometime soon," he said and reached out to shake her hand again before he departed the office.

"Hey, deputy, how about unlocking my door? Dinner is being served and I wouldn't want to miss it," Bianchi called out to a passing uniform as he stepped out into the hallway.

"Vonda, who was that guy? He's good looking and charming. His face seems familiar and I know I've heard that name before."

"Yes, I'm sure you have." I guided her out of the office, locked the door behind us, crossed the hall to the elevator, and reached out to push the down button. Since I was treating her to dinner, I figured that would make it a perfect evening.

"Oh, my God!" Edith suddenly exclaimed as she turned to face me directly. "I just shook hands with the Hillside Strangler! I shook hands with him twice! Oh, my God, I may be sick."

"Yep," I said, smiling in anticipation of our dinner yet to come in the ODR.

I knew Edi would never see my job the same way again.

CHAPTER 12

DOUGLAS DANIEL CLARK: THE MAN WOMEN LOST THEIR HEADS OVER

Suddenly it was autumn again and I had survived. My yearlong internship was completed and I would be taking the Psych Boards in a couple of weeks. With the license in hand, I would have new options. Then I would have to decide whether or not it was worth working the additional two years to earn the retirement.

The exams are given twice a year and must be passed before sitting for the orals. The verbal portion didn't scare me; it was the written test that I dreaded. I have dyslexia and have trouble reading. In test situations, I become so anxious that my mind literally shuts down.

This problem has bugged me all my life and I barely made it through my Master's degree by taking copious notes at the lectures.

Before starting the Ph.D., I contacted the reading program at California State University at Long Beach and told the interviewer that I couldn't read and needed help. When she asked if I had made it through high school, I was delighted to tell her that I was starting a Ph.D. A few days later, a tutor contacted me and, with her help, my reading improved.

Now the push was on to spend every free minute studying.

I had just shut my office door and opened a book when Ron stopped by.

"Can you see Daniel Clark today?"

"The Sunset Killer?"

"Yes. I'm worried about him. He's refusing to eat, might be suicidal."

I have to admit, I'd been stalling, not wanting to have him in my office. The visual image of him shooting women in the head while they were on their knees giving him a blowjob made me sick to my stomach.

It was difficult to reconcile who I was with what my job entailed —and a constant struggle to maintain a non-judgmental attitude.

I put the books aside and headed to Clark's cell.

Walking down the halls with killers housed on both sides was like walking through a zoo where wild animals are caged. Except these men were not as gracious as animals; they killed for their own selfish pleasure.

The inmates were alerted to my presence with the clattering of my high heels on the cement floor, and would come to their cell doors to watch me as I passed by. Their faces framed by the small windows made them look even more ominous and frightening. When I first hired into the jail, I wondered what they were fantasizing about; now I knew what was on their minds.

Clark's cell was located along the short corridor leading into the Forensics unit, about twenty feet from my own office.

Peering into his eight-by-ten cell, I found him sitting on the edge of his bed, dressed in white cotton underwear, staring absentmindedly at a crack in the wall. I stepped back from the door, reluctant to engage him, as if inviting him to speak would somehow unleash an evil spirit.

I bumped into Ron, who had walked up behind me. He grabbed my arm to keep me from falling.

"Vonda, have you asked a deputy to break Clark out?"

"I'd thought about interviewing him here at his cell, through the door."

"You need a face to face with him."

This is my job! I have no choice!

Ron nudged me back toward the door.

On the far wall, to the right of Clark's mirror, was a picture of a small tiger-striped kitten playing with a ball of pink yarn. This picture should only hang on normal, good people's walls, I thought. He had tortured and killed; he couldn't be normal and didn't have the right to anything that was normal.

A metal bed, covered with a thin mattress to provide minimal comfort, sat positioned in the middle of the room. The metal supports of the bed were buried in the non-polished concrete floor and a stainless steel toilet was similarly anchored.

He had the same jailhouse pallor that the rest of the high-profile inmates had. They weren't allowed on the roof for exercise— there weren't enough deputies to protect them from the general population who use it. The jail is a high-rise building in the middle of downtown L.A., and there's no room for another exercise yard.

Appraising Clark's soft looks, it was easy to see why young women didn't feel threatened by him. With his light brown hair, pale eyes, slight build, and serious, but kind face, he didn't look like a killer. He looked like a young doctor or minister.

I thought back to an evening when I worked for Orange County Mental Health in Santa Ana, and a group of us girls went down to the Velvet Turtle for drinks. It was a Friday night, after a hard week. A couple of attorneys—Dan, tall and good-looking, and Fred, short and weasely looking—joined us. We all laughed and relaxed; the men were friendly and pleasant to talk with. At the end of happy hour, Dan asked if anyone could drive them home. He said his car was in the shop and Fred's was at his place. No one offered to help and, having been in that kind of situation myself, I felt badly for him. Then, too, to be honest, I liked the idea of being with two attorneys and doing them a favor. Dan immediately took me up on my offer to help. I felt honored that these educated men would be interested in me; at the time, of course, I didn't see myself as being used.

We drove south to Laguna Beach, up to the top of the hill, and parked in front of a beautiful palatial home. I'd seen the house from the highway below but never dreamed I would be invited into it.

We enjoyed several drinks, and then Dan offered to show me around the rest of his house. Fred was nowhere in sight, so I assumed he had left.

Dan directed me out onto a wooden deck that surrounded the house. Lights twinkled far below and waves crashed on the beach, making me feel like I was in a magical dream. A warm, pleasant breeze surrounded us and played with my hair. Dan began to kiss me gently, tenderly, and then slowly guided me through the French doors that led into his bedroom.

He suggested we undress and go into his hot tub. Because the liquor was doing its job, it seemed like a great idea and I agreed. Dan excused himself, and I started undressing.

"She's…her clothes,   let's…" mumbled voices were coming from somewhere in the house.

The hair on the back of my neck suddenly stood up. *Danger! Fred hadn't left!* I had to get out of there. I dressed quickly, trying to reorient myself. *Where was my car?*

"I thought we were going in the hot tub," Dan said as he walked back into the bedroom.

"It's late. I have to go."

"Vonda, you've had too much to drink. It's not safe for you to drive. You've got to sober up some." Dan put his arms around me, trying to kiss me. I pushed him away.

"It's okay, honey. I just want you to relax."

My head was spinning, and I was unsteady on my feet.

"You'll feel better if you lay down for a little while," Dan said, pushing me down across the bed.

Momentarily, I gave into the comfort of the soft mattress. It felt good to be horizontal. Anyway, how could anything bad happen to me? He was an attorney, living in an expensive home, and my friends had seen us leave together.

Instantly, Fred was in the room. Everything began happening too fast. Dan lay across my chest, holding me down, while Fred ripped my pantyhose off and began thrusting his fist up into my body. The pain was sharp, excruciating. I heard someone screaming in the distance. It startled me. The voice was somehow familiar. Several seconds passed before I realized it was me. I started kicking wildly, hitting and screaming, fighting like a wild animal. I was off the bed, backing up against the wall.

"Goddamn you bastards! You hurt me! You fuckers get away from me!"

Neither moved. I must have been a sight, because they both looked startled. I had the vision of myself as a cat with my claws full out and the fur on my back standing straight up.

Walking toward me, Dan yelled at Fred to get out of the room.

"Don't you come near me, you fucking asshole."

I ran past him and to my car. He didn't follow.

Somehow I managed to drive down the winding road, my tears almost blinding me.

Later, I talked to an attorney and asked about filing charges. He advised against it. "You went there willingly."

I had been assaulted and there wasn't anything I could do about it!

———◆◆◆———

Clark's victims were emotionally needy, vulnerable young women, making them easy targets. He charmed them, gained their confidence, and talked them into going back to his place. That's where his charm ended. I could certainly identify with his female victims, having been victimized myself. But somebody up there was watching over me.

Now, for a little good news to end my story: I ran into Fred—the one that looked like a weasel—a few weeks later in the same bar. After confronting him in a very loud voice, the other patrons knew what he had done to me, and he slithered out quietly. I never saw either of the men again, but I didn't miss a chance to badmouth them every chance I could to anyone who knew them.

———◆◆◆———

"Vonda, you're still here." Ron was standing beside me. "I've had time to walk down to the nurses' station and back with coffee, and you're still staring at the cell door. Are you alright?"

"Just got lost in thought. Thanks."

I walked down the hall to get a john wayne and asked a deputy to bring Clark to my office. There was no reason to keep avoiding the inevitable.

When Clark arrived, he sat in a rigid position and stared at the wall behind my head, reluctant to answer my questions. Fortunately, I was able to glean enough from him to ascertain that he didn't present any suicidal ideation or any signs of schizophrenia; his thoughts were coherent and he didn't suffer from auditory or visual hallucinations. It would have been easier to understand his abhorrent behavior if he had been mentally ill. We'll probably never know what motivated him.

I finished with Clark, called for a deputy to return him to his cell, locked my cell door, and leaned back in my chair, rocking slowly.

Clark was sadistic, getting pleasure out of torturing the women before he finally released their souls to heaven. Necrophilia was one of his favorite perversions, and he liked to joke about how the women couldn't complain of a headache.

The police suspect that Clark killed between 50 and 100 people, but they couldn't prove it. His girlfriend and accomplice, Carol Bundy, said he admitted to her to killing 47 people. The D.A. may have wanted to believe her story because there were many unsolved murders in Los Angeles. If they could tie any of the victims to Clark, they could close some of the cases and file them away.

Like Bianchi and Komerchero, Clark doesn't look like a killer; that's how the public gets fooled. We all have preconceived notions of what the bad guys look like. In the movies, you can always tell the difference—the good guys wear a white hat, and the bad guys wear a black one. Unfortunately, that's not the way it is in real life.

Clark had been arrested for the murders of six women and

judged guilty on numerous counts of mutilation of human remains, mayhem, and murder. His trial now over, he's awaiting sentencing.

Clark, like Jeffrey Dahmer, had a desire to have complete control over his victims. They each wanted to have sex with their mates as long as they wanted and not to be refused anything.

Ron knocked at the door. "You okay?"

"Come on in."

"Remember, we hired you to keep these killers safe—and to keep us off the hot seat."

I remember!

Ron was quite unaffected by the killers. I thought he could have just as easily been dealing with the people who live in Mr. Rogers' Neighborhood. Except here, Mr. Rogers' neighbors littered their lawns with corpses.

CHAPTER 13

HOME AGAIN

County Office
The State Board Exams

Ten crowded rows of desks were lined up across the front of the room with ten desks in each column reaching to the back wall. The room was close to exceeding the fire department's capacity, and the air in the stuffy exam room was ripe with fear. Anxious ghosts from previous doctoral candidates still lingered in every corner of the space and darted between the fluorescent overhead lights.

We all knew that only thirty percent of the people sitting in this room would pass and go on to take the orals to become licensed. Several of my friends had already taken the test and failed it. One man I knew had taken it five times without success. They warned me not to be disappointed if I didn't make it on the first try.

Rubbing my fingers along the weathered wooden desk saturated with perspiration from previous candidates, I prayed to succeed and never have to sit for these exams again. My prayers joined the prayers of all the other hopefuls surrounding me.

The examiner handed out the test booklets and my heart began to race. After opening it and reading the first question which was, What type of neural integration of postural and locomotor movements is carried out by the pyramidal tracts? I spaced out. My anxiety so high that the intellectual portion of my brain was gone. It fled back to the time when my life was full of dreams and happy expectations.

I was back in Needles, California, where I grew up, to a place where I was relaxed and had little responsibility. As a kid, I knew there was more to life than having babies and taking care of a husband and a house. And I wanted more! I wanted to be a psychologist, in my own practice, able to set my own hours and make enough money to never have to worry about paying the bills. Although my dad never had problems holding a job, we were always in debt. I would often hear my parents' worried voices sitting around the kitchen table, discussing getting another loan from a finance company. I didn't want my life to be like that.

From a young age, my mother had me convinced that I wouldn't be capable of taking care of myself. My heart was weakened from the rheumatic fever, and I was a flighty child with problems concentrating on anything. Mother felt I lacked sufficient health or emotional substance to make good life choices. She wanted me to marry a mature man that could take care of me. Jay hadn't been her first choice, but she thought he would provide me with a good life.

From the place I am standing now, I see her in a very different light. I believe she wanted me to have opportunities she had never had. Marrying at fifteen, becoming a mother at sixteen stopped her from seeking her own goals. My father's life became her life. She dropped out of school in the seventh grade and Dad dropped out in the fourth. Although I became a college graduate, my parents were better read and knew more about what was happening in the world than I did.

I wanted to marry a man who kept regular work hours. Because of his job, my father was rarely home for Christmas, Thanksgiving, or my birthday. Also, I wanted a husband that would rescue me from Needles.

As often happens in life, fate stepped into mine when Ernie Pelto walked into the Chinese café where I was working. Although I was still wearing Jay's engagement ring, I fell in love with Ernie at first sight. I realized that these feelings were very different than the ones I had for Jay.

Before the week was over, I returned Jay's ring and explained that we weren't going to make it. Happily, he agreed with me, and we parted as friends.

Ernie was a good looking man; a young William Holden, tall, handsome, calm, introverted. He was twenty-seven and I was seventeen. He saw me as a giggly, teenage flirt, which I readily admit to now.

I invited him home for dinner; he said no. I invited him to church; he said no. He said no! no! no! to my every invitation! However, tenacity happens to be my middle name, and I had decided to marry him.

Ernie always came in with a library book to read while eating. So I contacted a friend who worked at the library and got a list of the books he checked out. She laughed when she heard my plan.

The next time Ernie came into the café, I casually mentioned what I was reading; he was amazed. After trading information on the books, we read for a while I invited him home for dinner again, and this time he agreed.

The appointed night came. Mom helped me fix dinner, and I put on my best Sunday dress. Time passed and no Ernie. He didn't show up and he didn't call to cancel. Angry and disappointed, I wanted to let him know how I felt without alienating him. I sent him a get well card in the hope of eliciting a response. A few days later we ran into each other.

"What's up with the get well card?"

"Well, I know you are too much of a gentleman to stand me up, so obviously you were sick."

The only requirement my parents had for us to marry was that Ernie be baptized in the church. He complied. We married ten months later and moved to Long Beach, California, where Ernie enrolled in college, and I went to work at the Long Beach Naval Shipyard as a keypunch operator to support us. Becoming a psychologist didn't seem to be in the cards for me now.

When we went home for Thanksgiving two months after we married, I cried and told my mother I'd made a mistake and wanted to come home. "Ernie's cold. He doesn't like me."

"Be patient," she said, "it's natural to be homesick, and it takes time to adjust to marriage. Give it some time."

Four years later he had earned a BS degree in engineering and I had given birth to two daughters.

Seven years later, I began to identify with Peggy Lee when she belted out the song "Is That All There Is?" The lyrics of the song echoed around inside my brain like an unrelenting mantra. My childhood dreams and fantasies of what my life would be had melted away like snowflakes. I had done everything God designed for me to do. But my dream wasn't fulfilled. I wasn't a psychologist.

It felt like my life was over.

To the outside world, we looked like Ozzie and Harriet, the ideal family with two daughters, a cat, a dog, and weekly attendance at the Baptist Church. We sang in the choir and taught Sunday school. My parents were very proud of me for having a good Christian home.

Inside our house, my life was very different. Ernie became reclusive, shut me out of his life. He spent endless hours in the garage talking on his Citizen Band Radio, coming to bed long after I was asleep. I felt alone, but afraid to leave him, believing I couldn't make it on my own.

Our biggest problem was that Ernie married a child and when I grew up, we didn't fit together anymore.

After eleven years of a marriage, devoid of love and comfort, the isolation and loneliness had become unbearable. Nothing helped, not even marriage counseling.

I was dying inside, but splitting up a family through divorce was not acceptable. My family and the church would be horrified. To raise the stakes against divorce even higher, my father held the position of Head Deacon in their church, and my mother was a State Sunday School worker. If you're not religious, you might have a problem understanding my feelings.

I couldn't leave him!

After sleeping in the bed with Ernie for an entire year and not being touched by him, I had an aching need deep in my soul. He was more amorous before we married. We would park out on the river road and do it like Bill Clinton and Monica did—you know, the Baptist way: do everything but put it in. When I married Ernie, I was a virgin. My mother had convinced me that if I wasn't, everyone would know and when I walked down the aisle at the church, maybe my dress would even turn black.

Ernie didn't drink or do drugs. He didn't run around with other women. He didn't beat me, and he earned a good living for us. He just couldn't handle an intimate relationship. So how could I consider leaving "such a good man"?

In desperation, I decided to either have an affair, which was contrary to my religious beliefs and training, or enroll in college and work toward my dream. I knew the latter choice would be a smarter option and much more acceptable to both my husband and my parents.

Ernie laughed when I told him about wanting to go to school to become a psychologist; however, he didn't know about my alternative plan.

"You don't know what you're talking about, thinking you could ever get a Ph.D. You won't be able to finish even one course, you are too disorganized." He went on to insinuate that I was an airhead. Much to my chagrin, I was afraid he was right. And there would also be many times in the future when I believed he was right.

"I could start with one class."

"It would be a waste of money," he said and laughed again.

My depression became so intense that I rarely left our home. I stopped functioning and would sit on the couch staring into space for hours, dead inside, unable to justify leaving. Nothing interested me. I started seeing Dr. Wilfred Broadbent, a psychiatrist, who gave me mood elevators and tranquilizers, which helped a little.

As I became more isolated, Ernie spent more time with our

daughters, taking them to the zoo, movies, out to dinner, and anything else that would please them.

One evening after Ernie left with the girls for dinner, I made my decision. I spilled out the Valium onto the bathroom counter beside a crystal glass we had received as a wedding present, and a full bottle of white wine. This seemed to me like the only way out of my pain.

I drank a glass of wine and downed a few pills, showered, put on a nightgown, and poured another glass of wine. Then I settled onto our bed, letting the pills and wine take affect. I poured yet another glass of wine and reached for more pills. Unexpectedly, the mental picture of Deanne and Tera finding my body the next morning flashed through my mind. Ernie always left early for work without waking me. I could visualize my children calling me to come for breakfast. When I didn't respond, they would come into the bedroom to find out what was wrong. They would walk to the bed and try to shake me awake. My God, what if they thought my death was their fault! I could see their stricken faces. I couldn't put them through that pain and trauma. After a lot of debate with myself, I put the rest of the pills back and drank enough wine to pass out. No one ever knew what I had done.

My children would be devastated if I killed myself, so I decided I was going to go to school regardless of what Ernie said.

Ernie finally relented and agreed to me taking an art class. Two of my married girlfriends—Inga, a tall German, and Celina, a short Mexican—enrolled with me, a naïve redheaded gringo, at Long Beach City College. We all had the same syndrome: We felt neglected and needed something else in our lives. Our kids were about the same ages, busy in school, and our husbands worked long hours and were preoccupied with their jobs.

Sitting around Inga's pool one afternoon, drinking wine and smoking cigarettes, we discussed our plights. Actually, I didn't know how to inhale and only puffed on my cigarette, wanting their acceptance. Inga, the most sophisticated of us, suggested for fun that we each choose a teacher to seduce. This was shocking, scary, and exciting. I was fascinated by the idea of having illicit sex but felt guilty that I could even entertain the thought. Would I be able to handle the guilt of being unfaithful? Would God punish me for adulterous behavior? My parents taught me that Jesus was watching me from above at all times, which was a very efficient way to control my behavior.

School didn't satisfy me. It didn't dispel my loneliness or blank out my desire to become a psychologist.

As Inga and Celina continued to reassure me that I didn't have to do anything I didn't want to, the idea sounded less frightening. In the final analysis, Ernie helped me make the decision, even though he didn't know it.

Our daughters were spending some of their summer vacation in Needles with Mother and Dad, which gave us an opportunity for a romantic evening.

Dinner was in the oven ready to serve, candles were glowing on the table, and fresh flowers filled the house with a pleasant aroma. As for me, I was dressed in a red, scanty baby-doll bought for the special occasion.

When I heard Ernie's key in the door lock, I ran to the couch to assume a sexy pose.

He walked in, saw me, and with a look of disgust in his eyes, said, "You're not normal; all you ever think about is sex. And if you ever think I am going to lick your pussy, you are crazy. Only low-class people do that. It's dirty. Now, go put on some clothes."

I sat frozen, feeling like I had been slapped. Was I evil? I slinked off to the bedroom to change my clothes, and then we had a quiet, awkward dinner before going to bed. The incident was never brought up again.

After Ernie's crushing rejection, I felt terribly unattractive and wanted validation that I was desirable.

Chris was the only straight man in my art class, and had made it clear on several occasions that he wanted me to go to bed with him. He was attractive and didn't pressure me—he just offered me the opportunity.

Week after week I spent my therapy sessions with Dr. Broadbent, trying to decide if I should go to a motel with Chris or not. The semester was coming to a close and if I didn't make up my mind soon, school would be over and Chris would be gone. This would be my last chance. I would go to my grave having slept with only Ernie. A week before school was out for the semester, Dr. Broadbent asked me if I thought other people ever had affairs. All of a sudden, I had my answer.

The last day of class I told Chris I wanted to go to bed with him. Ernie thought I was going to meet some of my classmates later in the evening for coffee.

It was already getting dark, pouring rain when I drove into the motel's parking lot and pulled to a stop beside Chris' car. The place wasn't a five-star; instead, it was one of those places that rent rooms out by the hour. Chris motioned that he would go into the office and get a key. I waited in the car, shivering.

The room was stark with a big bed that looked like it had a firm mattress, one night stand with a green chipped lamp sitting on it, and a fifteen-inch TV on a small wooden stand.

I excused myself and headed for the bathroom. I got my diaphragm in place and then started worrying about messing up the curly wiglet sitting on the top of my head. Ernie might notice if I came home all disheveled. Then I let out a nervous giggle, realizing how scared I was.

I finally took my curls off and set them on top of the lamp. Then we had sex! In the missionary position! And it wasn't much different from doing it with Ernie.

It was a good thing it didn't take long because when I lifted up my hairpiece, it was getting singed. That hairpiece got a lot hotter than I did. The evening wasn't romantic, not anything like in the movies, where the camera zooms in on the girl, crushing a flower in her hand and the music swelling in the background. This was nothing! The sex was nothing! Most surprising to me, I didn't feel guilty, didn't feel anything! I never saw Chris again and never told Ernie what I had done.

After the experience with Chris, I thought about what Celina and Inga had suggested and decided to pursue the idea.

I was fearful of taking academic classes so continued with art. But since my instructors were gay, taking art classes made it difficult to choose a likely candidate. Inga and Celina, however, didn't have the same problem. Inga chose Bill, her history teacher, and Celina chose her political science teacher, whose name was also Bill. Since I was seeing Dr. Broadbent, he became my target. Coincidentally, his name was Bill, too. The song "Marry Me Bill" became our theme song!

We lounged by Inga's pool several times a week, discussing our progress and planning the next strategies. It was great fun. After being raised Southern Baptist and having such a restricted life, this was like Heaven—well, maybe that's not an appropriate comparison.

Celina went on to marry her Bill several years later, and is still married to him. Inga denied that she ever slept with hers, which Celina and I didn't believe even for a minute.

Dr. Bill Broadbent spent a couple of afternoons a week at County General Hospital in downtown L.A., teaching psychiatric interns. On his way to work, he would pick me up at the Carson Street Bowling Alley parking lot and drive us to the hospital where I would drop him off. I would then drive off in his big black Fleetwood Cadillac and go to the flower district to shop. At a prearranged time, I would pick him up, and then go by a liquor store to buy some snacks and Hublein canned vodka tonics to enjoy while driving back to Long Beach.

Coming back from the hospital, we would often drive over to the Virginia Country Club and crawl into the backseat. One afternoon while we were in the throes of it all, Bill lifted up and said, "Don't look now, but the gardener is headed this way." Fortunately, the gardener was accustomed to this type of carrying on by other members of the country club and was too much of a gentleman to disturb us.

Bill once told me that I seemed very complicated when all

I really needed was to be loved. And I did feel loved by him. Unfortunately, he wasn't available because he was married. We never discussed him leaving his wife. I didn't want to destroy his marriage, and felt I wasn't taking anything away from his wife as long as we were very discreet and I didn't make any demands. Now I realize if my husband had an affair with another woman, I wouldn't tolerate it.

After one year, my affair with Bill ended when he met Nancy and moved in with her. In spite of being shocked and hurt by his choice, we remained friends, but never lovers again. After living with Nancy for a year, he was still torn with guilt over leaving his wife. One evening he took me out for a drink and talked about his feelings he asked me what he should do. I couldn't give him an answer. All I could say was that if after a year he still felt guilty about leaving his wife, what made him think he wouldn't still feel the same way a year from now?

As far as I know, his wife never knew about me. She and I became friends and spent time together after Bill left her, and me. Sometimes I wanted to laugh when I was comforting her over her loss. It was one thing for him to betray his wife, but to betray his mistress, too? What a jerk! Later, Bill went home to his wife; she accepted him back, and they left town. She was an amazing lady.

Ernie and I separated a short time later, and I was determined to make it on my own! Financially, the timing could not have been worse for me; but emotionally, it was a tremendous relief.

Thirty-three years passed before I learned that Ernie suspected me of having an affair. It happened after my mother's death. Among her receipts and birthday cards, I found a letter addressed to her from Ernie. He had written that he suspected I was carrying on with a guard who worked at North American Aviation where he was also employed. It's always been a mystery to me where he came up with that idea. I never had an occasion to go where he worked, much less get to know someone there well enough to have an affair. Ernie went on to say that he called my psychiatrist, Bill, and asked for his advice, wondering if he should talk to the personnel office and report the man he suspected, or confront me with his suspicions. Bill told Ernie that it wouldn't be a good idea to confront either of us; instead, he advised him to let me end the affair when I was ready. Since I was actually having the affair with Bill, I would love to have heard that conversation.

I don't know why Ernie thought a guard where he worked was my lover. But I didn't ask him. Thank God he didn't follow through with the plan and get some poor, innocent man in trouble.

Had Ernie confronted me I would have told him the truth.

Now, as I look back, I see how immature my behavior was. I was a coward and have always been sorry that I didn't separate from him much earlier. I never confessed the affair to him; seems confession is only good for the person having the affair, because it helps them resolve their own guilt feelings. Spouses really don't want to know about an affair, it's less painful.

"Time! Pass your test booklets to the front," I was brought back to reality, and was barely three-quarters of the way through. I was frantic and started filling in the bubbles as fast as I could, hoping to make some lucky guesses.

Vonda, what in the hell is wrong with you? You let your mind wander instead of concentrating on the test. You're not going to pass! Next time, you have got to keep it together!

CHAPTER 14

BACK TO THE GRIND

On a Saturday morning three months later, the test results finally arrived. My hands literally shook, holding the letter with its official seal stamped in the left-hand corner. It was literally a notice that could change my life. When my eyes fell on the first line, my heart sank. In very polite but official language, the form letter read: "We regret to inform you that you have failed the California State Board Exams. Please contact the agency to obtain information regarding the next scheduled exam. The phone number is..." I really wasn't surprised about the results, tears blurred my vision and I couldn't read the rest. I walked to the kitchen and poured a glass of wine. Over the past few months, I had ignored my children and my life and had not been successful. I returned to the living room and dropped the letter on the coffee table, not even bothering to note the phone number. I didn't want to think of the next time. Right now I wanted a hot fudge sundae, my favorite comfort food.

———

It was Monday again and time to go back to the jail. Passing my neighbors' houses on the way to the San Gabriel Freeway, I joined the other commuters already in the process of driving to work. The traffic turned out to be typical stop-and-go as I drove north into the city, even though the Eye In The Sky helicopter hadn't reported any accidents.

Reaching down, I twisted the radio knob on, hoping to catch a traffic report. In case of an accident, it might be necessary to take an alternate route.

The traffic slowed abruptly, redirecting my attention back to the road, and I hit the brakes just in time to keep from rear-ending the car in front of me.

The radio announcer was finishing a story about Ken Bianchi: "In the Hillside murder case, today Judge Ronald George stated that he will announce his findings next week after closing arguments from the defense's motion to exclude all hypnosis-induced testimony from the murder trial of Angelo Buono. Bianchi, thirty, told authorities he and Buono committed the ten sex-related murders and offered to testify against his adoptive cousin in order to avoid the death penalty in the two murders he had committed in Bellingham, Washington."

As I sat in the bumper-to-bumper traffic, I recalled that when Bianchi's mother was young, she had few skills to make a living. Out of desperation, she went into prostitution, and Bianchi was born out of one of those unions.

During grad school, when I was desperate for money, I was dating William Newhauser, a V.P. with the accounting firm of Arthur Anderson, a firm that only dealt with the whales of business. He was fourteen years older than me, sophisticated, and rich. His fingernails were manicured. And he wore Ferragamo shoes. We dined at fancy, exclusive, pricey restaurants—the best that the Los Angeles area had to offer. Certainly places I could never otherwise afford. Usually, I would eat a sandwich before dinner so I could take a doggie bag home to my girls.

William taught me which fork to use and introduced me to caviar and escargot. He even took me to La Costa, an expensive resort, for the weekend. He exposed me to a new world. I grew up a lot while dating him.

William knew I had limited funds and for that reason, he suggested we skip dinner on our next date, meet at a hotel, and he would give me the cash instead.

I wasn't quite sure how I felt about his suggestion, and was too embarrassed to ask my girlfriends what they thought. But after shuffling through my bills spread out on the kitchen counter, I decided to go along with his suggestion.

The night arrived that we were to meet. I pulled on the most expensive black nylons I could afford, hot pants, black shining high heels, caked on the makeup, looked at myself in the mirror, and saw a prostitute staring back at me. I didn't like the image and was glad my daughters weren't home to see me.

The chiming clock announced that it was five o'clock. I grabbed my purse and drove to the Airporter Inn, where he would be waiting with a bottle of booze.

When I grew up, we didn't have Nancy Drew mysteries, Tom Sawyer adventures, or Elizabeth Barrett Browning in our home. Mom was sixteen when my brother was born and she didn't have time to read the classics. Her reading consisted of True Story, True Confession, and True Romance magazines, the same as mine. I knew what was expected of a prostitute.

William and I had been making love together for several months. I tried to convince myself this wouldn't be much different. It was like a dress-up game. My parents certainly wouldn't approve, but the money was so tempting.

William would probably pay me about the same amount he spent on our dinners out, I thought, and they always cost at least one hundred dollars—sometimes even more.

He opened the door of the hotel room, wearing only his white underwear, his body odor permeating the air.

Tonight he treated me differently, rougher, and more demanding; not at all concerned about my needs or comfort. This wasn't making love. This didn't feel good. I didn't understand why this was so different.

He wanted me to do things he had never asked me to do before. I felt I had to comply. After all, he had paid for me!

After he was satisfied, I felt dirty, ashamed, and desperate to get away from him. At the door, he pulled out his billfold and laid two tens and one five dollar bill on the palm of my hand. I looked down at the bills and then up to his face. He seemed satisfied with our arrangement and wanted to set up another date. I made no comment. Our whole relationship was a fraud. I was only worth twenty-five dollars. I wasn't even a first-class hooker to him.

Standing under the hot shower, tears ran down my cheeks as I struggled to wash the odor of his body off my skin.

Ken Bianchi's mother must have felt like I did the first time she prostituted herself. Desperate and ashamed! Luckily for me, I was getting an education and would have many options in life. I vowed that night to become self-sufficient—and to never be at the mercy of another man, ever again!

CHAPTER 15

LONG DONG HOLMES

It was a Monday in early December. I remember that day in particular because that's the day I met John Holmes, the King of Porn, for the first time.

I had learned the routine of gaining entrance into the jail. Stand patiently for admittance in and out of the sally port, pick up the key, and wait for a deputy to ride with me up to the second floor. It took ten minutes to complete the process, but I didn't feel the same impatience. I understood who held the power, and didn't fight it.

When the elevator doors pulled open again on my floor, the sound grabbed the Hillside Strangler's attention, who was talking on the pay phone just outside my office. It seemed Ken Bianchi spent more time out of his cell than in it.

"Good morning, Dr. Pelto, can you see me right away? It's real important," he asked. Before I could answer him, I heard my phone ringing, rushed to the door, struggled to get it open, and pulled the receiver off the cradle on the fifth ring.

"Dr. Pelto, this is Deputy Jerger in 1700. Holmes says he's got to see you as soon as you get in; sounds urgent." Holmes had been arrested the week before, accused of bludgeoning four people to death in Laurel Canyon, California.

The morning was off to a fast pace. I hadn't had my first john wayne, and things were already popping.

I called back over my shoulder to Bianchi, saying he could come by later, and took the elevator back down to the main floor.

The first pornographic film I had ever seen starred John Holmes. It was while working at Orange County Mental Health back in 1977. At the time, there was still a lot of concern about mental health professionals being able to handle any type of sexual material presented during a therapy session without registering embarrassment. Patients needed a comfortable atmosphere in which to discuss any topic.

The administration wanted all of the clinicians to be shockproof. Even free love and open marriages were still being practiced and discussed. Couples involved in wife swapping and multiple partners during group sex often found they couldn't handle the situations and sought counseling. When they requested our help, we had to deal with them with complete aplomb.

To become desensitized, our staff shut down the psychiatric day treatment program every Friday afternoon, sent the psychotic patients home, and settled down to watch what were considered training or desensitization films. The administration felt the best way for us to become immune to explicit sexual material was to be flooded with it. This type of film was also being shown at the American Psychological Association conventions. The showings were always well attended.

Let me tell you, when they suggested we watch the porn films, no one argued, This was some fun time to be working in the mental health field!

The county hospitals kept pornographic films in their libraries for this purpose. A man working with us had a friend at Orange County Medical Center where they had a great library of these "educational films." Each week, he picked up a few for our training. Sometimes, after a long hard week, we included wine with our training sessions.

John Holmes was our favorite. He was made famous because of his God-given endowment. Thirteen-and-one-half inches long! His adult films made the male staff feel intimidated and the female staff extremely impressed. Many of his films can still be seen in the kind of movie theaters that make raincoats available for your use, along with your ticket.

Now Holmes was housed one floor below me, and I was on my way to meet him. I could hardly believe it, and wondered if I would find out if the films depicted his true dimensions or if they had been doctored or enhanced in some way.

"You Aint Nothin' but a Hounddog" blared out. I felt strange, tingly, and wanted to laugh while walking to the door of 1700.

Deputy Jerger opened the outer door to the High Power module after my third knock, allowing me into a room that resembled an air lock, dimly lit, measuring about four feet wide and five feet long. Each end of the enclosure was sealed with a locked metal door with a small window embedded in it. The second door opened into the main cellblock after the exterior door was secured. This is the most secure area in the jail, and houses the majority of the High Power inmates.

"Thanks for getting down here so quickly," the deputy said. "The Wadd has been bugging me since five a.m."

"John Holmes?"

"Yeah, Johnny Wadd, long dong? Trouser trout?" He watched for my reaction as we walked to the deputy's booth. I kept a poker face.

"That's what you call him?"

"Yep. That's some of his AKAs. If you've ever seen any of his films, you'll know what I mean." I knew what he meant. "Do you want to look over Holmes' log first?"

Yes, I would love to. I nodded and followed him into the glass-enclosed deputy's booth.

"You want a cup, babe?"

"You betcha. Make it a john wayne." The uniform poured the coffee and set it down on the desk beside me.

"Shit, Holmes is restless," the deputy said. "You'd think he was still snorting coke." I figured he still was—he probably got better stuff in here than he did out on the street.

"He bragged to one of the night shift guys that he had a real expensive habit on the outside, and offered the deputy some big bucks to smuggle some in."

"What did the deputy say?"

"Well, of course he told Holmes that wasn't possible." After hearing of the prevalence of drugs in the jail, I wondered if the deputy had refused him, but I wasn't going to say anything.

I put the coffee aside and perused the log. It reported that Holmes didn't sleep well and was having a difficult time adjusting to incarceration.

I walked over and added some hot coffee to my cup.

"He's been crawlin' the walls since the day he got booked in here. He's been whining, saying he'll go crazy if we keep him locked up."

"He gets time out of the cell everyday, doesn't he?"

"All these perps do. Twenty minutes a day freeway time, but that wasn't enough for the Wadd. He wanted to jus' walk around the module whenever he wanted. We told him no.

"He doesn't believe in following the rules. Thinks he's hot shit since he's got that monster schlong." I wondered if I'd ever see it. My early Baptist training and my female curiosity were at odds.

"Long Dong started pushing to be a trustee. Finally, we gave in. Shit, we were just plain tired of listening to him bellyache."

"He calm down then?"

"Yeah, but damn if one of the other jokers didn't attack him; tried to gouge Holmes' eyes out with a pencil."

"Was he hurt badly?"

"No. But scared the holy shit out of him. He's real nervous, now. We locked him down again for his own protection."

"The letter Holmes wrote to Lieutenant Chandler demanding more time out of his cell made the rounds upstairs."

"John's a crazy man, offered to clean the toilets if it meant more time out of his seven by nine. We caved! Gave him a push broom to sweep the enclosed freeway in front of his cell—hope that works off some of his nervous energy."

Before I had a chance to ask if that helped, the phone rang.

The deputy jerked it up and spoke loudly into the receiver.

"Yeah, who do you need? Oh shit! They didn't get him on the bus this a.m.? What time's his hearing? Shit, what do you want me to do about it? Sure, sure. I can handle that. Don't get your sphincter all puckered up. I'll call Transportation and get Buono over there by one o'clock."

The deputy made a few calls, nodded an apology to me for the interruption, and left the booth, slamming the door behind him. I didn't know if the door locked automatically. The room was brightly lit with reinforced glass on three sides, and anyone inside was easily visible to the rest of the module. It felt like I was on display, like a piece of meat hanging on a meat hook in a food locker.

"Hey, sweetcheeks, you wanta fuck?" An inmate I didn't recognize had extended his arms into the open window, pointing his middle finger at me. Feeling vulnerable, I looked around the area, hoping to find a place of safety in case he tried to come in. There was no safe place. Trying to calm myself by ignoring him didn't work. My heart was pounding wildly.

At last, two deputies came into view, escorting Angelo Buono. The offending inmate walked away immediately. I wanted to tell the deputies what he had done in the hopes he would be punished. Then I remembered this is a men's jail. We females are just tolerated. Taking a deep breath didn't slow my racing pulse.

Buono, the Hillside Strangler, looked smaller and meaner in person than he did on the television news reports. He was on my list of high-profile inmates, but I had stalled setting up an interview with him. He looked like a gray, bloodless snake.

As Buono walked past the booth, we made eye contact and I could have sworn he hissed at me. Obviously, my imagination was working overtime.

The deputies exited the cellblock, with Buono handcuffed, walking between them. Deputy Jerger returned to the booth, and I relaxed a little. I didn't know if I could stand this job much longer.

"That guy is a real adam henry," the deputy said as he sat down and engaged the computer screen. After a few false starts, Angelo Buono's file came into view. "Shit, sure enough, court date's right here. Night staff must have been jerking each other off and didn't notice he had a date with the judge this a.m." The uniform didn't face me, and seemed to be talking to the air.

"Asshole has a hard-on for everyone, and don't talk to anyone except his attorney. Sits in his cell all day and broods. Doesn't even want to come out for his freeway time. Hope they fry Buono's ass!"

I sneezed and the uniform turned to face me, suddenly aware of my presence.

"You ready to see Holmes?" he asked a little sheepishly.

"Sure." I didn't make eye contact.

"Follow me. Take a look for yourself. You be the judge."

I didn't have time to finish reading the log. I could do it later.

I drank the last of the coffee, dropped the Styrofoam cup in the wastepaper basket, and followed the deputy out of the booth, my high heels pounding on the cement floor. We walked past the interview room and through another locked door into a darkened hallway with one-way windows that extended along the entire length. It allowed an uninterrupted view of the seven cells that lay beyond. The inmates were housed in standard jail cells, with a wall of bars opening onto another narrow corridor, which ran parallel to the one in which we were standing.

"Have you met Holmes yet?"

"Not personally. I am, however, familiar with his artistic work."

The deputy gave me a knowing look, and I immediately regretted allowing this virtual stranger into my private life.

"Holmes kept a family of cockroaches in a little box, and a pet rat, until it got away. Another inmate caught it and for spite, flushed it down the toilet. Holmes offered ten dollars to anyone who would catch another one for him." It was strange thinking of a famous porn star being lonely enough to want a rat and a cockroach for pets. "He took good care of them, even shared his meals with them," the deputy said.

"Holmes is on edge. If he's convicted, he could face the death penalty.

"The killer, or killers, whatever, used lead pipes and baseball bats to beat these four people to death. The victims' heads had striated patterns from the pipes on their skulls. And the house was a bloody mess. This is a special circumstances case: multiple murders and murders committed during a robbery."

"Do you think he'll be convicted?"

"Can't say, but there's a hell of a lot of evidence stacked up against him. He's gonna be with us for a while 'cause he's been denied bail."

Judge Mayerson granted a two-week delay in Holmes' arraignment. His court-appointed attorney, Howard Gillingham, needed some time to become familiar with the case. Holmes wouldn't be entering a plea until December 22.

I watched through the window as the porn star frantically wielded a push broom up and down the length of the narrow hallway. Holmes was tall, lanky, and looked like a prisoner of war with hardly enough meat to cover his long bones. His eyes and movements were intense, as if he had ghosts in his head propelling him back and forth. He was oblivious to the catcalls and lewd remarks being shouted at him by the other inmates housed in the block.

Having watched some of his films, it was difficult to believe that he could be capable of such horrible murders. His portrayal in the movies showed a rather comical character playing a detective; he didn't come across as a violent person. I didn't trust my judgment anymore. We all have the capability of hiding our dark sides. Not even the most insightful therapist in the world can uncover our secrets if we don't want them to.

"He'll sweep that floor for hours," the deputy said, interrupting my thoughts. "Or until we lock him back down in his cell. He's high energy…guess you could say frantic."

We stood watching Holmes propel the bristle broom back and forth, amazed at his concentration.

"Have you seen enough, ma'am?" The deputy walked to the door and was turning his key in the lock.

"I'd like to talk with him now." My pulse sped up at the prospect.

We left the observation room, and the deputy escorted me back down the hall to the interview room and unlocked the door. I entered the brightly lit space, which also doubled as a barbershop, walked over to the wooden desk that faced the concrete wall, sat down, and waited for the deputy to return with Holmes. I felt keyed up and edgy. I didn't want to look unintelligent with this famous person. Then I reminded myself that he was an inmate, accused of violent murders, and I was the professional. But I fluffed my hair up anyway and then laughed at my vanity.

The deputy arrived with Holmes a short time later, the uniform leading the way. Holmes entered the room with a casual air as if he were walking onto a movie set, turned to me, and flashed a rakish grin.

"Okay, homeboy, in the chair," the deputy's voice was brusque. "You know the drill."

Holmes gave the deputy a puzzled look as he placed his foot on the metal stair and stepped up into the barber chair. He adjusted himself into a comfortable position and looked around the room.

"Give me your wrist."

Holmes smiled at me like this was all a big joke.

The deputy didn't seem amused. Instead, he pulled his cuffs and brandished them toward Holmes as if they were a gun.

"Mr. Holmes, put your left wrist on the arm of the chair."

Holmes reluctantly extended his wrist, giving the deputy a cocky smile. After the uniform efficiently cuffed John down, he retreated from the room without a word to me, and shoved the windowless metal door hard against the wall. The sound echoed through the cement room.

Holmes didn't know the drill yet, but in the months ahead, he would become familiar with it.

I warned him that whatever we discussed wouldn't be confidential since the door was open and the deputies would be stopping by to listen. John waved me off with a dismissive air.

"No problem."

He sat in a relaxed position with his long legs spread wide open. He had several days of whisker growth and needed a shave. Soft sandy-colored hair lay in ringlets around his forehead and his blue eyes shined out from a gaunt face, giving me a carnivorous look. Starting with my black pumps, his eyes moved slowly up my crossed legs to the soft, pale blue jersey dress to rest on my breasts. I felt unnerved.

"Dr. Pelto, you're an attractive woman. How do you see yourself on a scale of one to ten?"

Was my face as red as my hair?

"The deputy said you needed to see me right away."

"What's your first name?"

"Dr. Pelto."

"Are you married?"

"Mr. Holmes, we're here to talk about you."

"Call me John. Doc, I'm hoping we can see a lot of each other while I'm here." He winked and flashed his cocky grin.

"Do you have kids? I never did. I'm kinda sorry now," John said.

"Yes, I do."

"How old are they?"

"My youngest..."

He caught me off-guard. We weren't on a date! I had to remain detached and not be seduced by his charm. Oh yes, he was charming in a cute boyish way. But he was accused of bludgeoning four people to death. I was behaving like a star-struck teenager. I took a deep breath, trying to slow my fast pulse and collect my thoughts. *Vonda, get a grip on yourself!*

"The deputy said you needed to see me right away. From the way he was talking, I thought you were in crisis. Are you?"

"Yeah," he gave me a seductive grin, "I wanted someone to talk with. I'm bored. It gets so lonely in my cell."

"You have inmates on either side of you to talk with."

"Shit, we have nothing in common. I enjoy reading. All those fuckers do is burp and fart.

They're crude. Those assholes are curious about me. Every time I walk over to the pisser to take a leak, they try to get a peak at me. They holler and call me names. They're always asking me what it's like to make love to all those women. I tell them that what I do in those films is acting; it sure as hell isn't making love. Actually, I've only made love to five women in my life."

"Only five women?" I raised my eyebrows and gave him a questioning look. "With all of the women you have known in and out of your films? Only five?"

Bullshit! I thought.

"Yeah. I just fucked all the rest. It wasn't making love. Sometimes, after we finished a shoot, we'd go in the shower and have some pretty good sex, but that's not making love, either. Shit, most women I met are real ball busters. Actually, I think they all are bull dykes. Believe me—it takes an Academy Award performance to keep it up with those bitches."

Before I had time to catch myself, I blurted out, "How do you manage to, ah, keep it, ah…?" *Oh, damn! Why don't you keep your mouth shut?*

"Up? Ah, hard-on? Ah, woody? Ah, boner? With my praying one-eyed monk? Is that what you're trying to ask?" I looked back at him just in time to catch his mischievous grin.

"You look real cute when you blush."

I broke off eye contact, shifted around in my chair to face the wall, and reached for an Intake Form. Let's face it—he was sure as hell lots more fun to talk with than the other killers I saw.

"Mr. Holmes, do you have any brothers or sisters?"

"Yes, Dr. Pelto, I have one sister and two brothers. I, myself, resulted from my parents having a real good fuck." *He loves to try and shock me.*

Dealing with him was like being involved in a tennis match.

I was here to make sure he wasn't suicidal. Anything we talked about helped me make a determination about his mental state.

I wanted to make him feel comfortable; funny, I was the one squirming around.

"Were you raised in an intact family?"

Holmes began to laugh. "Come on, Doc, what's your first name?"

"Doctor."

"Now, don't be offended. I'm just trying to be friendly. Look, I know what I do for a living may not be acceptable to you, but it's what I do."

"Mr. Holmes, I have no negative feelings about you or what you do for a living. How did you get started in the adult film business?"

"I needed the dough. Dropped out of high school before graduation and joined the Army, served three years in West Germany. Afterwards, I came out here to California and kinda bummed around with a bunch of different jobs, ambulance driving, warehouseman, and door-to-door salesman. In my third year at UCLA, I got an offer to pose for some nude shots. I did. Shit, why not? I knew my schlong was real impressive. The pay wasn't great, but it helped my budget."

"How did you transition from nude photographs into making films?" John reached up and pushed several curls out of his eyes.

"An adult film producer saw some of my shots. We talked for a while, then he wanted a look at my credentials." John looked down at his crotch. "He liked what he saw and hired me on the spot, impressed with my talent." John broke into laughter. "So impressed that he wrote a three-page script that night. Can you believe it? He made a film starring me the next day. After that, I was making a film a day."

"Did you finish your degree?"

"Got it in English, but I liked making films a lot better."

"It sounds like you've had a lot of success in your career, and that you're proud of it."

"Have you seen my work?"

"Yes," I said quietly, hoping he wouldn't ask me if I enjoyed watching him, because I did. Holmes gave me a knowing smile.

"I've been in the biz about thirteen years and made more than two thousand films. Worked with some of the top female sex stars and made two thousand bucks a day. It's been good for my ego." He began to slap his legs together. I didn't know if he was getting excited, but I was.

"When I was in junior high school gym class, some of the other guys would look at me and say I had a bigger cock than their dads did. That bothered me back then. Guess it made me shy, and I never had many friends growing up. Guess you could say I was a loner."

"John, do you ever get so depressed that you think of injuring yourself?"

"No. Are you kidding? Honey, I'm not going to kill myself, if that's what you're worried about. I've got too much to live for."

"Are you nervous about the murder trial?"

"I'm innocent, so why would I be nervous?"

I kept a straight face. *Right, you're innocent!*

"Excuse me, ma'am." A deputy hit the office door with his hand and stood leaning against the doorframe.

"Dr. Pelto, Mr. Holmes' attorney is here to see him. Could you see Bonin while you're here?" *Thanks for not calling me babe.*

The deputy released the cuff from John's arm and placed them in his belt. Holmes stepped down from the chair and stretched. He walked slowly to the doorway and swiveled around.

"Dr. Pelto, will you see me again soon? I really do need to talk to you."

I nodded in the affirmative, and the Wadd strolled out of the room.

CHAPTER 16

DOC, YOU'VE BECOME
REAL POPULAR

"Deputy, bring Bonin on in whenever you get a chance. I have time to see him." I walked over to the deputy's booth and tapped on the window to get someone's attention. After the Senior unlocked the door, I stepped in and poured a cup of coffee.

"So, what do you think about the Wadd?" he asked.

"Well, he's an interesting dude and quite a flirt."

"I suppose he told you he's innocent." Both of us started laughing.

"You up for Bonin today?"

"Sure."

"He's been wanting to talk with you. Pelto, you're real popular with these perps."

"Right now, I'm just waiting for Deputy Jerger to break him out of his cell."

"Have you met him?" the deputy asked.

"This will be my first interview with him."

"He's a real mutha. Unbelievably cruel. He grudge-fucked those kids."

"I haven't heard that expression before. What's that?"

"Bonin would upend a kid and then cobhole him without any lubrication. The kids would bleed. That animal tore them all up. He got off hearing them scream." The deputy's face contorted. "I hope that sucker burns in hell."

Me too!

I exited the booth with my john wayne and began to pace back and forth in front of the interview office. I identified with Holmes, needing to move around a little, stretch my legs, and clear my head.

The media blared out the news that Bonin was accused of multiple homicides, and had sodomized, tortured, and killed as many as forty-four boys in Los Angeles and Orange County over the last two years. Fear reigned throughout the southern portion of California, and the manhunt for the Freeway Killer had been rigorous. Now, with his trial coming to a conclusion, he was close to learning his fate.

As with any group of people, there is a pecking order. Not surprisingly, the jail is no exception. Sexual molesters are on the bottom of the food chain and are often abused by other inmates. Usually, the deputies keep a man's crime a secret, especially the ones involved in sex crimes. The general population considers these men slimeballs. I'd heard of a few times when a deputy let it leak out—accidentally, of course—that a perp was here on a charge of child molestation.

Not long before I hired into the jail, a Mentally Disordered Sex Offender (MDSO) was murdered by a group of inmates. It happened during the deputies' shift change. The inmates saw the man headed down to the showers and followed him. Apparently, they had been waiting for an opportunity to get him. They cornered the guy in the shower and took turns grudge-fucking him first. Then they beat him. They killed him by ramming a spoon up his rectum. He had bled to death internally before anyone knew, and was found lying in a pool of blood.

I turned to see Bonin closing in on me, with the deputy walking slowly behind. He moved to the side and allowed the deputy to pass in front of him to unlock the door.

Bonin didn't look like what I expected. I guess I envisioned him having horns or "serial killer" written across his forehead. He just didn't look like a killer. However, when he talked about the murders later, he sounded like one and gave me a queasy feeling.

Bonin was a beefy man, standing five-feet-ten-inches, with unkempt brown hair and a heavy mustache. His stride was slow and deliberate, with his rounded shoulders slumped forward. He walked with his head down, studying the cold cement floor.

When he arrived at the doorway to the interview room, I stepped aside to let him pass in front of me. He reeked of body odor.

The deputy trailed us into the claustrophobic room while Bonin went directly to the barber chair and, without instruction, stepped up into the brown leather seat, settling himself down gingerly. He positioned his left arm and waited quietly for the deputy to pull his cuffs and anchor his wrist to the chair. The deputy efficiently clamped them shut and exited the room.

The office was stuffy and the bright light from the overhead fluorescent tubes made the room seem even hotter than it was.

Bonin turned to where I was seated. Both of his eyes were blackened, his face had multiple contusions, and his nose was broken—the results of a harsh beating. With each of his movements, he winced with pain.

The pounding had occurred while Bonin was in a holding cell at the Criminal Courts Building, under the sheriff's protection. He had been taken there for the final arguments in his case, along with Angelo Buono, the accused Hillside Strangler, and John Stinson, a reputed member of the Aryan Brotherhood. The three men were placed in the same cell.

"Mr. Bonin, I'm Dr. Pelto. I work in the Forensic Outpatient unit on the second floor. I don't have anything to do with the court or legal system. I'm here for you to talk with, about anything you'd like. However, we don't have the privilege of confidentiality." My whole canned spiel. He nodded, letting me know it was no problem.

"Shit, it doesn't matter what I tell you now. I've already been convicted. So go ahead and ask away. Ask anything you like." His attitude surprised me.

"The deputy said you had fallen and might want someone to talk with."

Bonin reached up and touched his blackened eyes.

"I didn't fall; that bastard beat me up! Stinson grabbed me and shoved me into the wall, and then he started punching me in the gut. He broke my nose. Blood poured out all over the place and I thought I was gonna be sick. I tried to defend myself. I couldn't. That Stinson must be workin' out, cause he's real strong."

"Didn't the deputies hear what was happening? Didn't they come to help you?"

"Nah! They don't give a fuck. While he was beatin' me, Buono, he was in the cell with us, he just lay there and watched, kinda smiling, like he thought I was gettin' what I deserved. That asshole didn't lift a finger to help me. Shit, Buono's no angel, either. He's up for killin' all those women. I read in the paper he tortured a bunch of 'em, too." I shifted in the hard wooden chair.

"I didn't really expect him to help me." Bill leaned down and rested his head in his hand. "In my life, I never had nobody to help me. My father used to beat the shit out of me. My mother never stopped him. She put me in one of those boy's homes, and I got raped by these older guys."

Bonin looked pathetic with his blackened eyes and bruised face.

"Why did you say you fell? Stinson should be punished for what he did."

Bonin smiled at my innocence.

"Look, Doc, that's not the way things go 'round here. When the deputy finally came by the cell, he saw me layin' on the floor, holdin' bloody toilet paper to my nose. He noticed Stinson's knuckles were bruised. He knew damn well what went down. Shit, he didn't do nothin' 'bout it. He probably thinks I deserved the beating, too."

"Are you okay now?" I struggled to keep my face immobile. Remembering what I had read about the killings, maybe he did deserve it.

"Yeah. They took me over to the County Hospital and x-rayed me. The doctor thought I might have a concussion, but I didn't. They said my nose would heal and I didn't have anythin' else broke. They sent me back to the jail. My whole body is real sore. I ache all over."

Bonin had been beaten up on several occasions and said that this probably wouldn't be the last time. Child molesters are on the bottom of the food chain in the jail. The lowest of the low are the men who violate boys.

"I guess all these assholes think they got some right to a piece of me. I'm bein' punished for what I did. I figure they want me to say I'm sorry for killing those boys, but how can I say that when I couldn't stop myself—I had to do it. It wasn't my fault."

I was stunned by his admission and didn't know how to respond. Did he want me to tell him he should be excused for killing those boys? As a psychologist, I understood the concept of being driven by poor impulse control to commit unbelievable acts; but as a human being, I couldn't pretend to excuse his behavior. It was hard to stay nonjudgmental, but I had to if I was going to be able to work with him.

I suggested to Bonin that he ask the deputy to put him in an individual cell the next time he went to court. Bonin covered his mouth. I thought he was about to cough, then I realized he was muffling a laugh.

Bonin said, "Doc, you're too much. They're not going to listen to me. They don't give a shit."

His attorney wanted the court to postpone his trial until all of the injuries were healed, but the court wasn't willing to wait that long.

When meeting with him, a sense of sadness washed over me. And at times, it was difficult to believe he had committed the horrific crimes he had confessed to. When he talked about being beaten by another inmate, I thought he would cry—not so much for the beating, but because no one came to help him. No one cared about him. No one comforted him. He was scared and alone. Listening to him, I shared some of these same feelings. Being single and working to support my two daughters while going to school, I often felt scared and alone, especially when there wasn't enough money to pay the rent and there was no one to help me.

Bonin let me see his vulnerable side—a human side—one that we all have in common. He was a damaged, lost child that hadn't gotten the care he needed while growing up. His parents were poorly equipped to raise their three sons. His mother spent most of her time at a bingo parlor. His father drank and beat the children and her unmercifully

I stepped to the doorway and called to a deputy to return Bonin to his cell and to let me out of the module.

"Dr. Pelto, would you see Billy Pugh?" Bonin called out as he was being escorted back to his cell. "He's real scared and needs someone to talk with. Tell him I said you were a good lady and he can trust you." Bonin sounded genuinely concerned about his co-defendant.

"I'll see him the next time I come down, Bill."

I walked to the exit door and waited for the deputy to take out his keys and unlock the door.

When I felt trapped, wanting a divorce from Ernie but not able to take the first step, I would lay in bed fantasizing about killing him by putting a pillow over his head. His death would save me from the shame and trauma of asking for a divorce. I could be free and not disappoint my family or our daughters. How could Bonin kill so easily? He killed kids he didn't know. I couldn't kill. But I wanted to! I was envious of him and filled with tremendous guilt for entertaining such terrible thoughts.

"You through for the day down here, Pelto?"

"I'm on my way back upstairs to open files on these guys and check the computer to see if there's anyone new that I should see. If you need me, you know my number."

The door slammed abruptly after I stepped out of the High Power module, the sound ringing in my ears as I started across the hall to the elevator. Blurred voices came from the right side of the hall. Turning toward the direction of the noise, I saw the deputies herding a fish line of inmates toward me. I had stepped directly into their path, and they were bearing down on me. I flew to the other side of the corridor and pushed the up bottom on the elevator panel.

"Yo, baby, you wanna fuck?" a loud coarse voice called out.

"Hey, mama, take me, forget that fat ole nigger. I'm the man! I'ze got the real goods. I gotta Louisiana Black Snake right here and it's all ready fer ya. You're gonna fall in love wid it; you'll know you been fucked fer real."

Out of the corner of my eye I caught a fleeting glimpse of the burly black man as he grabbed his crotch. Other inmates were laughing and making lewd remarks.

Why don't you go to hell? I stood silent, giving him a dirty look, and waited for the elevator. The line of inmates stopped and the deputy bringing up the rear of the line walked to the man who had addressed me.

"Yo, deputy sir, you gonna do me ugly?" the inmate asked with an arrogant voice. From his attitude, I figured him for a fish. He hadn't learned to keep his mouth shut yet.

"On the wall, blue!" the uniform yelled out.

The deputy pushed the inmate's head hard up against the wall with his flashlight and leaned close to the inmate's ear. The perp fell silent.

The deputy returned to the end of the line and gave a signal to the lead deputy.

"Okay, ladies, get the lead out of your asses."

The line crept silently on down the hall.

I looked back at the elevator, trying to will it to open. Finally, with a whooshing sound, the doors opened and I stepped in with a feeling of relief. I pushed the up button and absentmindedly leaned back against the urine-soaked wall of the car.

Suddenly, an inmate slipped through the closing doors. He got on so quickly that I didn't have time to escape from the car

Two weeks ago two inmates had shoved a deputy into the elevator on the first floor and started beating him. Another deputy saw what was happening but couldn't get on the car before the inmate pushed the button and the doors closed. When the elevator doors opened again, it was on the third floor, med surg. There were no deputies within visual range to see what was happening.

One of the inmates pushed the down button and the doors closed again. The two perps continued beating the uniform until the car's doors opened again on the ground floor. This time, several guards were ready and grabbed the perps and dragged them out. Now the same thing might happen to me. I should have waited for an escort.

I eyed the inmate, stepped closer to the door panel, and pushed the second floor button again. I stood very still, praying to be safe. The man's face wore a bland smile under his dark beard. He didn't say anything, just kept staring at me through granite eyes, all the while inching closer. I was trying frantically to figure out what to do to protect myself. The ride was taking forever. My heart pounded in my ears, and I was fighting hard to stifle a scream. I was panicked! He continued moving toward me, and then put his hand out. I was beginning to raise my arms to defend myself when he pushed past me, hitting the elevator button for the third floor.

After an eternity, the elevator doors opened on my floor. Sweating profusely, I took a big breath, exhaled, and tried to calm myself. I was shaking like a dried leaf, close to falling apart.

I was fearful of the inmates but, yet, I had to work with them. I had to gain perspective.

I bypassed my office and went straight to the hospital kitchen for a john wayne. The area was deserted. I poured a cup with shaking hands and stood, leaning against the counter. My heart continued to thump hard against my chest wall, and it was difficult trying to catch my breath.

It was lunchtime and most of the staff had already gone down to the ODR. I didn't feel like eating and knew I could always check the hospital kitchen later for leftovers.

I needed to get the rest of the personal data on Holmes and Bonin off the computer in order to open their cases.

Luckily, Lupe was taking a late lunch and sat hunched over her computer.

"Excuse me, Lupe. Could you pull up Holmes, John Curtis for me? I need some personal data on him." She was much quicker than I was using the computer. It still intimidated me.

"Give me a sec." Her fingers flew over the keyboard, and the screen with Holmes' booking information came into view.

Name:	John Curtis Holmes
Booking #:	6413230
Location:	CMJ
Module:	1700
AKA:	Harry Huge, Long Dong, Hung Lowe, Crotch Rocket, Johnny Wadd, Trouser Trout, Too Juicy
Sex:	Male
Age:	37
DOB:	8-8-44
Height:	6 foot 2 inches
Charge:	187
Martial Status:	Married
No. children:	none
Birth Place:	Piconey, Ohio
Social Security:	000-00-0000
Occupation:	Actor
Booked:	12-5-81
Court Date:	12-22-81

I jotted down the booking information and looked over the screen for any other information that might be helpful to me when dealing with Holmes.

Holmes had been arrested December 4, 1981, in Miami, Florida, on burglary charges and receiving stolen property. The theft was rather trivial, involving a word processor and a power booster, but a bench warrant was issued for his arrest. He had been successful in evading the homicide detectives for four months. He was escorted back to Los Angeles and incarcerated in the L.A. County Men's Jail.

The authorities used the robbery warrant as an excuse to return Holmes to L.A. They were interested in what part he had played in the Wonderland Avenue Murders. Holmes was suspected—as were Eddie Nash and Gregory Diles—of bludgeoning four people to death in a home in Laurel Canyon. A fifth victim survived the beatings; luckily for her, the killers left her for dead. But she was beaten so severely that when the police questioned her she had little recollection of what had happened that day. The only description she could give of the killers was that they appeared like shadowy figures moving around the room.

The coroner's report revealed that from the look of the striated pattern found on the victims, a lead pipe had probably been used as one of the murder weapons. Police Chief Daryl Gates believed the slayings occurred in retaliation of a robbery that had taken place at the expensive home of Eddie Nash, owner of the Starwood Nightclub.

John was a friend of Eddie's.

I walked back to my office with my coffee and read the information obtained from the probation department on the famous porn star. It reported that Holmes had a long history of drug abuse and involvement with Eddie Nash.

John's wife, Sharon, disclosed that he admitted being in the house hours or minutes before the murders were committed. The authorities believed that Holmes knew who had committed the murders but was unwilling to disclose the information. The Los Angeles Times said that John Holmes was fearful for his life and had told a friend, "Please tell everybody I'm not talking. No matter what people say out there, I'm not talking."

I sat thinking about Holmes as I watched a lazy cockroach wander across my desk. It stopped occasionally to check out some crumbs and bits of sugar cookies left behind from an earlier snack.

John didn't seem to me like a man capable of bludgeoning four people to death, but then I reminded myself that I would have dated Ken Bianchi if I had met him socially.

CHAPTER 17

I DIDN'T THINK I COULD DO IT!

In the undergraduate psychology program, I took my first required statistics course with a pass or fail grade. I have never been good at math—actually, I have a math phobia. Very soon I began to fail the course, and I knew there were several more statistics classes ahead as well as a major research project to obtain the Ph.D. I panicked, believing I wasn't capable of completing the degree. In desperation, I begged the instructor to just give me a passing grade and I'd forget about becoming a psychologist. He did, and I did.

I changed my major to social work to obtain a BS degree. I hated the field but I was broke. For the next six months, while still working as a waitress, I looked for a job. But everywhere I interviewed, I was told that an MS degree was required.

A short time later California State University in Long Beach started a new Masters program in Community-Clinical Psychology. I was four years older and decided to take another chance and confront my fear of math. At the time, I was also dating a statistics professor at the college.

During the two years it took to earn the MS, there were many times when I barely had enough money to make the house payment. But throughout my life I have had a guardian angel bringing me help from the most unexpected places.

My house taxes were due and there were no funds to pay them.

Tired of kids and money problems, two friends and I went down to the Golden Sails for a drink. The place was crowded and we ended up sitting at the bar where an obnoxious drunk sat down beside me. He started making lewd remarks and unwanted advances. Even though I worked hard to ignore him, it was impossible. Finally, after an hour he left. When he did, I noticed something crumpled up on the floor. I reached down and discovered it was a wad of cash. Now I knew from my Baptist training that I should have chased after him. But I was desperate and justified keeping the cash by telling myself I had had to put up with his bad behavior. I don't remember now how much money it was, but it helped me pay the taxes.

Before I turned forty, I enrolled in United States International University to begin my Ph.D. It was a private school located in San Diego, California. It was in the fall of 1979, almost exactly thirty years after I first dreamt of becoming a doctor of psychology. I didn't know how I would pay the ten thousand dollars a year tuition, but I was determined to manage it some way.

USIU, or as we called it, USIOU, had weekend classes set up for working people, offering two classes that started on Friday night and ended late Saturday evening. Although the school was a two-hour drive from my home, it was the only one that would allow me to work full time and do a Ph.D. The quarter system allowed me to go to school year round, which allowed me to finish the degree in two years.

Because of my B grade point average and low test scores on the SAT, the school admissions office admitted me on a probationary status. The first quarter I got all As. I often made the two-hour commute from Long Beach to San Diego twice a week. Sometimes I was so tired driving home, I was afraid I would fall asleep.

Halfway through the Ph.D., I was worn out, positive I couldn't complete the degree. I was so afraid of failing. It felt like I couldn't go forward with anymore classes, and I couldn't stop because I had already spent so much money. I took a week off work and enrolled in only two classes the next quarter.

Two years later I sat at my IBM Selectric typewriter, looking down at my dissertation, the last requirement to complete the degree. After reading through it, I wanted to jump out the window and kill myself, but we lived in a one-story house. I feared that my research was flawed and that my conclusions didn't make sense. I couldn't start all over, I was too tired, and the cost was overwhelming; the dream was over.

I thought back to when I was introduced to pot and wished I had a joint to smoke. When our class of thirteen students finished the MS degree in psychology, we had a graduation party at a spa where a classmate worked; we stripped down to our birthday suits and went into the hot tub. One of the forward-thinking students brought baggies of marijuana and we all lit up. All of the stress of getting the degree went up in smoke. It was wonderful. Now, all of my sources had dried up.

I called my dissertation chairman and explained my failure. Dr. Harris yelled at me. "There's not a thing wrong with your work. Now get the final draft to me and cut out the crap." She called me a few days later and told me the work was more than acceptable. I couldn't believe it was over. The only thing I needed now to become licensed was fifteen hundred hours of supervision by a psychologist.

Upon finishing the Ph.D., Ernie's invitation to my college graduation topped the list, and I made little effort to hide my gloating when I handed it to him. He slid the embossed invitation out of its envelope, glanced over it, but made no comment. He merely called to the girls to hurry up and grab their things so they could spend the evening with him. He didn't attend my happy day, either.

As I put on my cap and gown, I overheard my father saying, "Momma, don't tell her, it will hurt her." Of course his words were tantamount to waving a red flag in front of me. I had to know what they were talking about. After a lot of coaxing, Mom finally said, "All of your life our family has felt sorry for us. They all thought you were retarded because you could hardly read." I laughed and thanked her for telling me the story.

My parents and my children attended the graduation and it was hard to tell who was crying the most. No one in our large extended family had ever obtained this level of education.

To me, there's something wrong with people who use age or anything else as an excuse not to reach for their dreams.

It had taken me thirteen years to earn the Ph.D., while raising children, and working full time, but I did it. After all, whether you try something new or not, you are still going to get old and eventually leave this world.

One thing I did know for sure: If I couldn't make it as a psychologist, I sure as hell could make it as a waitress.

CHAPTER 18

JAMES MUNRO:
THE MAN WITHOUT A CONSCIENCE

Ron encouraged me to take time to prepare for the next Board exams, but so far the books were getting dusty piled high on the beat-up file cabinet in the corner of my office. Problem was, there wasn't any free time, too many inmates to see. An even bigger problem was that the jail was overwhelming and it was difficult to keep my mind focused on subject matter that didn't have any relevance to my job, or to my life. Who gives a damn about how the hairs in our ears conduct sound when you're trying to figure out how to keep a serial killer alive?

My next chance at the Boards would be coming up shortly, and my anxiety was already building.

After my interview with Holmes, I was freshly aware that, like many patients, these men wanted someone to listen to them. Most of them wouldn't feel comfortable talking openly with their attorneys, and they couldn't be straightforward with their fellow inmates because of the snitch system. If you snitched, you might obtain a lesser sentence, but you might also obtain a lesser life span.

Later in the week, I walked down the hall looking for Jim Munro's cell. He was whining about wanting to see me.

A deputy had told me approximately where his cell was located. Rounding the corner, I had to sidestep a gang of inmates down on their hands and knees polishing the cement floor. The floors were cleaned and polished, and the walls were scrubbed weekly, but none of these efforts reduced the stench. My heart pounded as I walked past the inmates.

"Hey, baby, you want to get it on?"

Why don't you piss off?

I was scared one of them might reach out and grab me. At that point, I figured they couldn't use me as a hostage to escape but they could severely injure me. There were no deputies in sight. They were probably down flirting with the nurses. Thank God I got by them!

Peering into the cells as I walked down the hallway, I saw inmates dressed in their underwear, sleeping on the hard metal cots with their legs pulled up in fetal positions. One was sitting on the toilet, watching me as I watched him. Others were pacing around their cells like caged animals.

Munro's cell turned out to be the third one on the right and was one of the few in 7000 that accommodated two inmates. The attorney general gave Munro a gay roommate to keep him happy. He didn't want him backing out of testifying against Bonin. Looking through the small window, I recognized him immediately. He used the phones outside my office on a regular basis, and always poked his head in like an old friend to say "hi."

I tapped on the window to get his attention. He smiled and came to the door.

I yelled, "I'm here to see how you're doing."

"I'm doin' okay. Not barfin' or drizzlin' the shits. Think I can see you today? I gotta lot of stuff on my mind, and I'm real stressed out."

"Let me set it up."

After returning to my office, I contacted a deputy and asked him to break Munro out. I pulled the visitor's chair up alongside the desk, then sat down behind the desk to wait for him. This young man seemed frail and vulnerable; I wanted to make him feel safe and comfortable with me.

I hadn't heard much about the role Munro had played in

the Freeway Killings, but I did remember young boys had been sodomized, mutilated, tortured, and killed.

Within twenty minutes, the tall, pale-faced boy arrived. He didn't appear capable of even thinking of such horrendous acts, much less committing them. He didn't look his twenty years, more like fifteen. His blue jail jumpsuit hung on his skinny frame like an oversized clothes bag and his straight hair fell into his eyes—he didn't bother brushing it away.

"You want me to cuff him to the chair?" the deputy asked as he stood beside the young prisoner with his hand resting on the restraints.

Munro looked sweet and innocent, but I didn't know him and wasn't willing to take any chances.

"Yes, please." I still wasn't comfortable meeting the inmates in my office without the handcuffs, even if they provided only minimal restraint. Then I thought about Ken who was in and out of my office all the time with no restraints. I saw so much of him that he seemed like an old friend.

James Michael Munro walked slowly to the chair, his footsteps barely audible. He stood quietly, waiting for the deputy to pull the cuffs. Upon a nod from the deputy, he dropped into the chair and automatically extended his arms.

In the meantime, I fumbled in my desk for a pen; I scribbled on a piece of scratch paper and found it was dry. I grabbed another pen and scribbled again. It took another try before I found one that worked.

Munro watched this process with a slight smile as if he wanted to make a comment about government-issue equipment, but stayed mute.

I set aside the manila chart with Munro's booking number neatly typed in the upper right hand corner and placed the Intake Form directly in front of me.

Looking past the man slumped in the chair, I spoke directly to the deputy standing behind him.

"You going to be around?"

"Sure, if you need me. I'll be out in the hall." He gave me a knowing smile and just before he disappeared, he closed the bottom half of the Dutch door and pushed the top half wide open.

"My name is Dr. Pelto; I'm a psychologist. Do you mind if I call you Jim?"

He smiled and nodded. "No problem, ma'am. That's my name."

His accent was Midwestern.

"I'll be available to talk with you whenever you're feeling down. Just let a deputy know and he'll contact me. Now, I need to open a file for our records. Do you mind if I ask you a few questions?"

He gave me an incredulous look. "Why would you do that? You gonna tell the D.A. whatever I'm telling you?"

"No, I won't be talking to your attorney or D.A. or anyone connected with your case. But we won't have any privacy." He seemed apprehensive and reluctant to talk, so I tried to choose my words carefully.

"Don't tell me anything you need to keep secret. This is not a therapy session...." I gave him my canned spiel about lack of confidentiality. "The Mental Health and Sheriff's Departments are concerned about you and want you to have some emotional support."

"Emotional support?"

"Someone you can talk to whenever you need to." I was purposely vague and hoped my brief explanation would satisfy him, not wanting to tell him we were only concerned he might kill himself and that the Mental Health Department, the City and County of Los Angeles, and the State of California would be embarrassed again. And my ass would be grass!

He responded with a blank stare.

"I was about eighteen when I hitchhiked out from Michigan to meet up with a friend and ended up living on the streets 'cause I never connected with him."

"How did you make a living?"

"Hell, I was makin' 'bout two, maybe three hundred a night fuckin' my brains out.... Oh, ma'am, excuse my language."

"It's okay." I smiled inwardly. This young killer was worried about offending me with his language. He didn't realize it was his murderous behavior that I found offensive.

"Well anyways, I'm bisexual, so I was fuckin' jus' anybody who'd come along and had the bread to pay for it. I finally gotta 'bout enough to get a place of my own, and I got rolled. Some asshole got to me when I was sleepin' and stole all my dough.

"I met Bonin when he was trying to pick up a trick.

"Bonin axed me if I'd like go to his house and do a little butt fuckin' with him. I didn't know him and shit, man, I wasn't in to givin' it away. I had to make me some more bread so I could get me a place, so at first I told him no."

"You did go with him eventually, didn't you?"

Suddenly, it was as if a dam burst. Munro began to spill his guts with little prodding from me. He was eager to have someone listen to his pent up feelings and what I assumed was his guilt over being a participant in Bonin's killing spree.

"Yeah, well, Bonin, he sez he lives with his mom and brother over in Downey. I stood there thinking. Hell, I thought 'bout it and I jus' figured anybody who lived with his folks couldn't be all bad. So I sez, 'sure,' and I grabbed my stuff and went over to his place.

"Billy, he was real good to me, gave me his van to drive and got me a truck drivin' job where he worked. His mom was a real good cook and it seemed alright with her that I bunked in. Billy and me had some sex together for a while, you know, like I'd suck him off or let him stick it up my ass, but then after a while I tol' him I was really inta girls and he sez 'okay.' I even got engaged to a girl over in Long Beach one time.

"Billy and me'd go up to Hollywood Boulevard sometimes and pick up some dude to party with. That way Billy got all the butt fuckin' he wanted without me havin' to do it."

"What was it like living with Bonin?" I asked.

"Well, ever' day we jus' got up and went ta work and then at night we jus' come home again. It weren't nothin' very excitin'. Then one day Billy sez, 'Do you wanna go out and pick up a hitchhiker and have sex with him and kill him?' Shit man, I was shocked, but I thought he was jus' kiddin', so I sez, 'sure.' I didn't want him to think I was some kinda pussy.

"Next night, we get home from work and Billy sez, let's go.' I didn't believe he was really gonna do it, you know—kill somebody. So I sez, 'no problemo.' I figure he was jus' seein' what I'd say."

"You did go along with him," I said.

"Well, yeah! But shit I didn't know what he was gonna do. Next thing I know, we go out and get into his big green bomb and take off. Billy's drivin'. He reaches out and puts the radio on one uh those shit kickin' western music stations and he jus' starts singin' away. He's soundin' real happy. Guess it was 'bout five-thirty, and since it was June it was still light out.

"We drives over to Hollywood Boulevard to do some crusin'. We drive up and down several times, lookin' for young dudes hitchin' or jus' standin', waitin' for a trick to come 'long so's they can make some bread. Billy tol' me to be on the lookout for a good one. He was still talkin' about findin' someone and doin' him and then killin' him.

"'Hey, Billy,' I sez, 'there's a kid over there on the right side of the street hitchin'. You wanna check him out?' So Billy pulls over to the curb and calls the kid over.

"'Hey, you wanna make a little money?' Billy sez to the kid. 'Sure, what do I have to do?' 'I was wonderin' about you and me and my friend, Jim here, going' over to my house to have a little sex party and then get somethin' to eat. You up fer it?'

"Billy was smilin' and soundin' real friendly to the kid. Then he axed him what he thought about gays. He always axed 'em 'bout that. Kid said he was bisexual, so it didn't matter to him.

"At first this kid, he seemed kinda nervous. I didn't think he was gonna go with us. Ol' Billy's smart, though. He reaches in his pocket and pulls out a twen'y. Then he waves it at the kid. Man, that kid lights up like a rocket and steps closer to the van for the dough. 'Hold on,' Billy says. 'Let's go for a little ride and have some fun first.'

"Billy leans over to me real quiet like and tells me to drive, 'cause he's gonna get in the back for a little suckin' and blowin'. He swings down out of the van, callin' to the kid to come over and get in. He waited real patient like for the kid to walk to the door and look around in the van before climin' in. Then Billy crawled in after him.

"I was kinda nervous, but I didn't let on. While I slid over to the driver's side, I was thinkin' to myself: Maybe he's jus' tryin' to shock me to see what I'd do. But then I sez to myself, well, maybe he really is gonna kill this here kid."

I looked up to see a deputy peering in at us.

"You okay, Pelto?"

"Yes, thanks. Any chance of getting some coffee?"

"Sure, I'll send a trustee over to see what you want."

"Let's take a break until we get our coffee." I needed a break. I glanced down at my watch; eleven o'clock. I wasn't interested in the time; I just wanted something to do while we waited for the trustee. I opened my top drawer and rearranged my paper clips out of Munro's vision to avoid eye contact.

When the trustee arrived, Munro ordered a cadillac, and I had my usual john wayne. The inmate returned shortly with the two coffees in Styrofoam, and a few cookies. I took a sip of the coffee, which set my stomach burning. I nodded for Munro to continue.

"It was gettin' dark, so I figured I'd head the van on back to Downey. I heard Billy call the kid Steve, so I figured they was gettin' real friendly. Then the kid screamed out real loud. Billy musta done him a fast shot up the ass. See, Billy, he really got off on that. I don't go for ass-fuckin' that much; it hurts like hell. What I like is pullin' a train."

Munro must have read the confused look on my face. "Ya know, pullin' a train, suckin' cock."

I tried for a face devoid of surprise, but didn't know if I succeeded.

Munro grinned at me, exposing yellow teeth. "I wanted Billy to trade me places so I could get a turn at the kid, but he tol' me I had to keep drivin'. Shit man, they was really doin' it back there. The van was kinda bouncin'. All that breathin' and groanin' got me to havin' a hard-on myself. I wanted ta have a little fun, too. Shit, man, I wanted to get back to the house so I could shoot my wad."

My jaws were aching from clenching my teeth.

"It was full dark by the time we got back to Downey. I pulled right up to the house 'cause Billy's folks was outta town for the weekend.

"'You hungry, Steve?'" Billy axed the kid. I figured he didn't want any trouble gettin' him into the house. Billy knew 'bout doin' that kinda thing, you know, to make you feel safe and that nothin' bad was gonna happen to you.

"'Yeah,' this here kid sez. 'I ain't had nothin' to eat all day.'

"'Cept my cock,' Billy sez, laughin'.

"So he sent me off to get some burgers. Shit, I was driving down the street and pulled over to grab a tape out of the glove compartment when this here cop flashed me the red light and pulled up behind me. He wanted to see my license. Shit, all I had was a learner's permit. He tol' me I shouldn't be drivin' unless I had a licensed driver with me and to get back home. After he pulled off, I went on down anyways and got the burgers."

Tragic, I thought, how close the police were and didn't know what was about to happen.

"When I got back to the house, they was undressed and really goin' at it. Whoopin' and hollerin'! I wanted to go in there, too, but I was hungry and wanted to eat my burgers before they was cold. I could hear 'em real good 'cause they were doin' it in Billy's mom's bedroom and that's real close to the livin' room where I hunkered down to watch some cartoons. I could hear 'em gruntin' and the bed springs squeakin'. I felt kinda left out, but I figured I'd get my turn."

I felt disgusted by Munro's matter-of-fact attitude then reminded myself to remain nonjudgmental.

"Billy come out to the livin' room door and told me to come inta the bedroom.

"'Stephen,' Billy sez, 'I got this here friend, who likes to have anal sex with a guy that's hogtied and naked. This guy is willing to pay up to two hundred bucks for it. What do you think? Can you use some extra cash?'"

The atmosphere in my office took on a sense of unreality. Munro's story was both appalling and riveting. Something in our emotional make-up fascinates us with tragedy. We crane our necks driving past traffic accidents looking for crash victims; pay money to see car races, more excited by crashes; and attend circuses to watch flyers on the high trapeze. We are voyeurs!

I took a sip of coffee and found it had turned cold. With my stomach burning, I swallowed the caffeine.

Jim's voice continued in his matter-of-fact tone, as he explained how cleverly Bonin talked Stephen Wells into being tied up.

"All of a sudden, the kid starts to yell and wiggle around. Guess he was gettin' scared and changin' his mind. Billy grabbed the kid's shorts and stuffed 'em in his mouth. Then he cinched up the rope from the ankles to the hands so the kid was kinda bow shaped. He was kinda funny lookin' with those shorts hangin' outta his mouth."

Munro's eyes were bright and shiny as he relived the murder. This was a game to him. There was no guilt or shame in him. Stephen Wells was an inanimate object to these two men.

"Billy told me to take the kid's legs while he grabbed his shoulders, so we could carry him out to the hallway. I almost stumbled over the guy's clothes layin' on the floor. I was bummed 'cuz I could hear the sound of my favorite show comin' from the livin' room, and I still hadn't got any sex or nothin', and now I had to help Billy carry this dumb ass kid all over the fuckin' place.

"'Jimmy,' Billy sez, 'let's go in the kitchen; I need a drink of water.'

"We walks down the hall to the kitchen. And I sez, 'When's the guy comin' over to butt fuck him?' Billy sez, 'What guy?'

"I thought someone was comin' over to corn-hole him, and that's why we hogtied him.'

"'Nah, that was just so we could get him tied up without too much trouble.'

"So, I sez, 'Well, when're we gonna let him go, then? We ain't really gonna kill him, are we?'

"Billy sez, 'What else can we do? We don't have no choice. We gotta kill him now, 'cuz he knows where I live. I can't have no witnesses.'

"We went back into the hall and Billy hit the kid in the chest with his fist, sayin, 'You're gonna do what I tell you to do.'

"Somehow the kid spit the shorts out and now he's screamin' and cryin' and beggin' us not to kill him. 'Please let me go', the kid's yellin'. 'I'll give you anything you want if you just let me go, please, please don't kill me.'

"I looked over at Billy, he's just smilin'. Then he went back into the bedroom and got the kid's wallet out of his pants and emptied it. When he come back, he sez to the kid, 'I'm just gonna knock you out, put your clothes back on you, and then leave you on a park bench somewhere.' Then he puts the kid's T-shirt over his head and 'round his neck. He told me to hold his feet.

"Shit, what could I do? I didn't wanna make Billy mad cause he might kill me. So I bend over and grab his feet, kinda hurt my back. Billy starts tightening the shirt; he's twistin' and pullin' it. Kid's wigglin' an strugglin', makin' these awful gaggin' and gruntin' noises. Almost made me barf. The kid just kept wigglin' and makin' these weird noises.

"'Billy,' I sez, he's jumpin' 'round too much. I can't hold him no more.'

"'You got to, I can't stop now.' Billy just kept twistin' and twistin' and pullin. Shit, I was gettin' really tired. That was hard work. Then I heard this noise like somethin' snapin,' and the kid was all limp.

"'What happened? Is he dead or somethin'?'

"Billy kinda laughed and said, 'Yeah, stupid.' Then he pulled off the T-shirt and threw it down the hall.

"'Yuk!' I sez. The kid's face was all kinda purple and puffy; he looked awful.

"Billy laughs and sez, 'You'd look that way too if you'd just been strangled. Haven't you ever seen a dead body before?'"

James Munro looked squarely at me with a toothy grin—he enjoyed having an audience.

I tapped my fingernails quietly on the desk to steady my nerves, feeling sick to my stomach.

It was a struggle to keep my face devoid of emotion.

Munro, unaware of my reaction, continued his story.

"No way I was gonna admit I hadn't never seen a dead body before, so I jus' shrugged like it was no big deal and sez, 'So what're we gonna do with him now?'

"Billy tells me to go and get a cardboard box 'cause we're gonna take the dude for a ride.

"I headed outside where it was dark with a little breeze. Felt good to be out, 'cuz I really worked up a sweat tryin' to hold that dude down while Billy choked him. I wasn't in no hurry to get back in the house with that dead guy in there; he was real disgustin' lookin', and he stunk real bad.

"I leaned against the van and began to feel a little nervous myself 'cuz I didn't know if Billy might think he had to kill me now, too. I decided first chance I got, maybe I should hit the road.

"I guess I was takin' too long, 'cuz Billy comes to the side door and starts yellin' at me to get my ass back in there and get the box out of his brother's room.

"When I get back, draggin' the box, Billy was back in the hall, jus' standin' there, lookin' down at the kid and smilin'.

"'Untie him, and help me get him into the box,' Billy sez.

"Shit man, I was gettin' tired of Billy orderin' me around, but I was scared of him and didn't want to end up like the kid, so I sat down on my haunches and tried to untie the knots. I couldn't get 'em undone 'cuz he had struggled so much the cord cut into his wrists and ankles. I go off to the kitchen and get a knife to cut the cords loose. I nicked him a bunch of times but he was past noticin'. I didn't like touchin' the dead kid, but I had to get the ropes off.

"Billy tells me to pick up his feet so we can get him into the box.

"I reach down there, and geez that slug had pissed and shit all over himself and he's really stinkin', and I can see it dribbled all over him. Man, talk about disgustin'. I tried to grab his legs without gettin' shit all over me, but his legs was slippery and I couldn't get a good hold. I dropped him, and he sorta slid around in the crud on the floor.

"Billy was laughin' at me. I didn't think it was funny. Finally, we drop him in the box with his feet stickin' up.

"Billy tells me to go out and back the van into the driveway so's we can carry him out the kitchen door into the van without no one seein'.

"When I get back, Billy's got the box waitin' for me where he slid it across the kitchen floor, and we gotta muscle it into the back of the van like we was carryin' a TV or somethin'. That sonofabitch was real heavy to carry.

"Billy grabs the keys and sez he'll drive. Didn't even give me time to wash the shit off my hands or turn off the TV in the livin' room. Billy was in some big honkin' hurry."

My jaws were aching now from clenching my teeth. I stretched and wiggled my feet under the desk to try to release some tension. Munro was watching me, enjoying my attention.

"Where we goin'?" I axed him.

"'We're goin' over to Vern's house,' Billy sez.

"I hadn't met Vernon before, but I knew he and Billy liked to play Dungeons and Dragons with a bunch of other dudes. But they played it for real, like they would really kill the guys.

"Billy drove us over to Vernon Butts' house, singin' all the way. Took us bout twen'y minutes over to Lakewood, where Vern lives. Billy had tol' me they was good ol' buddies. Said he met Butts at a bowlin' alley shortly after Billy got out of jail the last time. Said Vernon was the one that got him inta killin' kids.

"When we get there, the house looks deserted. Looks like blackout shades on the windows. We back into the drive anyways, and as soon as I open my door I can hear acid rock music comin' outta the house.

"'He's home,' Billy sez, 'go knock on the back door.'

"By the time Vernon opened the door, Billy had come up beside me and we went right in.

"Shit, Doc! You shoulda been there."

Munro looked at me and slapped his free hand on the desk.

"You shoulda' seen him. This here guy is all dressed up like Darth Vader, out of Star Wars, with a black hood and cape and ever'thin! We follow him inta the livin' room and he's got these here great red and blue and purple strobe lights flashin' in time with the music. He has a bitchin' sound system."

Had, I thought. *Had!* Vernon Butts was dead. Vernon Butts' suicide was the reason I was here, listening to this now.

"All the shades was drawn down. It was bitchin'. The furniture was shit, but Vern, he had this great fuckin' coffin right there in the middle of the livin' room. Billy tol' me later, that's where he saw Vern fuck a boy one night.

"Billy was all 'cited and talkin' real fast to Vern, tellin' him ever'thin' we done. They was laughin' their heads off. Then Billy sez, 'We got it out in the back of the van; it's a good one. Come on out and see it.'

"Vern gave us a couple of brews and then sez, 'Let's go see the stiff.' He sweeps past me, across the room with his black robes flyin' out behind him. We follow him back outside. I pull open the van doors and get back outta the way. They crowd into the back and Vern leans over and pokes at the kid. Then he sez 'Great job, Billy, you really did good.'

"I stayed back 'cause I didn't need to see it again. Then we stood 'round a while longer 'til Billy axes what we should do with the kid's body. Vern sez, 'Just drop it off somewhere along the freeway, unless you wanna keep it around for a while to remind you of what a good job you did. You guys really did a good one tonight; I'm proud of you.'

"Billy sez he don't wanna keep the body, 'cause he can always get him another one. Ol' Vern and me laughed cause we thought that was pretty funny.

"We piled back in the van and headed down toward the beach. I had to open my window 'cause the place was really beginin' to stink. We went past a cop on our way and Billy sez to him, quiet like. 'Hey, mista pig man, you oughtta see what we got here.' Then he laughed and laughed. But he drove real careful, so we wouldn't get stopped. We cruised down Pacific Coast Highway to Huntington Beach.

"We found this here closed gas station. Billy sez, 'That's perfect.' He drives over there and pulls to a stop behind it. After we take a piss and look around to make sure no one sees us, we unload the kid and leave him behind the station.

"Billy sez to me, 'We've had a good night; let's head home.'"

Stephen Wells was trusting and so naïve. If only he had run at that time, he would still be alive at home, safe with his parents. My daughters' faces flashed before me. I prayed they had learned to be cautious. I couldn't imagine what it would be like to lose one of them—especially the way Stephen Wells was lost to his parents.

When Deanne was a senior in high school, she had a very serious car accident. She and a girlfriend had gone to lunch at the local park. When she pulled back onto the main road, she was broad-sided by an oncoming driver. I have never been so frightened in all of my life. I came face to face with my fear that something horrible could happen to one of my children. I didn't think I would want to live if one was lost to me. During the forty-five minutes it took me to drive to the hospital, I was on the verge of panic. When the nurse finally let me see Deanne, I began sobbing uncontrollably. Her femur was broken, which was serious, but not life threatening. My mother said, "No parent should ever lose a child." I can only partially feel what Stephen Wells' parents felt when the police showed up on their doorstep and took them to identify their child's dead body.

"Dr. Pelto, are you about finished with Munro?" I nodded yes.

Deputy Gonzales' welcome face looked in.

I didn't know if he had been outside listening, or just happened to be walking by—I just knew that I appreciated his timing. I was ready for James Munro to be out of my office. His callousness was making me sick.

"Yes, please take him back to his cell."

"I ain't really done yet," Munro pouted. "I still gotta lota stuff I want to talk to you about, Doc."

"I think this is enough for today," I said. There were no symptoms of depression or suicidal ideation in Munro. "We'll have plenty of time to talk some more," I told him. "Let's not try to get it all done in one day."

"Yeah, I guess you're right, Doc."

I wanted him out of my office. Munro was emotionally dependent and not bright. Bonin didn't have any trouble getting Munro to go along with the killing; he took advantage of Munro's weaknesses. I wondered about Jim's culpability in the crime. But I sure as hell wasn't going to say anything to anyone.

Munro smiled as the deputy got out his key to release the cuffs.

I looked down at the file, trying to remind myself that Munro was part of the human race. I closed the manila folder, put it in my top drawer, and sat quietly watching Deputy Gonzales release the cuff on Munro's arm.

This had felt like watching a horror film — as though the whole scene was only the creation of a screenwriter's fertile imagination.

Munro stood by the chair and stretched. He rubbed his wrist where the cuff had left a red mark and turned slowly to walk away. At the door, he paused and turned to look back at me.

"Nice talkin' to you, lady. Hope I can see you again real soon."

During the time that Wells was being killed, the police department was setting up a surveillance team to watch Bonin's house located at 10802 Angel Street in Downey. The team arrived one hour before Munro and Bonin returned home after dumping Stephen Wells' body behind the filling station in Huntington Beach.

I had studied case histories of sociopaths in textbooks, people who have no conscience or empathy for other people. Now, academic theory was reality. Munro was a classic sociopath, detached from the youth's suffering, but acutely aware of his own: He wasn't getting any of the sex; he was missing his favorite TV show; he was hungry and didn't get to eat; he had to dirty his hands when they lifted Stephen Wells' lifeless body into a box; he was afraid Billy might turn on him. Totally narcissistic!

I got up, leaned over and tried to touch my toes, without even getting close. I stood up again, took some deep breaths, and tried to decide whether or not I was going to throw up. Just in case, I headed down to the bathroom to wash my face. I had to disengage from the horror and inhumanity of this killer.

"Autumn Leaves" was playing. My body felt agitated and on edge. I passed Ron's office and saw him sitting hunched over his desk. I thought about going in to talk with him and decided I didn't want to relive the crime. I walked quietly past in my rubber-soled shoes and entered the FOP unit, going directly into the bathroom.

I looked in the mirror. I didn't look any different, but I sure as hell felt different.

"Hi, Vonda." I turned toward the voice.

Sherry had entered the bathroom to find me wiping my face with a wet paper towel.

"Hey, little buckaroo, you okay?" She was mothering me, even though she was my age.

"I'm not sure. Just interviewed James Munro, one of the Freeways. He described in detail how he and Bonin killed a young boy. I don't know if I can stand continuing to work with these assholes."

Sherry smiled sympathetically and shook her head. "Sweetie, you've got to get stronger. If you don't toughen up, you won't make it in here. All of us have gone through the process. In time, you learn to separate out from all of this. Just don't let yourself feel sorry for any of these fuckers."

I kept the towel over my face, embarrassed.

"When I hired on seven years ago, I felt sorry for some of the young bastards and they manipulated me. They're clever. They'll take advantage of you, especially if they think you feel sorry for them. You've got to depersonalize these creeps in order to do your job."

This idea went against all of my training. My education placed a great deal of emphasis on having an empathetic, nonjudgmental attitude. Did I want to dehumanize these men in order to work in this job? *Wouldn't I become just like them?*

"They'll beg you to get them cigarettes or make phone calls and try to make you feel guilty for not meeting their needs. You got to learn to protect yourself."

I nodded, because I knew she was right, but it didn't feel comfortable to me.

"We call whites 01s, blacks 02s, Mexicans and Asians 03s, and the mentally ill dings 'cause these labels help us depersonalize them."

Munro and Bonin had depersonalized Stephen Wells by calling him "it" or "kid." Now I was learning to do the same. I dried my face, tossed the paper towel in the trash, and gave Sherry half a smile.

"Now," she said, "are you ready to go down and face the blue plate special, AKA the mystery food, in the ODR?"

I had to laugh. "After this today, I can face almost anything— except, maybe, the stew."

CHAPTER 19

WHY DID SHE HAVE ME ARRESTED? I ONLY RAPED HER!

I was barely coming out of my stupor from the day's events when the clock registered four-thirty; time to escape. The jail was more difficult than I could have ever imagined.

Tired and frazzled, I thought about the work that lay ahead. The State Boards were coming up again soon.

Gray clouds covered the sky, blocking out the sun, making the four-thirty hour seem later than it was. The dreary weather mirrored my internal mental state and felt comforting to me. Long shadows from the jail linked with the parking garage, forming an ugly shroud overhead. The cement walkway between the buildings was encompassed with desert-type dirt, and it swirled around my ankles willingly with the slightest breeze as I walked past the concrete parking structure.

I fired up my Fox and followed the other privileged staff cars out of the lot, around Denny's restaurant and past the cop bar, where the deputies hang out after work, made a left turn just beyond it, and drove the short distance to the freeway.

One thing you can always count on, especially on weekday afternoons: The Santa Ana Freeway, heading south out of downtown Los Angeles, will be bumper to bumper. On many days, that was a blessing. Crawling along at five miles an hour, I didn't need much energy to concentrate on keeping my car between the white lines.

I switched on the radio for company. I didn't want to think about the staff's attitude, the inmates, or the jail anymore tonight.

I pushed in a cassette tape to blank out the news, wanting Neil Diamond to transport me into a safe and more pleasant world.

He launched in with "Sweet Caroline" and I sang along. But in spite of my efforts, my mind kept returning to the interview I had had with Jose Rodriquez.

After lunch, I had gone down to 1750 to see William Bonin. Little did I know that a call in advance would have saved me from the ride down in the urine-soaked elevator.

"Sorry, babe, Bonin's in court," a deputy said as he admitted me into High Power. "Probably won't be back until the late afternoon bus. You want a cup?"

"Sure. I need to check Bonin's log."

As we walked to the booth, I caught him giving my legs an appreciative look.

"How do you like it?"

"I've learned to take it black, too much trouble trying to find cream and sugar."

"Is that the way you like your men, too?" the black deputy asked as he handed me a cup.

"Thanks for the coffee," I said, ignoring his comment. Sexual innuendoes came with the territory.

We were alone in the booth, and I didn't know this uniform. The jail is a man's world and I was well aware that I was an interloper, but it wasn't wise to alienate a deputy—they were our only protection.

I grabbed the log and started thumbing through it quickly. It didn't look like Bonin was showing any signs of depression.

I leaned back in the chair, finished my coffee, tossed the cup in the basket, and then turned to the deputy standing by the desk sipping his. "Well, I'll head back upstairs. Would you let me out, please?"

"Sure you wanna go, little momma? Maybe you're up for a little quickie? No one's using the interview room."

I put on a saccharin smile, and bit my lower lip. "No thanks."

The deputy pulled his keys as we walked to the exit door. "You sure, baby? You're missin' out on a good thing." He glared at me, attempting to judge my reaction to his proposition. I continued to force a smile, not willing to give him the satisfaction that he had gotten to me.

"Call me when Bonin returns and I'll come back down if it isn't too late."

"Excuse me, Doc," Deputy Briley called out as he came running up to where we stood at the exit door. "I know you don't usually see anyone other than the high profiles, but we got a guy named Jose Rodriquez in here who seems real crazy. Maybe you can figure out what's going on with him. You got time?"

"Sure," I said in spite of wanting to escape. "What's going on with him?" I turned my back to the offensive deputy.

"He goes from cussing and running around his cell to sitting like a statue looking through the bars with a blank stare."

"Recent booking?"

"Yeah, but sure as hell not his first. We all know him. Never been so strange before, though. Few months ago he was up on charges of being a contract killer. He beat the rap. The system didn't have sufficient evidence to convict. None of the witnesses were willing to testify against him. Go figure."

"Why is Rodriquez in High Power?"

"Got a lot of enemies in general pop, and the D.A. suspect he's one of a gang of contract killers, and hopes he'll turn State's evidence to cut a better deal for himself. They'll probably offer him a plea bargain to get out of his current beef."

"What's he up for now?"

"Rape."

I looked at the deputy but didn't respond. He studied my face, taking note of my hesitation.

"You want to see him?" *No I don't, but I will!*

I recalled being raped by the two attorneys. Since then, maintaining a professional neutrality with a rapist had been difficult.

I nodded to the deputy to break the inmate out and walked pensively to the interview room's entrance, steeling myself for the meeting.

A few minutes later the inmate arrived with a deputy following closely behind. The prisoner looked like a member of the Mexican Mafia, with tattoos of snakes encircling his long thin arms. Tattoos were also visible where his blue jumpsuit came to a V at the neckline. Dull, black hair pulled back in a ponytail tied at the nape of his neck, revealed his swarthy facial features. The long, bound hair hung over his right shoulder down to the breast pocket. As Rodriquez swaggered toward me, he fingered his straggly mustache.

My neck and shoulder muscles tightened.

The two-man procession walked past me into the interview room. Rodriquez walked straight to the brown leather barber chair. Even before the inmate had a chance to get comfortable, the deputy pulled his cuffs, ready to anchor him down. Rodriquez gave the deputy a defiant look. *Was the uniform nervous this guy would make a break for it?*

I loitered by the room's entrance. Eventually, the deputy turned, walked back toward me, and nodded that it was safe to enter.

I could feel Rodriquez staring at me as I made my way past him, smelling his strong body odor.

After I got as comfortable as possible on the hard wooden chair, I looked directly at the inmate. His eyes staring back at me were so dark that the pupils were indistinguishable from the colored portion.

I took a shallow breath, introduced myself, and started my canned spiel about the lack of confidentiality.

"Who gives a shit? I ain't done nothin' wrong." He pulled his mouth into a sneer.

I ignored his comment.

"How are you getting along?"

"I been here before. No big shittin' deal," he answered with a bland smile.

I worked hard to maintain eye contact.

"Are you having any problems?"

"That cunt!" He shouted and pulled his ears back.

I tried not to appear as surprised as I felt. "Excuse me?"

"It's all her fault I'm here."

"Who?"

"If she didn't wanna have sex with me, how come she didn't fight me? Just tell me that."

I was gritting my teeth.

"Do you want to tell me what happened?" I asked.

His voice continued to rise and fill with anger.

"I did that bitch a favor. This is how she repays me." He only half closed his mouth over his crooked teeth.

Rodriquez explained that he had found the woman's purse in the park and returned it to her, hoping for a reward. "I shows up on her doorstep, hand it back, and she starts gigglin' and jumpin' around, she's so happy 'bout gettin' her stuff back. I thought she was gonna piss herself."

I found myself distracted by something moving on Rodriquez' right shoulder under his hair. He was oblivious and continued talking.

"That bitch, she invited me in to have a cup of java. I would'a rather had a beer, but I don't say nothin'. She took me inta her kitchen. I was sittin' there watchin' her, thinkin' I'd gone through a lot of trouble and figured she owed me."

Rodriquez was agitated and shifting around in his chair. I caught something moving again out of the corner of my eye.

"Then I don't know what happened, but next thing I remember, I had this here knife up against her neck and we was goin' to her bedroom."

"Did you rape her?"

"I guess. Anyways, that's what she tole the cops. Muthafucker! I got arrested. That cracker called 'em soon as I split. Shit, she wasn't even that good lookin'. I been with a lot better looking chicks."

I bit my tongue.

"Was she frightened of you?"

"I guess. There was some blood. So I musta cut her."

Rodriquez reached up with his free hand and pushed his ponytail to his left shoulder.

"But why did that pale face bitch turn me in? It's all her fault that I got arrested. She should'a said no if she didn't want it. That bitch cunt!"

"Then what happened?"

"Don't know exactly. All of a sudden, I was home." He pursed his lips.

"Did you black out?"

"Don't know. I didn't fall down on the floor or nothin', if that's what you mean."

"It sounds like you lost some time."

Movement again. This time I was paying attention. A big gray rat stood up on its hind legs, balancing itself on the inmate's shoulder. It looked around and then scampered to the back of Rodriquez's neck and reappeared on the other side. Soon the rat disappeared down the front of the inmate's jumpsuit. A string tied around the rodent's neck kept it from getting away. I surmised that the inmate had the other end tied to his jumpsuit.

It seemed fitting. A rat for a rat! Perfect!

"Does that happen to you often?"

"What?"

"Losing time?"

"I guess. I wake up sometimes and don't know how in the hell I got there."

He shook his head from side to side with a puzzled look on his face.

"Yeah that stuff happens to me sometimes."

Was Rodriquez trying for an insanity defense? Did he blank out and not know what he had done?

"Do you ever find more or less money in your pockets than you remember having? Or find yourself in different clothing and don't remember changing?"

"Yeah. So?"

"Have you ever talked to anyone about these incidences?"

"Nah. Why should I? It's no big deal.

"Look, lady, all I know is this here Twinkie was tryin' ta pretend she didn't want me. A lot of these bitches wanna get fucked but they can't admit it."

"You don't think you should have been arrested?" I wanted to scream at this man. I wanted to tell him that he had probably ruined this woman's life, and for what? I kept biting the insides of my cheeks.

"Shit no. It's that cunt's fault." His voice rose to a shouting pitch. My ears started ringing and my blood pressure shot up. *Go to hell!*

"If she didn't want it, she should have fought harder. I tell you that goddamn bitch, she wanted it! Then she just comes up with this here rape story 'cause she got scared her boyfriend would get pissed." He was yanking at the handcuff. I prayed it would hold.

Suddenly, a deputy stepped into the room.

"Doc, you okay?"

"I'm okay," I said with relief. "Would you hang around for a couple of minutes?"

I turned back to the inmate. He was slapping his legs together, a favorite way of massaging the penis that can be done in public without being arrested.

"Do you ever hear voices in your head when no one else is in the room with you?"

"Shit lady, I ain't mental!"

"Are you feeling suicidal?" I needed to cover my backside.

"Nah. I'd just like ta get at that bitch."

Maybe he dissociated and didn't remember it being a forced act. I wondered if I should alert his attorney that he might be eligible for an NGI plea. *Nah!*

Rodriquez lacked any suicidal ideation, and I felt sure he wouldn't harm himself. I told the deputy that Rodriquez was angry about being arrested and yelling at the woman he held responsible; overall, he was stable.

My mind returned to the present; I had lost time and was barely aware that I was at the off-ramp for the San Gabriel Freeway. A fine mist covered my windshield, distorting the lights from the oncoming traffic, making me feel like I was in a strange dream.

A lot of the other eastbound traffic turned north at the divide as I turned south. Traffic picked up speed, and I arrived home fifteen minutes later in the pouring rain.

I began my turn into the driveway and had to slam on the brakes. Deanne and Tera's cars were parked there, blocking my entrance into the garage. I pulled back out onto the street and parked at the curb. Damn those kids! I grabbed my purse and made a mad dash for the front door. By the time I walked up the three steps, I was soaking wet and ready to chew them out royally.

Inside the house, the rock group Queen blasted out "Tie Your Mother Down" and almost drowned out their shrieks of laughter. Initially, I was further annoyed by the noise. But as I watched the house full of giggling girls, my irritation dissolved and the scene turned to a pleasant distraction from the jail with its horror.

"Mom, you look like you're in shock." I struggled to orient myself to the scene of laughing girls and loud music in my living room. Queen was a relief from the elevator music.

"Did you forget about Cindy's bridal shower tonight?" Deanne asked. "Earth to Mom." She waved her hand in front of my face. "You look out of it."

"You should have reminded me, but its okay, sweetheart. You guys have a good time."

"Mom," Tera yelled out over the music as she walked across the living room toward me.

"Some guy name David called."

"Did you get a number?"

"No. Said he'd call back later. Is he the guy you met at the singles' party last weekend?"

"Yes."

 "He didn't waste any time calling you. He's interested."

"I hope."

"You still got it!"

"Thanks. I'm going to grab a bite to eat and hide out in my room to watch the soaps. You remembered to set the VCR, I hope," I called out after her.

She didn't answer.

In the kitchen, I put together a bowl of corn flakes, sugar, hunks of banana, and a glass of milk that I would pour over the cereal after I got settled in bed. I hate soggy corn flakes.

It had been a long time since I'd dated anyone seriously. I'd met Jack during grad school one evening when a couple of us girls stopped by a happy hour after work. He offered to buy us a drink, and I invited him to join us. He seemed like a nice guy. Told us he was a V.P. at Security First National Bank, and in the process of getting a divorce. We talked easily, had fun, laughed, and he asked for my phone number. After trusting the two attorneys and being raped by them, I was skittish about going out with anyone. I explained this to Jack. He said it would be great to just meet for drinks. I learned to trust him, and we dated for about eight months.

Jack's job required him to make numerous business trips to New York. During a school break, he invited me to go along with him. He booked us into a first class flight on a redeye out of L.A. where the booze was flowing freely. We made out for a while and then he invited me back to the restroom where he made me a member of the Mile High Club. When we came out, a man waiting to use the facilities gave us a high five. It was a real kick.

Unfortunately, Jack wanted more than I could give—marriage. After my divorce from Bob Fife, husband number two, I didn't want to marry again. The four-year relationship with Bob had been a tumultuous one. Bob couldn't commit to our marriage and after we separated, he couldn't let go. I was grateful when he moved away.

And besides, I was married to my Ph.D. and wouldn't let anything distract me from it. I only wanted to date Jack without any strings or commitments. He said he understood, but he was hurt and soon stopped calling me after I turned his proposal down. But nothing was going to deter me from my goal.

That was two years ago and I hadn't dated anyone since. I missed Jack. Textbooks don't keep your feet warm at night, and mine were real cold.

The possibility of a new relationship was exciting. It was hard coming home alone every night and not having someone to talk with and hold me. I was lonely and wanted someone in my life. The girls were busy dating and had their own lives.

I set the tray with my dinner on the dresser and pulled on my flannel nightgown. The scene in my living room was a welcome distraction. The girls' biggest worry was what to wear to the upcoming wedding. Their lives were just opening up. Many jail inmates' lives were at a dead-end. Their poor choices would haunt them for the rest of their lives.

Looking at my reflection in the bathroom mirror while washing off my make-up, I thought about what my parents had taught me about having a forgiving spirit. I couldn't believe that anymore. The men I dealt with were capable of unthinkable acts with no feelings of guilt. I felt no empathy or forgiveness for them. The idea of the death penalty was still unresolved in my mind, but I was leaning more favorably toward it. My parents were against it, which is the way I was raised. One day I would take a mental vote with myself and make a decision.

Freud believed that all people were basically evil and, given the right circumstances, were capable of murder. Maybe he was right.

I made my usual rounds, checking the windows throughout the house, making sure everything was secure. I didn't feel safe in my home anymore knowing that everyone I saw in the jail had friends on the outside.

I walked back into the living room.

"Tera, be sure and tell the girls to lock their car doors when they leave tonight, and to walk to their cars with the keys in their hand."

She gave me a strange look.

"You've gotten so weird."

"I know. Tell them anyway, okay?"

"Sure, I will." The mental picture of her patting me on the top of my head flashed through my mind.

Back in my bedroom, I munched down the cereal and then searched my purse for David Eagleson's phone number. David looked like a Superior Court judge, and could have been sent out from central casting: tall, slender, with a serious face, the right type of glasses, and fine gray hair, with a stylish cut.

I met him at a singles' party given by a woman whom I would much later learn was his fiancé.

David and I spent the evening together, talking and dancing while Cece, the hostess of the party, looked on. He explained that he had been widowed a couple of years after a long marriage and lived nearby. We were relaxed with each other and found conversation easy.

Having been single for several years after divorcing Bob, I had become cynical about the men I met. My rule of thumb was to get the man's phone number, and call his home when I knew he would be at work. If a woman answered, hang up; if the answering machine picked up with a recorded woman's voice, hang up; if the answering machine blurted out a message announcing that they were not home, hang up. If none of these scenarios was present, it probably meant he was single—although I've learned that even all of these precautions are not always foolproof. I grabbed the phone off its cradle, crossed my fingers, and dialed the number.

After three rings, a recorded message came on informing me that the Lincoln-Mercury Service Center was closed for the evening but assured me that it would reopen at seven a.m. What? I hung up, rechecked the number, and dialed it again very carefully. The same message came on the line.

I looked at the phone with disbelief and dropped it as if it were a hot potato. "Damn, that rat is married," I said aloud.

I slipped on my robe and started for the kitchen to pour a glass of Chenin Blanca. I didn't make it out of the bedroom before the phone started ringing.

"Hello."

"Hi, David here."

I didn't answer immediately. I was taking a vote whether or not I wanted to confront him.

"Hello, Vonda?"

I choked out a hello, filled with disappointment and suspicion.

"Is that you, Vonda?"

"Yes."

"It didn't sound like you."

"I hadn't realized how hard working in the jail would be. I should be able to do this." The words seemed to tumble out.

"Well, that is no place for a woman to work."

Typical male attitude.

"Why did you take the job? Couldn't you find something more suitable, like adoptions or children's services?"

"Well, I am a psychologist, and I've been trained to help all types of people."

"Vonda, I've worked in the criminal justice system for many years, and it's been my experience that," his condescending attitude was irritating, "you don't change these men. I hope you didn't take this job with the idea you could."

"Some of the inmates don't look old enough to be out of high school. Even Jim Munro, one of the Freeway Killers, is just a skinny kid that was at the wrong place and became involved with the wrong person. Maybe if someone had been there and warned him, he might have made better choices."

"I've worked juvenile court for a long time, and I've found that when these kids get involved in crime at early ages, there isn't much hope for them. I impose the longest sentence allowed when they come before me. My thinking is, keep them out of society until they have time to mature and then hopefully they will make better decisions for themselves."

"I saw Rodriquez, a rapist and contract killer today."

"Alleged rapist and contract killer," David interjected.

"Rodriquez has been tried for several murders and managed to escape prosecution on a technicality each time. Now he's incarcerated for raping a woman and blames her for it. This is a tragedy. If he hadn't been released, this woman's life wouldn't be ruined. She was an innocent."

"Well, unfortunately the legal system isn't perfect and sometimes these guys do slip through. But you have to remember: It's better for us to err on the side of letting a guilty man go than locking up an innocent one."

"I have a difficult time maintaining a nonjudgmental stance toward these men. I want to tell them what horrible people they are. Guess my facial expression doesn't give away my feelings or they don't care, because it doesn't deter them from talking to me."

"How are you going to handle these inmates?

"I'm not sure."

"How's the studying?"

"Slow, having trouble concentrating. It's hard trying to learn how the taste buds on our tongues distinguish between sweet and sour, when I don't give a damn. I'm thinking about how these inmates go out and brutally kill people without feeling some remorse."

"I'm sure. Well, this is a hard population to work with."

I nodded as if he were sitting next to me on the bed. "You're right. It's a lot harder than I imagined. The air in the jail is stale; that stench stays with me all the way home, and I never want to see another mustard-colored wall as long as I live."

"How about lunch later in the week? I can pick you up at the jail," he said.

"I would enjoy that." I wondered why he didn't invite me out to dinner and hoped I didn't already suspect the reason.

"Friday is a light court day for me, is that good for you?"

"It'll be a nice way to end my week."

We said our goodnights and he wished me sweet dreams. My dreams weren't sweet anymore. In fact, I often laid in bed fighting sleep, dreading the nightmares that would come.

CHAPTER 20

TRICK OR TREAT

Halloween arrived with cold and drizzly weather. Temperatures typically stay in the mid-eighties in Southern California until Halloween night when the kids dress to go out trick or treating. Then the weather turns cold as if to spite the little ghosts and goblins and their chilled guardians, who stalk the streets in search of goodies. This year the weather turned wet and dreary well before Halloween, mirroring my tumultuous mental state.

This was my second Halloween in the jail and I was afraid I was going to start screaming and not be able to stop. The jail was killing my spirit. There still were no other jobs available and I couldn't make enough money to support us as a waitress. I had to do something to survive.

As a kid, I was the instigator, the one who came up with crazy ideas to have fun. Not a beer bust, not that kind of party. I didn't start drinking until my neighbor introduced me to vodka tonics when I was twenty-five.

One of the craziest ideas I ever came up with was while I was engaged to Jay. He took me to my junior high school prom along with four other couples. Traditionally, couples went to SearchLight, Nevada, located less than one hundred miles from Needles, where you could get liquor, cigarettes, or anything else you wanted. The little city had a red light district where our football players went after the games. My father said he would skin me alive if we went up there after the dance. But the idea of just going home afterwards was boring; that's when I came up with the idea of going to the mortuary where Jay lived and worked. The other couples agreed. We ended up making popcorn, fudge, and roaming around, checking out the embalming room and the caskets, and then we turned up the music in the chapel and rocked out to Fats Domino and "Blue Suede Shoes."

When Jay took me home at four a.m., the lights in my house were ablaze. I panicked and knew I was in trouble! Dad had gotten home from a railroad trip and was out looking for us. Mom fixed us all breakfast and when Dad got back an hour later, she calmed him down, assuring him we didn't go to SearchLight.

At the morning staff meeting, I suggested we have a Halloween party. Their initial reaction was one of shock. They had never done anything like that before and didn't respond too enthusiastically to my idea. Then Pat joined in, saying it would be fun and that we should also wear costumes. Ron didn't say much, but he didn't object.

The secretaries decorated the conference room for the party, stringing up orange and black crepe paper from one side of the room to the other, and they hung pictures of ghosts and black cats on the walls. Pictures of the serial killers would have been more frightening.

On the day of the party, we gathered in the conference room at noon and took an extended lunch hour. Deputies Johnson and Gonzales joined us for the party and came dressed as deputy sheriffs.

The party was potluck. What a relief!

We were spared from eating the cafeteria food and the extras the inmates hid in it. Since I don't like to cook, I picked up fried chicken from the Colonel. My culinary expertise extends to frozen dinners prepared in the microwave. I rarely burn or undercook one.

As soon as everyone got their plates loaded and were seated

around the steel tables, Sherry clapped her hands to get our attention.

"Did you hear the latest?" she spoke loudly. "Some perp got brought in last night for screwing a horse. And it was a virgin. But the funniest part is, the horse belongs to a deputy that works down in the reception center."

"Come on," Lupe spoke up. "How in the hell could anyone do a horse?"

"The dude got up on a box, dropped his drawers, lifted the horse's tail, and started banging away on her, or maybe him. Shit, I just thought about it—this may have been a gay relationship," Sherry said.

I could see it.

Bobbie joined in the conversation. "Well, if it's a girl horse and she gets pregnant, they may have to have a shotgun wedding. The other horses will really be embarrassed for her. She might even get kicked out of the herd."

We all laughed. Man, that felt good! Some relief from the horrors in the jail.

Gonzales said, "I wonder who the baby, or should I say the colt, will look like? I heard the perp is so ugly that he has to wear two bags over his head in case one falls off. Hope the newborn looks like its mother."

"Ron," Bobbie asked, "what's the jail time for knocking up a horse?"

"Beats me. I've never been asked that before."

"A fireman friend told me a great story about a call they got late one Friday afternoon," I said. "They were dispatched to a car accident on the southbound Santa Ana Freeway. It was a single car incident. A Ford Falcon had crashed into a bridge overpass.

"The firemen arrived and found the driver passed out cold. Alone in the car, the man appeared unhurt. Sitting beside him on the passenger's seat was an empty gallon jug of cheap wine. Looked like he had gotten drunk and let the car get out of control.

"The man was wearing a loud Hawaiian shirt on top and

absolutely nothing from his waist down, except a pair of red socks. The firemen couldn't believe their eyes. The driver had a full-grown fryer; you know, a real chicken, with feathers and all, mounted on his penis, and the poor hen was gasping for its last breath. There were chicken feathers and bird shit all over the car. When some of the firemen started laughing, the other firemen looked at them as if they were crazy. They wanted to see what the joke was.

"He said he'd never seen anything so funny in all his life. Not funny for the chicken or for the other five dead ones they found thrown in the backseat, either. That dude had a strange idea of having fun."

The jovial mood felt good and for a little while I forgot I was in jail.

Lunch was great! Reminded me of a Baptist potluck dinner with all of the different dishes: enchiladas, chips and dips, meatloaf, fried chicken, scalloped potatoes, and apple pie. A staff member let out a loud burp as I walked back from the urn with a cup of coffee.

"Okay, ladies, and I use that term lightly," Pat called out as she walked to where I sat with Gonzales. "It's time to put on our Halloween costumes. Gotta see who gets the prize for the best one. "Hi, big guy," Sherry said to Gonzales.

"Thanks, but how did you know?" Gonzales asked playfully. "Come over here, babe." He reached out and pulled Sherry in between his legs. He leaned in close to whisper in her ear, almost out of my hearing, but not quite. "Hey, babe, you gonna think of me tonight when you're having your third orgasm?"

They both laughed. I turned away, pretending that I hadn't heard the comment.

Although I felt uncomfortable about actually going trick or treating, I loved the idea of doing something outrageous.

I walked back to my office and pulled the red and white striped flannel nightshirt over my street clothes.

I got back to the FOP unit after the rest of the staff had finished changing into their costumes and walked over and sat down by Ron on the cold steel seats.

Only a few of the staff members wore costumes, but they didn't want to go trick or treating with Pat, Sherry, Bobbie, and me. Ron didn't participate. He just sat, watching with a bemused smile.

Wearing a nun's habit with a big cross hanging around her neck, and a big hat that made her look like the Flying Nun, Sherry won the prize. Lupe wore a black penoir, and Bobbie dressed in tight black leather pants and a jacket with zippers and silver buckles: a realistic-looking biker chick. "Come on, little buckaroos, get the lead out. It's time to go trick or treating," Sherry said as she walked over to where I sat. She handed me a paper bag full of candy and cigarettes to give out to the inmates. This had initially seemed like such a good idea but now, I wondered what in the hell I was doing.

We stepped out of the unit and stopped at the first cell— Douglas Clark's.

"Trick or treat," Pat called out as she banged on his door. No response.

"Yo, dude, you in there?" she called out again.

The Sunset Killer walked to the door and glared at us. Then he raised his hands and cupped them under his chin, as if his head were floating on a platter. My breath caught in my throat as a cold chill ran down my spine and I recalled a Bible story I had learned in Sunday School. It was about Salome, a wicked woman, who danced for the king and then asked him for the head of John the Baptist to be delivered on a silver platter. Stepping back from the cell door, I flashed back to the story I'd heard about Clark having his girlfriend put make-up on the severed head of one of the woman he killed. I had goose bumps!

Sherry, unaffected by his depiction, called out to him again, tapping her foot loudly while waiting for a reply. Clark continued staring out at us with a frozen smile, and didn't utter a word.

"He's a shithead!" Sherry barked out, probably loud enough for him to hear. "Come on; let's go. He's OTR."

"Yep, on the rag!" Bobbie said.

The nervous tension had gotten to me. I felt giddy and started to laugh uncontrollably.

"Yo, Pelto, it wasn't that funny." Bobbie thumped me playfully on the head.

We continued on down the hall, stopping at several other inmates' cells to trick or treat. The cigarettes were by far the most popular.

A few steps further down the hall, we arrived at Ken Bianchi's cell.

"Vonda, you go up this time." Bobbie gave me a nudge. "Kenny's got a crush on you."

He didn't have a crush on me, he just liked coming by for hot coffee and someone to chat with.

Peering into the cell window, I found Ken facing his toilet, his back to us. I moved back, hoping he hadn't seen me, embarrassed catching him in the process of urinating. I was looking into a man's cell, his home. My parents taught me to respect other people's privacy. Should I show him respect? He tortured twelve women and participated in their deaths, does that mean he has no rights?

At that moment, I didn't feel like a professional. I felt like a woman that shouldn't have the right to such access into his life. But he was the Hillside Strangler. Thoughts were racing through my head. Do you lose your rights if you torture and kill people?

"Vonda, why didn't you say trick or treat?"

"He's...."

"Masturbating?" Bobbie said and laughed.

This is a disgusting job!

"No! He's ... I guess you'd say, using his bathroom. Let's wait a few minutes and give him a chance to finish up."

"Why? That adam henry doesn't deserve jackshit," Bobbie said.

"He hasn't been convicted yet."

"So what! He's guilty as sin."

"Trick or treat," I said loudly to make him aware of our presence as I approached his door again, slowly this time. "We have Hershey bars and cigarettes. Which would you like?" I was in my flannel nightshirt, standing outside the Hillside Strangler's cell.

This is bizarre!

Ken Bianchi pressed his nose against the window.

"How about one of each. Is that allowed?"

"Sure." Accidentally, I dropped the Hershey bar and it broke into pieces.

"I'm sorry. I can get you another one."

"Nah," the Hillside Strangler said, "I'm just going to chew it up anyway."

Then, as he instructed, I stepped on the pack of cigarettes to flatten them enough to slide under his door.

"Thanks for coming by. You're the best looking trick or treaters I've seen in a long time."

"See you next year." *What did I just say?* Well, that was the object of this party. The inmates were our world. I reminded myself that common responses were not appropriate here.

We had barely turned toward James Munro's cell when Ron approached us.

"Vonda, we just got a call from Captain Jenson. We have an emergency situation out in 4500 and he wants us there ASAP. Come on, let's go."

I was relieved to get out of further trick or treating. Little did I know what was to come.

I jerked my nightshirt off, handed it along with my candleholder to Sherry, and tucked my blouse back into my slacks as I ran toward the elevator. Ron was already several feet ahead of me and had reached out to push the down button.

"What's happening?"

"The deputy didn't give me any details, just said someone had been killed and the cellblock was on the verge of rioting."

It was unusual for a serious problem to break out in 4500. These inmates are seen on the psych line on a regular basis by the psychiatrist as well as by our FOP staff. Most of them are on enough psychotropic medication to keep them relaxed.

We almost ran down the long hall, past the lieutenant's office to the wide, dimly lit corridor that connects the new jail to the old portion.

"How's the filing project coming along?" Ron asked between pants.

"Slow. The staff isn't happy about working on it and are digging their heels in. I feel like I'm pulling a ton of bricks behind me, trying to get it finished."

"I'll speak to them if you want me to."

"No, but thanks. I just have to be firmer. If you step in, the staff will never listen to me. I'll work it out."

We arrived at the cellblock five minutes later, out of breath. Ron pounded on the steel door with the palm of his hand, at the same time pressing his body close to door to show his full face to the deputies through the tiny square window.

Angry shouts came through the locked door.

"Fuck you, you cocksuckin' greasers; you killed him and you're gonna pay."

"Back at you, you fuckin' niggers. He had it comin'. We'll teach you to mess with us."

"All of you, back in your cells!" A deputy's voice rang out above the foray.

"Ron, what's happening?"

"From the names they're calling each other, my guess is that it's a gang retaliation between the Crips, a black gang, and the Mexican Mafia."

"What are we supposed to do?"

We were there to debrief the deputies, and help them calm down. They live in constant fear of being taken hostage, injured, or killed. In these hot situations, their blood pressure shoots up like a pressure cooker with a full head of steam and no way to release it. I think that's why law enforcement officers have such a high rate of divorce, alcoholism, and suicide.

This cellblock was reserved for the mentally ill. I learned that the Sheriff's Department had tried an experiment and put a few of the gang members in with the dings. They thought there wouldn't be enough of either gang to cause a problem. The theory was a good one, especially now, with the jail being so overcrowded.

Overall, the Sheriff's Department does a good job of keeping these gang members apart to avoid this type of war, but there are so many gangs in here that it's impossible to keep them all separate.

The block was comprised of forty cells arranged in upper and lower levels. The two tiers of cells lined the opposing walls with the deputy's booth running through the center of the room between them. The booth was a long, narrow, tube-like room with large plate glass windows on each side to allow a full view of all of the cells at one time. Two inmates occupied each cell. The electronic cell door controls and the two-way loudspeaker system were also enclosed in this cloistered environment.

I stretched to peer through the small opening and watched the inmates milling around. Some were on the cement floor below, and others were running back and forth on the second-tier catwalks, yelling obscenities and banging their cell bars with metal objects. I could barely make out the deputies' voices over the inmates' shouts.

The deputies stood at attention with their batons at the ready, their bodies rigid, the noise deafening. I couldn't make out all the words the inmates were screaming, but I heard a lot of "fuck yous."

"Get back in your cells immediately," a deputy's stern voice shouted out again over the speaker system, which had been cranked up to a higher decibel level.

With that command, a line of deputies spewed forth from the booth with their batons raised.

The inmates stood, still screaming obscenities, defiantly facing the law enforcers.

My heart pounded in my temples. What would happen if the inmates didn't back down?

"Put your hands on your heads and get back to your cells," came another shouted order from the booth. The line of uniforms walked forward now with their batons raised higher above their heads. I held my breath, praying the inmates would obey.

After what seemed like an eternity, but was probably only a couple of minutes, the inmates began to back away from the deputies, moving slowly to their cells. The gates stood open.

I felt a rush of relief.

With the inmates back in their cells, and the grinding sound of the cell doors closing still echoing through the cavernous area, a uniform came with his keys in hand and allowed us entrance into the block. A doctor and nurse had joined us. Our little group traversed the short landing quickly and was ushered into the long, narrow deputy's booth.

As Ron talked with a deputy to get the details of what had occurred, the doctor and the nurse, accompanied by a deputy, left the booth and descended the cement stairs to the lower level. I walked to the window, leaned my forehead onto the cold glass, and looked down.

On the hard cement floor below lay the crumpled body of a nude, black male. His age was indeterminate. The top of the man's skull was missing. Red streamers formed by bloody parts of his brain intermingled with black hair, spread out from his ruined head—the darkening blood a striking contrast to the gray concrete.

The room began to swirl and I thought I was going to pass out. This feeling reminded me of the Technicolor film we were shown in gym class, showing a surgeon removing a cancerous lung, a propaganda film against smoking. The movie was shown in a hot, crowded room, and when the doctor made the first cut into the man's chest and the blood oozed from the wound, I passed out cold. When I came to, I made it to the bathroom barely in time to throw up my lunch. At that point, I knew a nursing career was definitely out.

Initially, my mind refused to comprehend what I was seeing laying on the cold concrete floor below. My logic told me that this must be a movie set and that the actors would jump up when the director called "cut".

A deputy looked down at the man sprawled on the gray floor. He gently nudged the still figure with his left foot. There was no response.

The doctor knelt down, lifted the man's limp arm, and fingered his wrist for a pulse, then he pressed the jugular vein in the man's neck. Then, without any more effort, he looked up to where we stood and shook his head.

Involuntary tears trickled down the sides of my face as I stood riveted to the scene below.

This was my world. Cruel and out of control. I turned my cheek to the cool glass in an attempt to steady myself.

Ron walked over to me and placed his arm on my shoulder.

"Are you okay?"

"I don't know." I stumbled out and turned my back to the glass wall.

"What happened, I mean why did this happen to him?"

"Word came through the jail grapevine that one of the Crips gang over in 2100 ratted out a member of the Mexican Mafia gang. The M/M sent word back to 4500 to take a Crips' member out in retaliation. They wanted to make an example of him to anyone else who might think about squealing.

"A couple of the Mexican Mafia grabbed a Crips' gang member, dragged him to the upper tier, stripped him, beat him, took turns raping him, and then hung him by his feet over the railing. They dropped him head first to the floor below. The doctor thinks he may have been semiconscious when he was dropped."

"Where were the deputies? Didn't they notice what was happening?" *Is anyone ever really safe?*

"This was a well thought out plan. The deputies think that the Mexican Mafia had been stirring the psychotic inmates up for days, getting them ready for this mayhem. Earlier today they riled them up even more. The dings hurled food, feces, urine, and burning toilet paper rolls from the upper tiers. They do this to our staff, too, when they walk the rows. The deputies were distracted and unaware of what was happening."

I wondered for a moment where the inmates got the matches, then remembered that they've got ways to smuggle in anything they want. I stood quietly, staring out at the raging inmates now safely locked back down in their cells.

I was grateful not to be assigned to walk these rows and prayed I would never have to. Give me the serial killers any day of the week. Unfortunately, we never know what lies in our future.

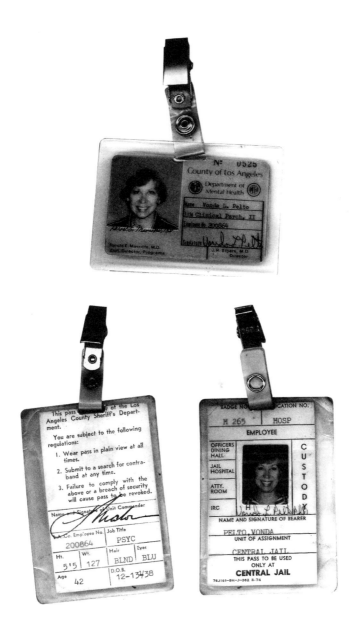

Vonda's employee badges from the Los Angeles County Jail

The Hallway at the LA County Jail outside Vonda's office
with Bianchi, Munro, Komerchero and Clark's cells

Vonda sitting on Charles Manson's bed

Halloween's Trick or Treat
Vonda at the County Jail

TO:
DOCTOR PELTO!

Happy Birthday
Happiness Always

I am glad I've This
oppor-Tunty to Thank you
For every Thing you have
done For me, and
most of all For The
very SpeciaL weekeNd
you have made by giveing
me The radio.
I wish you many more
happy Birthday's in years
To come and all The BEST.

Where did you learn
that lovely way
Of always being nice —
Of doing
extra-thoughtful things
And never thinking twice?
Well, don't know
where you learned it
But one thing's surely true —
You're a very special person
To send birthday wishes to!

Eli Komerchero

Birthday card for Dr. Pelto
from Eli Komerchero, The Trash Bag murderer

Vonda and Jim's blind date
1990

Jim and Vonda's wedding day with family

CHAPTER 21

BONIN'S FATE

Bonin had made me promise to see him as soon as the judge handed down his sentence. He suspected it wouldn't be favorable, and he was right.

Watching television one Friday evening while having dinner, I heard the NBC nightly newscaster make the announcement.

Today Judge William Keene sentenced William Bonin to die in the gas chamber for the murder of six young men and boys. "He had a total disregard for the sanctity of human life and the dignity of a civilized society," Keene said when pronouncing the sentence. "Sadistic, unbelievably cruel, senseless, and deliberately premeditated. Bonin is guilty beyond any possible or imaginary doubt."

I had the weekend off, and made it a point to see Bonin the following Monday when I returned to work. That would be one of the last times I spoke with him before he was shipped off to Orange County to stand trial for four other murders. I vividly recall that meeting.

I arrived at work, took the elevator up to the second floor, dropped off my purse, relocked my door, and walked back across the hall to push the down button. Bonin was housed in High Power. Being a child molester, he was especially vulnerable to attack by the other inmates.

Riding down to the first floor, I tried to figure out what to say to Bill. I felt at a loss; what do you say to someone who has been sentenced to die? Nothing in my life had prepared me for this situation. I thought of the enormity of what Bonin had been told and tried to understand what he might be feeling. I couldn't get myself to that place. He was going to die; he had been told his life was going to come to an end at the hands of others.

The elevator doors pulled open and I reluctantly walked the short distance to 1750. I knocked on the heavy metal door and waited to gain admittance. A line of inmates being herded like cattle down the long mustard-colored hallway came toward me, their leg irons scraping along the concrete floor with each step they took. I shuddered inside, wanting to get into the module before they reached me.

After knocking repeatedly, I heard the sound of tumblers engaging and the door lock being released. A deputy pushed the outer door open just as the inmates arrived and I quickly stepped inside.

"Doc, you okay? You look kinda shook up."

"I'm fine. Thanks for asking, though."

The cellblock was eerily quiet that morning, making me shiver, even though I was perspiring. Most of the inmates housed in the block were involved in their own trials and had been herded into jail buses and transported to the various courts where their cases were pending. With almost all of the inmates absent, the deputies had free time and were gathered in their booth talking over donuts and coffee. The deputy who admitted me extended an invitation to join them.

Bonin lay on his metal cot, sleeping, and didn't see me walk by.

"Hey, babe, you down here to see Bonin?" Bob, the Senior Deputy, recognized me and knew I saw Bonin on a regular basis.

"I caught the news on Friday that the sentence had been handed down. No surprise that he received the death penalty." I walked over to the hotplate, poured a cup, and grabbed a maple bar. There weren't any napkins so I pulled a tissue out of my pants pocket and rested the sticky pastry on it.

"We were just talking about that." Bob said. "Looks like that adam henry isn't getting away with it this time. He sure as hell beat the legal system more than his share."

I sat down on the only empty chair in the office and took a bite of the sweet bun.

"Gotta go. Let me know when you're ready to see Mr. Bonin and I'll pull him out," Bob said as he exited the booth.

I chatted about the Freeway Killer and the problems the legal system has getting these killers off the streets with the four other deputies sitting around the booth. We indulged ourselves in the "what if only" game, and acknowledged relief that Bonin wouldn't ever be released again. I was stalling, because I dreaded seeing Bonin today.

Finally, I couldn't put it off any longer. I finished my pastry and signaled the deputy. My coffee had gotten cold and tasted bitter. I tossed the cup in the wastepaper basket and walked across the hall to stand in front of the interview room.

I was shifting my weight back and forth from one foot to the other when the deputy returned with Bonin walking slowly in front of him. Bonin walked as if he was in a daze, his feet shuffling along the cold concrete floor.

The deputy unlocked the door to the windowless interview room and flipped on a switch that allowed garish light to escape out into the hallway. The interior room reminded me of a crypt, with its gray cement floor and thick cement walls.

After the uniform pushed the heavy metal door fully open, he moved to the side, stepping in front of me, and allowed Bonin to walk in front of both of us. I was relieved that Bonin couldn't accidentally touch me as I waited for him to pass by.

Bill walked the few steps to the familiar barber chair and without instruction, stepped up into the brown leather seat and waited quietly for his right wrist to be cuffed to the arm of the heavy chair. He kept his eyes diverted from mine, his pale face devoid of expression.

I sat down opposite of him, laid my notepad and pen on the

battered wooden desk, and tried to conjure up some moisture for my dry mouth, wishing I hadn't thrown the cold coffee away.

Remnants of Bonin's breakfast stained the front of the uniform he wore, a uniform that strained to cover his stocky build. Greasy brown hair fell in his face and his heavy mustache needed a trim. His flabby fingers, lengthened by dirty nails, dangled limply from the ends of the armrest. He was disheveled and grimy.

Staring at his pudgy hands and grubby fingernails, I thought of how he had used them to wring the life out of twenty-one young boys.

I couldn't imagine what the families must have suffered when the dead bodies of their children were found like pieces of trash, thrown carelessly along the freeways.

Sitting motionless, I waited for Bonin to speak, my heart pounding so hard that I thought it might be audible in the tomb-like room.

Dead eyes gazed out at me from under thick eyebrows. An uneasy silence filled the room.

Oh, God! I don't want to be here!

William Bonin broke the deadly quiet.

"Judge Keene sentenced me to death on Friday." His voice was hollow, and I could barely detect his lips moving as he spoke.

"I know. I caught the announcement on the news."

"He told me I was sadistic and guilty of monstrous criminal conduct." Bonin's voice began to rise. "If you ask me, I think that pompous Judge Keene is the sadistic one."

Bullshit! I bit my tongue and took several deep breaths to compose myself.

I finally said in a low voice: "Bill, I read about the murder of Darin Lee Kendrick, and it sounded monstrous to me."

I watched Bonin's face, wondering if I should have said anything. He stared at me without speaking. My palms were clammy, and I felt apprehensive, waiting for him to react to the confrontation. In our previous meetings, I'd never even hinted that I knew what he had done. My job didn't entail helping him to gain insight into his behavior. My role: Be supportive and watch for suicidal ideation. But I had grown tired of hearing Bonin, as well as the other killers I worked with, refuse to take any responsibility for their crimes.

I don't know what prompted Bonin to describe Kendrick's murder to me. But after a long pause, Bonin turned to look at me, cocked his head to the right, and with a distant look in his eyes, began the story.

He spoke easily to me, as if we were sitting in an outdoor restaurant sipping tea and discussing the latest car models.

"I went out drivin' around one night, lookin' for a kid to pick up. I felt horny and restless. I couldn't sit still. I had to get out and do somethin' to relax, you know, come down. I went cruisin'. I'd 'bout decided to give up and head back home when I spotted this here kid in Lucky's Supermarket parkin' lot. You know, the one out close to Knott's Berry Farm? He was roundin' up shoppin' carts. I sized him up and he looked just right. I made a U-turn 'cause I was on the wrong side of the street, and pulled into the shoppin' center. I come up close to the kid and leaned out the window and started talkin' to him. I ask him 'bout comin' over to a friend's house to party with us. At first, he wasn't interested. Shit, I was 'fraid the night was gonna be a total bust. Then I offered him some drugs; that changed his mind."

I reached my hand up and squeezed the back of my neck hard, trying to short-circuit the growing tightness.

Bonin's expression changed again and a smile crept across his face as he relived the events of that evening.

"He got in and I pushed down the car door locks so he couldn't try to escape, and headed straight over to Butts' apartment.

"Sometimes when Vern and me went out together, he'd drive so I could crawl in the back of the van and butt fuck the kid. He didn't mind drivin' cause he got off hearin' the kids scream out when I shot 'em a fast one up the butt."

I'm a psychologist; I have to maintain a nonjudgmental attitude.

"Vern and me had been talkin' for a while about doin' somethin' different. We had got some of that chloral hydrate, you know — that stuff that's in knockout drops. We'd been wantin' to try it out, you know, see what would happen when we gave it to somebody."

Bill reached up and scratched his head, then pushed back the hair that had fallen over his right eye.

"Didn't take me long to drive back to Vern's apartment. Parked the van and me and the kid walked in like old buddies. Neighbors didn't pay no attention to us.

"I knocked on the door and when Vern opened it up and saw the kid, shit, his eyes lit up. I was happy 'cause I could tell he was pleased with me. We went in and Vern grabbed us a couple'a cold ones. We settled down on the couch natural like to get acquainted — wanting the kid to relax. I asked the kid if he was gay, he said, 'Shit, I don't care. I can go either way if the money's good enough.' We jus' sat there talkin' and listenin' to some music for a while. Then I don't know what happened, but the kid suddenly jumped up and said he wanted to leave. We had the stuff hidden, so he couldn't have saw it. But somethin' spooked the kid, and he started for the door. Fuck, we weren't gonna let the punk get away. Took both Vern and me to wrestle him to the floor. We had to hit him a few times. Shit that kid fought us, but we finally got his clothes off and tied him up. By then, me and Vern were breathin' hard. Vern decided to have another beer. I had a Coke. I sat relaxin' and thinkin' 'bout how good it would be to have the kid suck me off."

My stomach tightened and I attempted a deep breath, without success.

"'Hey, Vern,' I said, 'you want to do him first?'"

Bill's voice had an excited quality as he continued.

"Yeah, last time I got sloppy seconds.

"Vern got up and started pumpin' away. I was gettin' real excited sittin' there watchin' 'em. Shit man, the kid started to holler real loud. I almost got off just hearin' the kid scream.

"We cranked up the stereo real loud 'cause he was makin' so much noise; we got 'fraid the neighbors might hear him yellin' and call the cops. But that wasn't real likely in Vern's neighborhood, anyways."

Bill's breathing was coming in short gasps; he was getting sexually excited.

He is disgusting.

"Then we decided to give the kid some of that knockout stuff to see what would happen. We had to force him to drink it. He tried to bite us when we was holdin' his mouth open, spittin', but we kept tryin' to get it inta him. He threw up all over the place. Shit, he got it all over his chin, his chest, his stomach. Finally, he quieted down. He stopped jumpin' 'round so much, complainin' he was dizzy."

I picked up my pen and started doodling out of Bonin's line of vision. *Vonda, calm yourself down.* He was wrapped up in his story and didn't notice what I was doing.

"The kid started fadin' out, jus kinda whimperin'. I don't like fuckin' some limp piece of meat. It's no fun if they don't let me know how it feels. Guess we give him too much of the stuff. Next time I figured I wouldn't use as much. Anyways, I'd gotten my rocks off and the kid was gettin' borin', no fun anymore, so I strangled him."

"Excuse me, Bill, I didn't catch what you said." His admission came out so easily that I was sure I had misunderstood him.

"Oh, I said I strangled him."

He's completely indifferent to the boy he killed!

Bill's voice had maintained an excited quality throughout his description of Darin Kendrick's murder. *Was he ignorant of the heartache he had brought to this boy's family?* I scrutinized his face, searching for any signs of guilt or remorse. I couldn't detect any. *Was I reading his expression right?*

"How did you feel after you strangled the boy to death?"

"Well...." Bonin looked around the concrete room, searching for words.

"Excited...guess kinda high, and not as tense. I got some good sleep that night." *Totally narcissistic! I couldn't respond.*

I'd read about the murder of Kendrick in The Los Angeles Times and had seen the picture that accompanied the article.

Darin's sweet, boyish face looked much younger than his nineteen years, much too young to have had his life ended!

Lord, give me the strength to deal with this sadistic killer.

After Bill and Vernon killed Darin, they put a plastic bag over his head, held in place by a rubber band, and carried the lifeless body into the shower, where they washed it in the hopes of destroying any evidence. *Sure as hell wasn't due to any concern for Darin.*

During the recounting of the story, Bonin continued to call Darin Kendrick "the kid," never referring to him by name. Bonin robbed Darin not only of his life but also of his identity. He was only an object to William Bonin and Vernon Butts.

The youth's nude body was found the next morning, discarded in an industrial park in the city of Carson near the Artesia Freeway.

Later, when I read the trial transcripts, I would find inconsistencies in Bill's story. The autopsy stated that there was no trauma to the rectum or semen found in it, indicating Vern and Bill hadn't engaged in anal sex with Kendrick. However, the probation report stated that the men had sodomized Darin. The probation report also said that the ice pick was thrust through the right eye. The autopsy said it was the ear. No chemicals were found in Kendrick's system, but there were chemical burns on his chest. I wondered why Bonin had lied to me, and then figured it didn't really matter.

Bonin's voice brought me back to the small room in which we were enclosed.

"Jury found me guilty of five or six counts of murder and guilty for as many counts of robbin' the kids. Shit, I don't remember exactly how many death penalties they gave me, but who gives a fuck. They can only kill me one time, anyways." Bonin let out a throaty laugh.

"Bill, how do you feel about the verdicts?" I asked, working hard not to react to the bizarre laugh.

He answered quickly, with a bemused smile.

"Well, I'm not surprised. That's what I expected. And what the hell, it makes me eligible for a ton of automatic appeals. Charvet, my attorney, he'll be right on it, you know, startin' to file my appeals. This ain't nothin' to get 'cited 'bout 'cause you never know what'll happen. I'll probably grow old before I run out of appeals. That pompous Judge Keene labeled my crimes 'a gross and revoltin' affront to humanity.' If you ask me, I think he's an affront to humanity.

"What the fuck, I'll probably outlive that asshole, anyways."

Bonin stared past me and spoke slowly. His voice had changed back to a monotone, and his face became as blank as an unused piece of paper.

"Why did you kill the kids?"

"I killed 'cause I like to."

CHAPTER 22

THANKSGIVING

Time in the outside world was running fast. Inside the jail it was as if time had stood still.

Thanksgiving arrived and I was holed up in the kitchen sipping on a mimosa while cooking one of the two meals I enjoyed preparing, the other one being Christmas dinner. Neither of my daughters was interested in learning the traditional family recipes and had abandoned me to watch a football game in the living room with their boyfriends.

I had hoped David Eagleson would join us for the holiday. He and I had been having lunch together several times a week, oftentimes with his fellow judge friends. David was the presiding judge in L.A., and I liked being with he and his powerful friends.

On a few occasions, I talked him into going to a sleazy bar to drink beer and shoot pool, which I loved. I would wear a see-through blouse with strategically placed pockets on my bra-less body. Unfortunately, the pockets didn't have to be very big to do the job. That was a time that braver women were going completely topless, but I never got there. Nonetheless, I still felt very racy. David was always concerned that some of the men he had sent to jail might recognize him. Fortunately that didn't happen.

David asked if he could come over one evening and make his favorite soup for our dinner. Afterwards, we sat relaxing on the living room couch talking. Apropos of nothing, he asked me if I liked to camp or had ever considered going to Africa on safari.

"I'm more the resort type," I answered, "slow room service to me is roughing it."

We both laughed.

"If we married, you could stay home and get out of that terrible job. The jail is no place for a woman to work. You don't need that license or to work at all. You could take up painting or anything else you would like to do."

I took a vote with myself and decided I'd made it on my own so far, and I wasn't going to give up my dream. My second husband had been a compromise. At that time I was so scared and didn't believe I could make it. That marriage lasted two-and-a-half stormy months. I wasn't ready to do it again with a third husband. Besides, David was fifteen years older than me and had too many shades of Ernie: serious, rigid, and wanting to tell me what to do. Been there, done that!

A week later I invited David for Thanksgiving.

"I don't know how to say this", he said, "but I guess there is no easy way. I'm getting married to Cece that weekend." He didn't sound cheerful, more like he was resigned.

"What?" I almost shouted at him.

"It's difficult for me to be single. I need to be married,"

David needed a hostess, a woman who would live in his shadow and demand little from him. That sure as hell wasn't me!

David became a California State Supreme Court Justice a year later and I flew to San Francisco to watch him preside over the court. Our affair continued on and lasted until I married my third husband three years later.

Standing in the kitchen I knew this would be the last holiday season Deanne, Tera, and I would be living under the same roof and was having a difficult time holding back my tears.

After saying grace, we stuffed ourselves with the bronze-colored turkey along with all of the trimmings, and then vowed to never eat again.

Deanne's wedding invitations had been mailed out and their engagement party was a success. Almost all of the preparations for the nuptials were in place. The bridesmaids were wearing burgundy satin and the groomsmen, gray tuxes. Deanne and Richard chose a patio setting, even though the event was to take place on the tenth of January, which is often the rainy season in Long Beach.

Richard is Jewish and his family was opposed to having their son marry a Christian girl in any church. I was opposed to having the nuptials take place at the county courthouse with a Jewish boy. His family was opposed to having the Wedding March written by Wagner played. Wagner had been anti-Semitic. I was opposed to being out of control of my daughter's wedding.

Deanne and Tera were raised with the same traditions that I was. And my dream was for each of them to walk down the aisle of a Baptist Church marrying a Baptist man to Wagner's wedding march. The same music that had been played at my wedding.

During this period of time, my tongue was often bloody from keeping my mouth shut. Even though the plans were not going the way I wanted I didn't want to cause Deanne any stress, but it was often difficult. Richard's parents, on the other hand, were equally upset about the interfaith marriage, but they didn't keep their mouths shut about it.

Well, bottom line: the kids loved each other and that was that! And I am most happy to say that in spite of us parents having different ideas about what our children should have done, the kids have a great marriage.

CHAPTER 23

MANIPULATION AND MAYHEM: KENNETH BIANCHI

All too soon it was Monday again. I grabbed the half-empty bottle of Valium off the bathroom counter and threw it, along with a new bottle of aspirin, into my purse and headed the car back to the freeway. Traffic was typically heavy and I felt drained before even arriving at work.

The morning started off with an unscheduled staff meeting. After picking up a john wayne, I walked to the conference room and had barely gotten settled with the rest of the staff before Ron came rushing in, late as usual, and, as always, out of breath.

"Good news! The administration has finally okayed a four-day workweek, and if any of you are interested, let me know." I wanted to jump for joy. *Far fuckin' out! You bet I'm interested.* One less day in this hell hole and one less day on the freeway. *There is a God!*

Ron had worked hard for this change; he cared about the staff and wanted to support us.

He continued on with other items of business, his voice a mumble in my background. I'd already had enough of the meeting. Usually, I came late to avoid as much bullshit as possible.

Sitting on the cold steel chair, I let my mind drift back to my most recent conversation with my future son-in-law. He feared it might rain, which was a legitimate concern since the facility didn't have an interior room large enough to hold all of the guests. Silly me told him not to worry. "I'm a witch and a long time ago an Indian friend gave me the inside track on how to control the weather." Richard gave me an incredulous look, wondering if I was off my rocker. "Trust me," I stated with confidence, "the day will be perfect." I hoped!

"Vonda! Vonda!" Ron pulled me back to the present. "Follow me back to my office, need to talk to you about something."

Stepping out of the FOP unit, I started laughing under my breath. I was absentmindedly humming "Red Roses for a Blue Lady." The elevator music had infiltrated my brain, just like Bobbie had said.

When we arrived at Ron's office, he held the door open for me. His shoulders stooped. I pushed past him, almost spilling the remainder of the coffee on my freshly ironed blouse, and got as comfortable on the hard wooden chair as possible. Almost immediately a pounding on the glass wall startled me, and I spilled coffee down my front. *Shit!*

"Can you see me later?" Ken Bianchi mouthed, leaning against the wall. "Sure," I mouthed back. His charm was growing thin.

"Ken likes you," Ron said.

"Don't know. I think he just likes coming in for hot coffee." I thought back to when I felt attracted to him, and was glad I had come to my senses.

"Well, you're doing a good job. None of these high profiles are attempting suicide. And that's why we hired you.

"I noticed you're making some headway on the filing, too. That room is looking a hell of a lot better. Any idea how much longer it might take?"

"Probably another month. It's a struggle. The staff's not happy about working on it, and I'm sure as hell not making any points with them."

Ron smiled and scratched his head.

"I figured. Actually, a couple of the women have been in here complaining about you. Said you were pushing them too hard. They don't like you cutting in on their coffee and cigarette time. Sounds to me like you're doing a great job."

"Thanks for your support."

"How's the studying?" Ron asked.

"Slow."

"On another subject, I'm going to be expanding your duties. I want you to start seeing the NGI and MDSO population."

"Not Guilty by reason of Insanity and Mentally Disordered Sex Offenders?"

"Yeah, forgot you used to work with weenie waggers, exhibitionists, and sexual molesters at Orange County Mental Health."

Yeah, almost eight long years!

"The staff there always kidded me about the perverts I hung out with."

"Well," Ron said, "you'll be seeing some of the same perverts here. These inmates have been sent to Patton State Mental Hospital in San Bernardino for treatment. At the end of their treatment, a panel of doctors evaluates them to ascertain the state of their mental health. If they are deemed cured, they are housed in the jail and returned to court to stand trial, serve jail time, or be released from custody and, hopefully, required to continue outpatient therapy."

I grinned! Ron noticed my expression.

"What's funny?"

"Cured? These perps? You're pulling my leg. I've worked with them much too long to believe they are ever cured." He nodded in agreement. Sadly, they just start killing their victims to avoid being identified and returned to jail. That's what William Bonin did.

"Some of these guys may be suicidal, so we have to watch them carefully. You can start the four-day workweek next Monday." *Sometimes, life is good.*

"Thanks. See you later."

I exited Ron's office and walked back to my office. Ken Bianchi was sitting on the bench and stood as I approached.

"Doc, I've been hoping you'd come back soon."

I fumbled with the key in the lock, finally got it open, pushed the door fully open, and went behind my desk to sit down.

Ken ambled in after me and sank down on my new chair.

"Hey, Doc, these chairs have cushions! Where'd they come from?"

"There's a rumor floating around that the deputy's booth is missing a couple of them. With their budget, they won't have any problems replacing them." I had gotten the hang of this place. Hopefully, the deputies wouldn't reclaim the chairs after I left for the day. I had lost several items from my desk, including a textbook. If anything of ours was missing, the deputies had it; and if anything of the deputies went missing, we had it. The inmates couldn't get away with taking anything because their cells were rousted routinely.

"You have some time to talk?"

"Sure." The paperwork and phone calls could wait until later.

"Some coffee and cookies would be nice," Bianchi requested pleasantly.

I stepped to the door to look for a trustee, didn't see one wandering the halls, and resumed my seat.

"Coffee on its way?" Ken asked more forcefully.

"I'm sorry, I'll try again." My second try was successful. *What in the hell is going on with me?*

"My problem now is that we're going to trial in a few weeks and I'm the star witness against Angelo."

"He is your cousin by blood, isn't he?"

"He's my mother's nephew; I'm not sure what that makes him to me."

"You did confess to the murders and agreed to testify against him in order to get out of the death penalty up in Washington, didn't you?"

"Well, yeah, but I wasn't there. I had to lie and say I was with Angelo so they would arrest him."

"What's the problem now?"

"I don't know what I'm gonna say. Soon as the attorneys start questioning me, they're gonna know I'm lying. When the cops interviewed me, I gave them some wrong details, and they didn't even notice. I didn't commit the murders in L.A., but I had to confess and pretend I was there to make sure they got Angelo. I'm not guilty."

"You were charged with murdering two girls in Bellingham, weren't you? Are you afraid of being convicted for those?"

"No. I don't remember anything about those girls being killed up there in Bellingham. I pled NGI. Figure most I'll get is some time in a mental facility."

I looked at him with half a smile. *Bullshit!* Didn't matter how many times he denied his culpability in the murders, I believed him to be guilty.

The coffee arrived and the trustee set the tray on the edge of my desk without ceremony and left.

Ken said that Dean, his attorney in Bellingham, came up with the idea for him to plead NGI. Bottom line was that Bianchi manipulated Dean. He had his attorney believing he was so distraught, even suicidal because he couldn't remember anything about the murders of the two girls. His explanation for pleading guilty to the murders was that there was so much evidence against him.

I'd heard this bullshit before, didn't believe it then, and didn't believe it now.

Ken kept telling me he couldn't have done anything so horrible. He said he did try suicide, but the jail staff didn't find any visible signs.

"I understand you tried suicide."

"I don't want to talk about that, it's too upsetting.

"Dean called a psychiatric social worker to see me and he thought I must be a multiple personality and that another personality came out and committed the crimes. But then that got tossed out."

Ken maintained eye contact with me. *What a cocky sonofabitch!*

"Ken, what techniques did they use to disprove the Multiple Personality Disorder?"

"They brought in this whole battery of doctors to interview

me, some of them brighter than others." His voice dripped with sarcasm.

"They convinced me to allow Dr. Watkins to hypnotize me. He thought he could put me under and speak with the other personality."

"What happened, did another personality emerge?" I smiled inwardly.

"Of course, Steve popped out, he jumped up out of the chair, started pacing back and forth and started cussing, saying that he hated Ken and his mother. Steve told Watkins that Ken walked in and caught Angelo in the act of killing a girl. Ken didn't know what was going on. Steve kept it hidden from him. You should have seen Watkins' face light up."

I bit the inside of my cheek to keep from laughing.He manipulated the authorities into believing he wasn't responsible, and implicated Angelo Buono in the murders at the same time.

"Sounds like you had the doctor convinced."

Ken looked pleased with himself.

"Yeah, Watkins bought my performance; it was the legal system that caused problems. They wanted another expert. They brought in that quack, Dr. Martin Orne."

I hoped my facial expression hadn't changed. Watkins, an expert in hypnosis, had little experience with the criminal population. His big mistake, naiveté: He assumed that all patients were honest with him.

Dr. Orne put Bianchi under hypnosis and used several tests to make sure he was in a trance. His goal, trip Bianchi up. And he succeeded! He proved Ken to be faking the hypnosis.

Dr. Oren's next step, disprove the multiple personality defense.

Ken claimed that his attorney had given him books on MPD and the movie Sybil was playing on TV, which he studied. The story was about a woman who had multiple personalities.

I didn't know his attorney, but it was hard to believe that he would aid in the deception. I wanted to confront Bianchi, but reminded myself that it was my job to be supportive and avoid another embarrassing suicide.

Before being arrested, Bianchi had taken several courses in psychology and actually worked as a family therapist. He rented office space from Dr. Weingarten out in the San Fernando Valley, put up fake diplomas, handed out business cards, and found several patients. He gave it up when he couldn't make enough money.

"You have no idea how easy it was. Well, anyway, if you are smart enough to figure it out."

He raised his eyebrows and smiled, obviously pleased with himself. *What a jerk.* I maintained a benign facial expression. He had contacted a friend back east, a guy he said that could get you anything you want, even a passport. He got Ken a degree in the name of Steven Walker from Columbia University.

I didn't know if Bianchi was lying to me, but it didn't matter. The newspaper reported that he had gotten the diploma from someone at California State University at Northridge, a local college.

"You are very clever, Ken." I wanted to ask him why he hadn't used that skill in more positive ways, but I didn't. Obviously, I was delusional thinking there were any words that could make him feel guilty for what he had done.

A self-satisfied smile spread across his face.

"After Dr. Orne proved you weren't hypnotized, how did he disprove your Multiple Personality Disorder?"

"That Orne, he's a crafty one. He offhandedly suggested that it was very rare in cases of MPD that only one other alter ego presented itself. Usually, he said, there were three or more. I bought it! My downfall, I produced Billy. That fucker had me!"

I maintained my professional face and bit my lower lip. *Gotcha!*

"Dr. Pelto, I never killed anyone," Bianchi said with emphasis. After repeating the lie to so many people so many times, was he beginning to believe his own story?

"I still don't understand why you confessed."

"Shit, I had to. Angelo Buono was the Hillside Strangler. The only way I could make sure he would be convicted of the murders was to say I saw him kill those girls.

"Angelo did them all by himself. I had to use this hypnosis thing to let the authorities know about him. That's why I let it come out in the 'trance,' you know, that Angelo did the killings."

Ken sure did let it "come out." Less than six minutes into his hypnosis session, he started telling how Buono had committed all of the crimes.

"Angelo's evil. He killed all those women."

"What makes you think he did?"

"Do you know much about him?"

"I've only seen him in 1700, talking with the deputies."

"That guy is cruel and sadistic. I lived with him for a while. That's how I know what he's capable of."

Ken yawned, stood, and stretched.

"I didn't get much sleep last night. Someone down the hall kept crying and yelling, kept me awake most of the night. It sounded like he was crying for his mother. You can't believe it; when the lights go out at night, I can hear the guys up and down the halls letting out these earsplitting screams. Sometimes they do it all night.

"Doc, you got enough pull to get me some more hot coffee?"

"Sure. john wayne?"

"No. Now I feel like a cadillac."

"I'll call a trustee."

As we waited for the coffee, I reflected on what I knew about Bianchi's background.

Kenneth Curtis Bianchi grew up in Rochester, New York, born to a young barmaid, and adopted at a very young age by an Italian family. At age thirteen, his adoptive father died, abandoning him to an overly protective, smothering mother. Ken was miserably unhappy after his father's death.

Ken didn't do well in school and at an early age began to get into trouble with the law. Shortly after high school graduation he married Laurie, his high school sweetheart. However, the tumultuous marriage was short-lived, lasting only eight months. Ken returned home one evening to find she had moved out without warning. He felt betrayed and suffered a second abandonment in his life.

At age twenty-six, his mother decided he would have a better chance in life with a fresh start in California. They contacted his adoptive cousin, Angelo Buono, who owned an upholstery business in Glendale. He agreed to give Ken a job and a place to stay. When Ken got out here, he found Angelo living the high life. Angelo wasn't good looking but he had the reputation of being a "chick magnet!"

As it turned out, Angelo's business couldn't support both men. Ken applied to California Land Title Company and got hired, which is where he met Kelli, the mother of his son. Ken wanted to marry Kelli. She refused, complaining that he couldn't handle money and he wasn't ready to settle down. In time, she relocated to Bellingham, Washington, to be close to her family. A short time later, Ken followed her. She hoped Ken would settle down if he got away from California and Angelo. Kelli felt Angelo was a bad influence on Ken and that they spent too much time together.

The trustee returned with our coffee and a small plate of cookies. I knew the trustee would expect some type of favor from me—probably for extra cigarettes or phone calls—for bringing cookies without being asked. That's the way of the jail.

Ken and I took a few minutes to enjoy the snack before we resumed talking.

"How was it growing up, Ken?"

"My biological mom gave me up for adoption. Guess she felt she wasn't ready to raise a child. But a year later, she had another son and named him Kenneth."

"How did that feel for you? She chose to give you up and then have another son, give him the same name, and keep him."

"Well, I guess she just couldn't handle me, but my adoptive mom really loved me and was good to me—she would even put my needs before hers."

Ken didn't want to deal with the rejection, but he had to be angry at being replaced so quickly, especially with the new son being given his name.

"After I got here to California, I told Mom I needed a car. She sent me the money for a down payment. It was a beaut. Cadillac. Two tone. Navy on the bottom and white on the top. Guess it looked kinda like a cop car in the dark."

He guessed it looked like a cop car...*that's why he chose it!*

"It felt great having my own set of wheels. Even Angelo, who thought of himself as the Italian Stallion, didn't own a car. He used his customers' cars when they dropped them off at his shop for an upholstery job."

"Sounds like you were making progress."

Ken chatted on about the car as I recalled details of his life I had gleaned from the media.

After Ken moved out of Angelo's place and got an apartment, money became tight for him. So he and Angelo started a new business. Prostitution! Angelo said, "We always got plenty of cunts hanging around here, why don't we start putting them to good use? Shit, we can make some good bread off 'em."

Bianchi and Buono became small time pimps. Because of his good looks and charming personality, Angelo put Ken in charge of recruiting the girls.

Their first girl was Sabra. Ken met her at a cocktail party and convinced her he had contacts in the modeling business and could get her five hundred a week. Her dream was to become a model. Since she was broke, she was easy prey. A petite blonde with large breasts, Angelo called her "choice."

"Ken, I read that you and Angelo got into the prostitution game. That surprised me. I've overheard you and Komerchero arguing about women and how they deserve respect."

His expression changed: His charming smile was transformed into an ugly frown.

"Well, I do respect women. I have a very high regard for them—anyway, for the good women, women who deserve to be treated right.

"Angelo showed me that there are different types of women. He told me that some women deserve respect and others deserve whatever they get. Some like to be roughed up. 'You gotta teach those cunts who the boss is!' He was always saying that."

Ken reached into the pocket of his blues, pulled out a tissue, and blew his nose. "My allergies are acting up. The dust in this joint gets to me."

He sneezed and blew his nose again.

"Go down to the medication line. The doctor can give you something."

"Not worth it. You have to stand in that line for an hour or more waiting to see the doctor. And I'm sure as hell not going up to 8100 to see Magic Fingers. My prostate is just fine, thank you."

I wondered if the story about Magic Fingers was really true or a jailhouse rumor. I didn't plan to find out personally.

Ken took a drink of his coffee and reached for a cookie.

"Dr. Pelto, have you been watching the news reports about what's going on in the Falkland Islands?"

"No, I haven't."

"I don't think we are going to have nuclear war in our lifetime, but our children might. The news said that the Russians have developed a mechanism to blank out our early warning devices in many areas, and this is the first move toward nuclear war."

I was amazed. The Hillside Strangler, rambling about today's happenings as if we were old friends sitting on the front porch swing, drinking ice tea flavored with mint.

My mind kept returning to what Angelo had done to Sabra. She was moved into his place and told never to leave without his permission. She disobeyed him. When Buono discovered this breach, he told her that if she ever tried that again, his Mafia connections would hunt her down and kill her. Feeling she needed to be taught a lesson, Angelo beat and raped Sabra. Then he told her that she would be working as a prostitute.

Could my daughters be in danger from a madman like this? My throat tightened. I leaned forward, hunching my back, trying to stretch out the tight muscles.

Ken continued to ramble on about political affairs.

Sabra was terrified of Angelo, believing he might have her killed.

Ken and Angelo beat her, using wet towels so as to not leave any ugly bruises. Bianchi admitted to enjoying it.

Sabra didn't attempt to leave again. Angelo had complete control over her life—using her sexually any time he wanted.

Ken reached up, rubbed his eyes, and yawned.

Angelo and Ken worked Sabra as a prostitute for a couple of months and then demanded she recruit another girl, which she did. They brought in a girl of fifteen, Becky, to hook for them. Things went well for a while. Angelo Buono abused Becky regularly, sodomizing her so brutally that he tore her rectum. She was so frightened of the two men, she didn't try to run away. Then one evening Angelo sent her out to a john named David Stewart. She broke down in sobs, telling him of the physical and sexual abuse she suffered at the hands of Ken and Angelo. Stewart felt sorry for her and gave her enough cash to escape. Angelo was pissed! He made threatening phone calls and harassed Stewart. Stewart didn't intimidate easily. Instead, he tired of Angelo's threats, and sent a couple of burly guys over to Angelo's place. They put the fear of God into Buono and he never bothered Stewart again.

Things went sour. When Sabra learned that Becky had escaped, she found the courage to run away, also. Ken and Angelo found another girl, Jennifer, to hook for them, but she didn't work out. She didn't comply as easily as Becky and Sabra did.

Things were going wrong and falling apart for Angelo. He became furious. First Becky, then Sabra got away, then he felt cheated by another woman with whom he did business. It was too much for Angelo to handle. "Did these cunts think they could get the best of Angelo Buono? The Italian Stallion? Think again, bitches."

Angelo sent a message to the woman that deceived him. "Nobody fucks with me and gets away with it." He couldn't kill her because people had seen them together. He decided to kill her friend.

Actually, Bianchi killed the woman, wanting to prove to Buono that he was capable of committing murder.

And so the killing spree began!

"But, Dr. Pelto, I couldn't let Angelo get away with them. I knew what he done." I watched Bianchi's face as he tried again to convince me of his innocence. It was like watching a stage actor perform. At one point, he hung his head and appeared to wipe a tear from his cheek, rambling on with the same rhetoric, sneaking a look at me from time to time to see how I was reacting to his story. He was a keen observer of people.

"Now I don't know if I should testify against my cousin or not. I shouldn't have lied and said I was there but I couldn't let him stay out on the street and kill some more innocent girls. Mom raised me Catholic and taught me about what is right and wrong."

He was trying out his story on me, wanting my reactions. Maybe he thought I would be subpoenaed to testify for him. He, the good Catholic boy, seemed to be trying to convince himself that he hadn't done anything wrong, that none of it was his fault.

Ken was adept at changing the subject when he didn't get what he wanted from me. I took a sip of my cold coffee.

"By the way, I understand your daughter is getting married in early January. How are the preparations going. I…"

Oh, my God! How does he know about the wedding? What else does he know about me and my family?

CHAPTER 24

BIANCHI AND KOMERCHERO IN FOR COFFEE AND COOKIES

"Hello, Dr. Pelto."

I looked up at the sound of Eli Komerchero's voice. He stood at my doorway, looking over the half open Dutch door. Ken heard Eli's voice, jumped up from the chair, and ran over to hug him. The two men embraced and patted each other on their backs. I looked on in amazement. They were displaying such human sides. They were behaving the same way I would with a friend. I wanted to believe these men had nothing in common with me. It was easier to deal with them, believing they were completely evil, one-dimensional.

"Hey, Ken," Eli said. "I didn't recognize you from the back of your head. Man, it's good to see you." Komerchero turned to me.

"Excuse me, Dr. Pelto. I'm not interrupting am I?" he asked as he made his way into my office. I shrugged.

"No," Ken replied, before I even had a chance to answer. "Not at all; in fact, I planned to ask Doc to have you come down to her office so I could see you before you get sent out to Camp Snoopy. Sit down, Eli! Take a load off."

At Ken's invitation, Eli sat. I looked on, uncertain how I felt about sitting with two killers.

Ken turned to me with his casual air, as if this was his office and I was his secretary.

"Think you could get us some hot coffee? Mine's gotten cold, again. You want some coffee, too, Eli?" Ken asked.

"Yeah, sounds good. It's a treat to get it hot."

"She'll get it for us," Ken said.

My emotions were running the gamut: from bewilderment to wonderment that the Hillside Strangler and Trash Bag Murderer were in my office hugging like best buddies, and ordering me to get them coffee. Neither one of them was wearing any type of restraint. I felt amused! Actually, I wanted to laugh. My office had become a coffee shop for these killers, a place to gather and catch up on the latest gossip. Maybe I should put in a couch, coffee table, men's magazines, and perhaps even a television set. *That'll be the day!*

I was doing my job!

I stepped out into the hall and hailed down a trustee to dispatch more coffee. Returning, I found Ken had turned his chair to face Eli and they were laughing and catching up on the latest gossip—an obvious bond of affection between them.

"Did you hear what's happened with Bonin?" Ken asked.

"What's the latest?" Komerchero replied.

"He's been convicted of murdering six boys here in L.A. County and still has to stand trial for four out in Orange County. Bonin's going to be sentenced right after the first of the year for the first six," Ken said.

"I'm glad they found him guilty," Eli said with emphasis. "I hope he gets the death penalty. He sure as hell deserves it!"

Ken gave a slight noncommittal nod and squirmed around in his chair.

"They should string him up by the balls after what he did to them," Eli continued. "You know, he tried to cut the balls off one of those kids. He should have a slow torturous death."

"I don't go along with putting him to death," Ken said, rubbing his chin. "The death penalty doesn't act as a deterrent to anyone else, and it just isn't humane. It shouldn't be an eye for an eye and a tooth for a tooth."

I thought of my own parents' attitudes about the death penalty and the fact that they would probably agree with Bianchi. I still hadn't made up my mind.

Komerchero's eyebrows shot up. "Why not? He didn't show those kids any mercy. Why should he get any?"

"Well, Bonin deserves to be punished, but he doesn't deserve to be executed."

"What do you think he should get?"

"Maybe life in prison."

"Are you shittin' me? They should kill that fucker," Eli retorted.

"It's society's fault that he ended up doing what he did. He had to kill those boys; he couldn't help himself." Ken's face was getting red and his hands were forming fists on the arms of the chair.

"How the hell you figure that?" Eli shot back, rising halfway out of his chair.

I sat quietly, trying to maintain a bland demeanor, even though I could feel my pulse throbbing in my ears. I was fascinated by their differing opinions and wanted to let them play it out. Ken might be headed for the death penalty himself.

Ken turned his back toward Eli.

"By the way, Doc, those drawings look great." The subject of Bonin was over.

Eli had a surprised look on his face and turned his attention to a plant sitting on my desk.

"Your plant needs some water."

"Eli, what do you think about women wearing make-up?" Ken asked.

"Makes 'em look good." Eli shrugged. "Makes 'em look even better."

"Well, I wouldn't date a woman who wears make-up. It makes them look cheap. I like the natural look," Ken said with a defiant look.

"You kidding me?" Eli asked.

"Ma'am, where do you want me to set the coffee?" The trustee stood in the doorway.

I pointed to the corner of my desk with one hand as I pushed the paperwork aside with the other.

His tray contained three john waynes, plastic spoons, a pitcher of cream, packages of sugar, and six peanut butter cookies. Ken played host and handed out the food, then resumed talking.

"No, I'm not kidding. I attended Catholic school when I was little and I hold women to high moral standards. I don't even think it's ladylike for them to wear V-neck sweaters or tight blue jeans."

Ken turned to me.

"See, Dr. Pelto knows how to dress. She looks like a lady."

I wondered what Bianchi would think of me if he really knew about my life. I had started dating right after Ernie and I separated, usually meeting men in bars when we girls went dancing.   One week I had five different dates and slept with them all, believing that if they bought me dinner and wanted to sleep with me, they must like me. It was hard to learn how to date after ten years of being with one man. I wasn't a virgin anymore and the men would say, what are you saving yourself for? Are you gay? Are you frigid? I didn't have any answers. And the problem was compounded because I had needs, too. I was afraid of being alone. That made me vulnerable. I became a wild little turkey, shaking off my Baptist roots. But I didn't like myself very much.

"Ken, you're full of shit." Eli didn't smile.

"Backatcha. And furthermore, I definitely think a woman should be faithful to the man she's with."

Ken was irritated and wanted to fight. I wondered if it had gone badly for him in court earlier today.

"Do you think men should be faithful, too?"

"Men are different. We have more sexual appetite than women do," Ken said.

"You really have a double standard, don't you, asshole?" Komerchero retorted, slamming his fist down on my desk.

My heart rate accelerated. Anxiety! I wished there was a panic button under my desk. I watched frantically for a deputy to walk past the door. No one in sight! Typical when you needed one.

I sat, trapped behind the desk in my crowded office, trying to figure out what to do. Why had I told the deputies they didn't need to cuff the inmates anymore? Or let these two men in my office at one time. *Stupid!*

I didn't think either of these men would intentionally hit me. Actually, I was more fearful of the dings because of their mental illness. But I didn't want to be a mushroom and be hit accidentally if they got into a fist fight.

I had to diffuse the situation before the argument escalated any further. I banged my fist on the desk. "Excuse me! Hey, guys, excuse me!"

They turned toward me, startled looks on their faces, suddenly aware of my presence.

"How about some hot coffee and a cookie?"

"Yeah, thanks." Eli leaned forward and grabbed a cookie, almost crushing it in his fist.

Ken picked up his coffee, finished it with one quick gulp, and reaching out easily, tossed the empty cup in the wastepaper basket sitting by my leg.

I sat quietly, with my fingers laced together, and watched their faces.

Then Bianchi smiled and asked, "How's the weather out today?"

I let out a breathy sigh, feeling suddenly drained.

"I think it's lovely," I said, as I pushed myself up from the chair to a standing position.

"Excuse me, guys, but the coffee break is over."

The men rose slowly and went toward the door. I followed them out. I was agitated! I needed to move around. Ken stopped at the phones and turned back to me just before he pulled out some change from his blues and picked up the phone receiver.

"Dr. Pelto, you didn't have to worry in there. I would never let anything happen to you. I know I don't have much to offer, but if there's ever anything I can do to help you out, please let me know."

Ken reached out and gently touched my shoulder. A cold chill ran through me. My blood felt like a river of ice. His affect and voice reeked with sincerity. I had no doubt this sociopath could pass a lie detector test.

"Dr. Pelto, could I speak with you? It's real important." I turned abruptly, not realizing Eli was standing behind me.

"Come back in, Eli. I have time."

Komerchero returned to the little room, pulled the chair formerly occupied by Ken up closer to the side of my desk, and leaned in close to me before speaking.

"I think Bianchi deserves whatever he gets after what he did to all those women!" I gazed at Eli and debated whether I should make any comment. Finally, I said with a diminutive smile,

"I know what you mean."

"Please excuse my language, but I really wanted to tell that asshole off. He just made me so mad! But that's not what I want to talk to you about. I want to talk to you about writing an article for the newspaper about snitches."

"About snitches?"

"Remember, I mentioned it to you the other day: the snitch system in here." *Part of the time, I couldn't remember my own name.* "I want people on the outside to know what it's all about. The deputies put professional snitches in our cells when the District Attorney wants information. These guys pump us about our cases and make up stuff we didn't say and then give it to the D.A.'s Office. The legal eagles offer these guys time off their sentences or better if they can get something on us. Half the time these maggots make up a bunch of garbage. Shit, nobody cares about the truth. They always believe the snitch. Most of these rats would give up their grandmothers for a smoke."

"Has this happened to you?" I asked.

"Yeah, I'm sure this guy they put in with me is a snitch. The D.A.

had been grilling me over and over about a man named Amann something-or-other. They think he's associated with the Israeli Mafia or maybe even the head of it. I told them that I wouldn't give them any information on this guy. I knew what they wanted, but I'm not willing to cooperate with them, and told them that.

"Do you mind if I have a cigarette?"

"No, go ahead. Do you need one? I have some of those non-brand type the Sheriff's Department furnishes us."

"Nah. Save those for the dudes who don't have any."

I pulled open my desk drawer and retrieved the ashtray copped from the St. Francis Hotel in San Francisco. I smiled as I set it on the desk. I had taken it while having a drink at the famous Nob Hill hotel. Some of us traumatized grad students went there to celebrate after the ordeal of sitting for the psychology Board exams. I wanted a souvenir. Given the right circumstances, I guess everybody has a little larceny in their soul. This souvenir reminded me that I had survived taking the Boards. I was only sorry that I hadn't passed them.

Komerchero reached in his blues, pulled out a cigarette, lit it, and inhaled deeply before exhaling slowly through his nose. The smoke created a haze in the small office, reminding me of the smog outside.

"A couple days after they questioned me, I saw this snitch walking down the corridor with a couple of immigration officers. They took him to a private office to talk."

"How'd you know this guy was a snitch?"

"Grapevine! That kinda news travels 'round real fast.

"A week later they moved us in together, put us in a two-man cell. Sure enough, he started pumping me—asked me if I knew this man, Amann something-or-other. The way he started asking questions made me feel even more certain this pump was a stoolie.

"Doc, people out there should know about these guys. It isn't fair for them to lie and say we said stuff we didn't say and then get rewarded for it. If I write an article, do you think you could get it published for me?"

"I don't have any contacts with the newspapers. But I'll get you the addresses of some of them. Send your article to them and see what happens."

"Thanks, I'll give it a try.

"I got to talk to you about Yehuda Avital. This has really been on my mind. I saw him a couple of days ago talking on the phone. He glared straight at me and gave me a look that scared the piss out of me. He's gonna try to kill me. Have you met him yet?"

"Not yet." Komerchero read the vacant look on my face.

"You remember who he is, though, don't you?"

"He's the man that chopped up the bodies in the Bonaventure, isn't he?"

"Yeah, used a meat cleaver and made me and Zakaria pack up their bloody parts.

"He said he would kill me. And I know he will if he gets a chance. He doesn't have nothin' to lose. They gave him a life sentence without possibility of parole. I got life, too, but I come up for parole in a few years. I'm scared. I made a big mistake turning State's evidence, but what the hell, can't take it back now. So I may be free one of these days, but what's that worth? He's connected. I'm afraid some of the guys who owe him a favor will get to me in here or anywhere I go. God I'm scared! I'm not safe anywhere."

Komerchero's hand shook as he reached out to pick up his coffee.

"You mind if I have another cigarette?"

Ordinarily, I tried to limit smoking in my office. Today I made an exception. Eli's fear was almost palpable.

Eli pulled out another cigarette, and attempted to light up, but his hands weren't steady enough to succeed. I took the matches from his trembling hands and lit it for him. He gave me a weak smile, then quickly inhaled and blew the smoke out. Today the smell of cigarettes was a pleasant change from the smell of urine. He was scared and wanted to know if there was anything he could do to protect himself. I suggested he let a deputy know about Avital's threat.

He was skeptical that the deputies would help him. I assured him that I would report the threat, too. The deputies do take this type of threat seriously. They don't want anything to happen to an inmate while they are in custody. Too much paperwork.

"Thanks, Doc, I feel a little better." If he felt reassured, it didn't register on his face.

Whooosh, the elevator doors opened and we heard the lunch trolley being pushed over the threshold even before we saw the trustee pushing it. Eli spun around.

"Guess I'd better head back to my cell," he said. "Wouldn't want to miss my five-star lunch. Gotta eat it fast 'cause I don't want the ice cream to get cold or the meat to get hot." He laughed at his own joke, stood, and walked out of my office.

My body felt tense and I needed a release. Walking usually helped, if I only had someplace to walk. I rose from the chair and followed Komerchero out of the claustrophobic room.

Standing in the doorway, I watched the Trash Bag Killer walk down the hall toward the deputy's booth. There was no place for me to go.

Ken Bianchi was still talking on the phone. He smiled and nodded in my direction. I pretended not to see him. I didn't want to encourage him to come back into my office. I retreated into the office, pulling the bottom half of the Dutch door closed, sat down behind my desk, and finished off the last peanut butter cookie.

"By the way, Doc," Ken was off the phone and leaning on the half-open door to my office, "I'm glad you got rid of that dented file cabinet. It was pit bull ugly. That wooden bookshelf is an improvement. You're a doctor and your office should reflect that."

He departed without any comment from me. Relieved, I shut and locked the door then reached into the file drawer to retrieve some study materials. Time to start studying again.

CHAPTER 25

CHRISTMAS COOKIES
AND KILLERS

"Good morning, L.A. This is J.D. at KNXT radio signing in. For all you dudes and dudettes just tuning in, the time at the gong will be six a.m., and I'm here with you, your sleepy guide for the morning commute.

"The weather in beautiful downtown promises to be clear and sunny after the fog burns off. For now, be careful driving out there on the freeways 'cause those puppies are slippery.

"Heads up, ol' buddies, we're counting down…jus' fifteen more shopping days 'til Christmas."

J.D. put "Winter Wonderland" on the turntable. It made me wonder what it would be like to have a white Christmas with a loving large family around me. Tears flowed down my cheeks as I drove past quiet houses and an occasional jogger on my way to the jail.

With gifts under their trees, happy families everywhere were spending time singing Christmas carols, and couples were toasting each other at holiday parties. Being privy to their lives was a constant reminder that I was divorced, alone, and struggling to work and raise my children.

I switched the radio off and thought back to the Christmas season almost five years ago when the holiday blues got to me. I was so depressed and lonely that I began to think that the divorce from Ernie was a mistake. Maybe we could make it now that we were both older and more mature. So I invited him home for Christmas dinner. He arrived on time and walked into the house, tall and handsome. I was immediately drawn to him, wanting the comfort of his arms around me. When I reached out to hug him, he pulled away.

"Where are the girls?" he asked.

Instantly, the old feelings of being rejected came flooding back. And I remembered why I had wanted the divorce in the first place.

It was eleven years before I married again. Bob and I dated for more than three years, never talking about marriage. I didn't think I would want to marry again. My older brother didn't particularly like him, said "he was a blow hard." Frankly, though, there are a lot worse traits a man can have. Later, I found that out firsthand.

One evening, after a pleasant dinner, I broached the subject. He said he would marry me if I got pregnant. He didn't want another child. He just wouldn't make a commitment without being forced.

I scheduled a tubul ligation as soon as possible. I didn't want any man marrying me through default.

After many break-ups, we married a year later. The neighbors got a big kick out of our relationship. Bob had beautiful bedroom furniture and he moved it into my bedroom where it stayed for two weeks until we had an impressive fight and I threw him and his bedroom set out. A week later he and the set moved back in only to stay for another week. We actually did this four times. After two-and-a-half months of marriage, we filed for divorce. The relationship wasn't over, though. After two weeks, Bob began to call me at three and four in the morning, begging to come back.

"Vonda, please just agree to have breakfast with me. I want to kill myself. I know what I did was wrong. I can't sleep, I can't live without you." Finally we went into therapy and were able to sever the relationship, but we still talk on the phone occasionally.

I already missed my warm bed and flannel nightshirt. The car heater shucked out warm air, but I wanted to be curled up under my feather comforter. My bunny slippers felt warm and soft on my feet and gave me some comfort, and I hated the idea of having to leave them behind. I didn't want to be in the jail.

I hadn't adjusted to my new work hours yet. Getting up at five a.m. was taking a toll on me, and leaving before the girls woke up made me feel more isolated.

Typically, I lingered in bed as long as possible, and didn't have time for breakfast, not even time to make a cup of coffee. Luckily, there was a McDonalds on the way to the freeway where I stopped and picked up a cup of caffeine.

The wedding was one month away and Deanne was getting excited about her upcoming nuptials. I was getting excited, too, but for different reasons. With each mail delivery, we were receiving RSVPs with the "Yes, I can attend" box checked. This was one of those good news/bad news stories. Good for the kids receiving all of the wedding gifts, but bad for me and my budget. I talked with Ernie, and he agreed to help me with the cost. I put my energy into having the weather be beautiful for the big day. After all, I had promised Richard it wouldn't rain.

The smell of burning fireplaces still hung in the frigid, early morning air. Store windows were decorated with Christmas scenes and fake snow. Red and green bows attached reindeer to the light standards. Even the blinking red and green stoplights seemed to hail the holiday cheer. While the outside world was preparing for Christ's birth and family gatherings, the world inside the jail stayed the same.

The traffic was holiday light and my drive was over too quickly. I pulled into the prized parking lot, changed out of my slippers, and walked slowly toward the building under a sky streaked with pale pink streamers. The air felt good. I dreaded being swallowed up, cut off from the world outside.

Christmas in the jail is a sad time, not only for the inmates, but for the staff as well. The deputies did their part by changing the elevator music to Christmas carols and the songs blared over the hidden speakers. The staff in the FOP unit put up a four-foot pine tree and hung dusty ornaments on it. Neither effort helped. Maybe decorating my office would lift my spirits.

I had picked up a leftover box of decorations from the FOP unit before I left last night and planned to hang some of them up. The box sat on my desk.

Lupe arranged a gift exchange and put a ten-dollar limit on it. We would exchange the gifts at the Christmas potluck on Friday, the thirteenth of December, which was also my birthday. Unlucky for some! But not for me.

Jail bookings would be up. During the holidays or extremely cold weather, the Sheriff's Department books in a large number of street people; they're brought in under the title of "mercy booking." It's a way to get some of the homeless people in out of the cold and provide them with three squares. The staff would be overwhelmed dealing with the influx of inmates and their seasonal depression.

Even though I didn't feel particularly cheery, I absentmindedly hummed "Jingle Bells" as I rode the elevator up to the second floor. I had to work until five on Christmas Eve and the commute would be murder. This made going home to Needles for Christmas impossible.

I stepped off the elevator opposite my office door and found Ken Bianchi with a foot propped on the bench beneath the phone, leaning forward, talking into the receiver. I walked quietly past him and stood in front of my office door, squirreling through my purse for the key.

"Good morning, Dr. Pelto."

Bianchi covered the telephone's mouthpiece and turned to address me.

"Dr. Pelto, I noticed you have a box of Christmas decorations on your desk. I'd like to help you put them…"

How did he know about the ornaments?

"Excuse me," he turned back to the phone, "I'll call you back later. Yeah, me too. Hey, give me a break, will ya? I gotta go."

He hung up abruptly and held out his hands.

"Here, let me hold something for you."

Ken took the grocery bag filled with candy canes and the small Santa Claus, leaving me free to dig for the key.

"Would you mind if I helped you put up the decorations? It's been a long while since I've had much Christmas spirit, and that would help. Maybe ask Eli Komerchero to help, too? I miss him; haven't seen him in quite a while, not since they rolled me up and put me down at the other end of the hall. We used to talk everyday."

I answered, "Sure," finally retrieved the key from the bottom of my bag, and inserted it into the unyielding lock. I was on the verge of swearing when I finally got the door unlocked and turned the knob. I vowed to ask Ron about getting the lock fixed for Christmas.

"Ken, I'll call you out as soon as I'm ready to start decorating." He nodded and followed me into the office, dropping the grocery bag on the desk. He stood watching me, an uninvited guest.

"Since they moved me to that dead end hallway, no one ever walks by. I'm isolated," he said. "It's real lonely down there."

Ken absentmindedly plowed through the box of ornaments. And I slumped down behind my desk.

"Are you okay? You seem down," he said.

"I'm fine, thanks."

"I like people! Enjoy being around them. That's how come I pretended to be a psychologist and tried to work in that field." He glanced down at me. "The Attorney General got me a television to keep me company, but that doesn't make up for seeing people." I nodded at him to show I understood. "He thinks giving me that TV is going to keep me happy. The A.G. must think I'm stupid. He wants to make sure I'll testify against Angelo. If he really cared, he'd have them bring me back to the main hall."

Maybe it was the Christmas season, I don't know for sure, but I started thinking about what Ken had said about needing human contact and shaking hands with his attorney. He felt like a kindred spirit; I longed for human contact, too. And Ken did pay more attention to me and was kinder than anyone else. I told myself that the only reason I was going to shake his hand was to help him feel better. As soon as that thought crossed my mind, I knew it was a lie. I felt a need to touch him, also.

I faced him directly and spoke. "Ken," I reached out rather timidly, "I'd like to shake your hand." My heart was pumping fast, and I could feel my pulse throbbing in my ears.

His face lit up and without a word, he extended his hand. His grip was warm and firm. He held my hand for a long time. His eyes filled with tears and his face softened.

"Thank you. You have made my day. This is the best present you could ever give me."

It had been a long time since I felt warm inside.

"Are you going to put up a tree?" Bianchi asked, as he dabbed his face.

"I don't think so. Probably just hang up some cards and maybe some tinsel." I stood up, preparing to lift the box of ornaments off my desk.

"Here, let me help you." Ken reached out for the box. "Where do you want me to put this stuff, Dr. Pelto?" He turned to me with a smile. "You shouldn't be lifting things."

I directed him to set them on the remaining empty shelf in the bookcase.

"Thanks, Ken."

"Let me know when you're ready to put up the decorations. I'm always ready to help you in any way I can. I think you already know that." Ken winked as he exited the office.

I sat back down at my desk, trying to understand what I was feeling.

Suddenly, my face burned hot and my stomach tightened. I was being sucked into Bianchi's game. "No shit, Dick Tracy," I muttered under my breath.

We're trained all through school to be compassionate and nonjudgmental. These qualities are necessary to work with patients, no matter how evil they might be. Right now, I was having difficulty maintaining a professional distance from the Hillside Strangler. He had become a real person to me. Then I reminded myself what Gonzales had said my first day in the jail.

"Babe, please be careful working with these guys. Especially Bianchi. He's a real smooth talker, but don't forget he's a killer. He's got twelve notches on his belt."

He sure as hell didn't care about Kristina Weckler or the other women he killed. *How could I have gotten sucked in so easily?* I found myself rubbing my hand against the underside of my desk as if I could free myself from his touch. *What was wrong with me?*

I was brought back to reality when I heard "I Saw Mommy Kissing Santa Claus" filling the hallway.

I ended up hanging the Christmas decorations alone. Bianchi was talking to his attorney in the visitor's room and Komerchero went to sick call. I didn't know if I wanted these two killers helping me, although they were my world and much more friendly than the clinical staff.

After I scotch-taped the cards to the wall behind my desk, I strung red and gold tinsel from one corner of the room to the other. I added a few tiny red and green balls to my philodendron, and sat the Santa Claus doll on the corner of my desk. I tore open the cellophane bag, pulled out the candy canes, and stuck them in a glass jar. The place looked a little more cheerful.

Sitting at my desk, I shoveled through the messages and memos Lupe had left for me the day before. There were requests from Bill Bonin, asking me to see him today. No problem, I thought.

"How are you, baby?" My ears perked up, listening to the inmate talking on the phone outside my office.

It was Eddie Nash, who, along with John Holmes, was accused of bludgeoning four people to death with lead pipes and baseball bats.

"I miss you, too, sweetheart," he said. "Yeah, keep your fingers crossed and say prayers for me. I'm sorry I didn't get to see you on Monday. The judge was sick, but maybe next week I'll get kicked out. Yeah, me too. Hey! Tell her to keep her fucking ass at home. Yeah, me too, baby. Gotta go." I heard the receiver being returned to its cradle.

Eddie was leaning on the bottom half of my Dutch door. He looked pale and gaunt. Said he'd lost thirty pounds. Rumor had it that he was worth three million dollars and snorted a million dollars worth of coke a year up his nose.

"Would you like a candy cane?"

He pushed the door open, walked over, and checked out the candy canes sitting on my desk.

"Do you mind if I take more than one?"

"No problem."

He reached into the glass jar and took several.

"You're the shrink, aren't you?"

"Yes. Would you like to come in and talk?"

"No. I'm getting along okay." With that comment, he turned and walked out of my office.

About half an hour later a couple more inmates showed up.

"Eddie told us you're giving away candy."

"Have a couple, if you want." Throughout the rest of the afternoon, there was a steady flow of perps in and out of my office.

I shuffled through the phone messages piled on the desk and returned the necessary calls. There was a bright yellow sheet of paper folded in with the other messages. Usually our memos were on white bond. A Christmas party, maybe?

It read:

MEMORANDOM

Date: **December 9, 1981**
From: **Lt. Chandler, Captain of the Jail**
To: **Uniformed and Civilian Staff**
Subject: Pilfering from the Hospital Kitchen

It has been brought to my attention that the staff is removing food from the hospital kitchen without authorization. This food is provided for the inmates only. The sandwiches are made for inmates' lunches when they are taken for court appearances.

Meals are provided for the uniformed and civilian staff in the ODR.

Pilfering from the hospital kitchen will not be permitted. This is a serious matter and is to be discontinued immediately.

Anyone found guilty of pilfering from the hospital kitchen will be disciplined to the fullest extent of the law.

NO EXCEPTIONS!!!!!

cc: All Service Chiefs

Oh shit! I felt like a kid who had gotten caught with my hand in the cookie jar. I didn't know it was illegal to take the food. What if the surveillance cameras in the kitchen had caught me on tape? I was sure that a deputy would be at my door any moment to arrest me. What if I get fired? I don't have a license yet. *Oh shit, oh dear!* I was learning to cuss, too! I jumped up and started toward the FOP unit to find out what would happen to us.

"Pelto, can I talk with you today?" Jim Munro was talking on the phone and called to me as I hurried past.

"Sure, as soon as I take care of something. Wait on the bench for me."

As I reached for the heavy door, Sherry, with Bobbie close behind her, pulled it open.

I held up the memo. "What does this mean? Are we in trouble? Can they really take criminal action against us?"

"It's okay, little buckaroo, relax. This is no big shittin' deal." Sherry patted my head "God, you're still a fish." I couldn't understand her cavalier attitude. *Why wasn't she upset?*

Ron had seen us from his office and came jogging over to join us.

"Did you girls see this? Do you know what this means? Do you realize what can happen to us?" he said with a mock-stern voice.

"Oh fuck, oh dear, I'm so scared," Bobbie said as she choked back laughter.

"Yo, boss, you want one court-line or two?" Sherry asked.

"I'm not that hungry," Ron said. "One will do. Can you manage a john wayne, too? And grab some cookies if they're fresh." He turned and stopped when he reached his office door. "I've got to go back to the FOP offices, so please deliver the contraband over there."

I looked at all of them in amazement.

"Are you really going down to the kitchen to get something to eat?" I asked.

"You betcha," Sherry answered.

"But what about the memo?"

"Ah, we get those all the time. They get on this economy kick every so often. Must be expecting an auditor soon. The joke is that they waste so damn much money with their big lunches and bar bills, the court-lines are nothing. The memo makes it look good to the auditors, like the department is doing something to cut costs.

"We just go underground for a little while," Sherry said.

"How?"

Bobbie filled me in. "We stick the sandwiches and cookies down our blouses. They don't care if we get coffee."

This exchange occurred as I followed them toward the hospital kitchen. We packed the court-lines and cookies into our blouses. After we got them carefully adjusted, we poured a john wayne and walked out of the kitchen.

Hiding the goods was easier than I thought! *What a lark!*

Jim Munro was still sitting on the bench, waiting for me. I pushed open the door and let him follow me in. Now I had a problem. The sandwich was bulging out from under my soft blouse. I kept my back turned to Jim until I figured out that I could fold my arms over the bulge and lean forward to sit down. He was oblivious to my concern.

"Dr. Pelto, me and Sammy made somethin' for you back in my cell. Can I go get it for you?"

Relieved, I nodded yes. He left and I pulled the sandwich out of its hiding place. The top piece of the French roll had slipped and an escaped slice of cheese was plastered to my side, just below my bra. *Holy shit, no one would ever believe that I'm a psychologist.* People always expect us to all be above such craziness. I never want to get that old or stodgy. I pulled the slice of Velveeta cheese off my side, put it and the bologna back between the French roll, and wolfed down the dry sandwich.

By the time Jim and Sam returned, I had finished my breakfast and was reading the newspaper.

"Doc, we're back."

I looked up to see them carrying a miniature two-story house into the office.

"Where do you want us to put it?" Jim asked.

"Set it there," I said, pointing to the wooden bookcase. "My God, that's great! How on earth did you guys build this?"

"We used playing cards for the walls and toothpaste to hold it together," Sam said. "See." He pointed to a line of toothpaste at the corner holding two cards together.

"Do you really like it?" Jim asked.

"Yes. It's great! You're very clever." Jim and Sam beamed.

The little house measured about two feet long, one-and-a-half feet wide, and twelve inches high. Inside, the two men had carefully pasted pictures of furniture, bathroom fixtures, kitchen appliances, rugs, and curtains, all cut from magazines. The house was incredible in its detail.

"We made it for you," Jim said.

"Good job! Thanks. I love it!

"Would you like some coffee?" I felt badly for not seeing Jim as often as he wanted. My caseload had grown, leaving me less time to spend with an inmate unless he was in crisis.

"Yeah, we been wantin' to talk with you anyways. Make mine a cadillac, and how about some cookies?" Jim asked.

"Me, too," Sam added. "With extra sugar."

I ordered the coffees and pulled out a plate of cookies from my desk drawer, sliding it toward the middle of the desk.

"I'll enjoy looking at it," I said.

The house showed real ingenuity. Amazing what they had done with toothpaste and a deck of cards.

"How about a pack of smokes? I'm out and dead broke," Jim asked. He's so predictable! Always wants something.

Jim kicked a chair back from the desk and sat down. Sam also sat down, uninvited. *Oh shit, these assholes have something to complain about.*

Sure enough, more bitching, but nothing I hadn't heard before. They took turns complaining about the deputies and how mistreated they were. I nodded at the appropriate times and tried to figure out what to pick up for dinner. We had already had McDonalds, Kentucky Fried Chicken, and Shakey's Pizza this week.

CHAPTER 26

CHRISTMAS PARTY

After Jim and Sam left my office, I walked over to FOP to see how the preparations were coming along for our Christmas party. Bing Crosby's mellow voice was crooning "White Christmas". I didn't feel mellow. I felt cheerless and needed something to pull me out of the doldrums.

Senicqua, the administrative assistant, was talking on the phone when I arrived at her office. In the past few months, we had developed a solid friendship. She was an attractive black woman, a single mother, about my age, and much more friendly than the clinical staff. We went out to the Velvet Turtle for lunch occasionally and would usually imbibe in a little white wine.

"What you up to?" Senicqua asked.

"I'm depressed. My birthday is coming up next week and I have no plans."

"What about Larry?"

"We're fighting. He wants to get married."

"Do you love him?"

"I can't handle being alone anymore. But I'm having trouble trusting any man."

"So get a good pre-nup."

"Senicqua, what do you think about us spiking the eggnog for the party?"

"We've never brought any alcohol in before."

"At Orange County, we always brought in booze. It really helped the parties. What could the department do to us?"

"Don't know. We're already in jail."

"You game?"

"Sure, why the hell not?"

"Is that bitch Mitzi coming?" I asked.

"You really don't like her, do you?"

"Don't trust her." Guess I don't trust anyone.

"How come?"

"She reminds me of Donna Gale, LCSW, the supervisor in the first job I had after earning my MS in psychology. Shortly after I was hired in, she scheduled me to interview a patient, while the rest of the staff observed from behind a one-way mirror. I'd never done anything like that before and wanted to watch someone else first."

"You ask her for more time?"

"She refused, saying it was part of my job. I didn't sleep the night before, I was so nervous. The interview was a nightmare. The female patient was extremely agitated, hyper-verbal. I couldn't get her to shut up and listen to me.

"A couple of days later, I overheard Donna and her pal Jan laughing about me and how I had screwed up."

"You don't like Mitzi because she's a social worker?"

"She comes on so sweetly, just like Donna did when I first met her. I thought I was going to get a cavity. I've never trusted anyone who comes on too saccharin. I always figure they have an evil side, to balance out all that sugar.

"Later, I went to a birthday party for the head of the clinic, hoping it would help me fit in better. I walked in and saw most of the staff sitting on the floor, doing lines of coke. I couldn't believe it. I'd never even seen cocaine before. Everywhere I looked, the staff was smoking pot and drinking. I didn't fit in and left as soon as it was polite."

"Vonda, can I use your office for a little while?" Sherry asked, poking her head into the office. "Jose is bringing a couple of dings up here for me to see. Says it's my Christmas present."

"Sure, no problem."

"Hello, ladies!" We turned to see Gonzales walking in. "What are you ol' douche bags jawing about?"

"None of your business, asshole! Even us sluts have our right to privacy," Sherry said, raising her middle finger.

"Just wanted to let you know I got your presents sitting out there on the bench. You ready for them?"

"Be right with you, little buckaroo." Sherry patted his butt as she followed him out.

"Sorry, I gotta run, too," Senicqua said as she pulled her purse out of the drawer. "There's a meeting over at Central."

I walked down the hall to check on the staff's progress with the filing. Thank God! The project was nearly completed. Three staff members sat smoking, talking, and laughing. No one was working on the files. They didn't hear me walk in.

"How's it going?" I asked.

"How's what going?" Felicia asked.

"The filing."

"Oh, that. No problem. We're gettin' it done. You got a problem?"

"No, just thinking how nice it will be to get this job off our backs."

A couple of staff gave each other a quick look and then rolled their eyes at me.

"Everybody ready for Christmas?" I asked.

Icy silence!

I wanted to return to the safety of my office, but it wouldn't be free for at least an hour. An inmate standing in the hall scratching his crotch studied me as I passed by on my way to the kitchen to get a john wayne. I leaned heavily against the stainless steel counter, sipping the hot coffee.

"On the wall, blue," a deputy shouted.

"Hey, man, don't do me ugly," the inmate answered back. The deputy put his flashlight into the perp's back and shoved him hard against the wall.

Earlier in the week a deputy had been injured when a ding in 4500 attacked him. The deputy's back was broken and he might never walk again.

Walking back down the hall past the two men, I prayed that I would pass the Boards on my next try.

"Hey, Doc, wait up," Gonzales called out to me. "I've been following you, watching you walk. Hope you're not offended, but I have to tell you: You're one woman built for speed and comfort." He was a bright spot in the dreary surroundings.

"Gonzales, thank you. I'm taking that as a genuine compliment."

"You gonna make it to the races tonight? I heard you've been doing pretty good."

"You betcha!" I smiled and reached out to pat his shoulder.

"See you later."

Even with the decorations, the conference room looked bleak. And the little Christmas tree was drooping from lack of water. I gave the tree a drink and sat down on the cold metal seat.

Most evenings Sherry Johnson, Jose and I got together to listen to the horse races. One of the other deputy's had a bookie and when they first mentioned the races to me and said we could lay down bets, I thought they were kidding. Thank goodness they weren't. The irony of making illegal bets from the jail was exhilarating.

After waiting an hour, I returned to my office to find the bench empty. Sherry was sitting behind my desk talking with an inmate. She had placed a wreath of gold tinsel around her head and dangled several gold and red balls from it, attached by paper clips. Each time she asked the inmate a question, she shook her head, putting the balls into motion. The inmate was oblivious to her crown. He answered her with a flat, lifeless voice.

I stood back from the door before I started to giggle, and caught a quizzical look on Gonzales' face as he walked toward me.

"What's so funny?" I pointed toward the office. He strolled over to the door, looked in, and rejoined me as he burst into laughter.

"Can you believe her?"

"She's a crack-up."

"I hear you guys out there. Get your butts in here," Sherry called out.

"Hey, babe, love your crown," Jose said, before he turned to the inmate who was wearing a dazed look.

"Okay, homeboy, on your feet." The inmate rose slowly. "Park it out on the bench."

The inmate walked out of the office, muttering to the voices in his head. He stunk of body odor and urine.

Jose winked at Sherry. "Well, babe, guess I'd better get him back to the ding tank where he belongs. Catch you later."

"You finished?" I asked.

"Yeah. It was great not having to walk the rows today," she said.

"How can you stand never knowing if you're going to get piss or shit thrown on you? I don't think I could handle what you do."

"Well, it's a job. Shit, I don't know how you can stand to be in the same room with all those fucking serial killers."

"It is weird. I have to separate them out from their crimes and see them as human beings. If I let myself think about what these guys have done, I couldn't work with them."

"Guess you're working it out."

Sherry exited the office, still wearing the tinsel. I thought back to my first impression of her and felt ashamed of being so judgmental.

I settled down at my desk, relieved to be able to see most of the inmates I was assigned to in my office or in the High Power unit. Walking the rows in 4500, interviewing the psychotics, sounded disgusting.

"How you doin?" Ken Bianchi walked into the office and plopped down on my new cushioned chair that made a whooshing sound.

"I see the aspirin helped."

I studied his face, trying to figure out what he was talking about. He reached out and touched my thriving green plant. Now I remembered: He had suggested putting the aspirin in it.

"You ready for the holidays?" he asked after some quiet time had passed. There was an air of sadness in his voice. Christmas Day wouldn't be any different for him than any other day. The inmates would cook a fancier meal, but the trustees would probably still spit in it before they delivered it to him. I would be home with my family and friends where presents lay under our well-decorated tree, and a turkey would be roasting in the oven.

Even though the inmates looked up to the serial killers, the trustees didn't spare them from any indignities.

"Doc, I'm sorry I didn't make it back here to help you decorate. I wanted to. Hope you didn't have trouble getting the things up." Ken raised his eyebrows and studied my face.

"Are you doing okay?"

"I'm okay, just tired."

"You're tired a lot. Maybe you need vitamins."

"I wondered if you could invite Komerchero and me down here to your office for some coffee and cookies. Kinda like a little Christmas party. I sure would like to see him before they ship him out to Camp Snoopy."

"Now, Ken, do you promise to behave this time and not argue with Eli?"

"Doc, I promise to be a perfect gentleman. Besides, as I told you, I would never let anything happen to you." Bianchi smiled with boyish charm.

"I can arrange it."

Ken stood to leave.

"Take a candy cane if you like."

"Thanks." He stuffed a couple in his pocket and walked out of the office. I felt sad thinking about what lay ahead for Ken's young son. He would never really know his father. Then I reminded myself what Ken had done to those twelve women.

"Did you hear the latest?" Gonzales was hanging on the bottom half of my Dutch door.

"What?"

"They just hauled Nash's butt up to 8100. Thought he was having a heart attack."

"Eddie Nash?" I asked.

"In here on drug charges. Probably the perp that offed those people with Holmes out in Laurel Canyon."

"I think you're right," I said.

"Anyway, the nurses had to do an EKG on him to see if he had a problem. They got Eddie up on the table all hooked up to the leads, fired up the machine, and nothin' happened. No power cord. Shit, they all started flailing around until some enterprising deputy found a string of blinking Christmas lights to use as an extension cord. Those little suckers were blinking up a fucking storm. When Nash turned over and saw them, he sat straight up on the gurney and yelled, 'What in the hell is going on?'"

"Are you pulling my leg?" I asked.

"That's what I heard. I wasn't there, but it's a great story."

I could see it.

"Shit, Eddie had some sharp looking attorneys. Looked like Mafia to me, with those expensive suits and all that gold jewelry."

He was right, they did look like Mafia, and they reminded me of a man I met while in grad school.

One afternoon a couple of girlfriends and I met at the Edgewater Inn in Long Beach for happy hour. Still early, the band had not arrived, and quiet music filled the dimly lit room. Except for three well-dressed men sitting at a table positioned close to the dance floor, the bar was deserted. One of them smiled, I smiled back, and they invited us over for a drink.

One of the three, Don Ross, was in charge—I could tell by the way the other men agreed with whatever he said. He was the moneyed one, and he was interested in me. I was wearing navy shoes and stockings, a navy crepe skirt, and a white long-sleeved crepe blouse with a sailor collar and a tie to match the skirt.

Don was Italian, raised in New Jersey, and sounded like Marlon Brando in "The Godfather." Although not as expensive as Don's, his two companions were dressed in nice suits as well, and were considerably taller and decidedly more muscular.

Don asked me out for drinks and dinner, never to a motel—and never alone. I was cute and perky, and he enjoyed parading me around in front of his friends. Often calling me at the last minute, he demanded nothing of me except to be there whenever he wanted. He paid for my babysitter and gave me money to help with my bills. He always carried a big wad of cash in his pocket. And although I never learned much about the business he was in, whatever it was, it did very well, and I knew better than to ask about it.

Whenever we went out, we traveled with his entourage and my girlfriends that he asked me to invite along for his business associates. One evening we all met down at Huntington Harbor where his sixty-foot yacht was berthed. About once a week we went to Don's favorite Italian restaurant, after closing hours, for dinner. The owner would reopen and make a special five-course meal, for us. That's when I learned to drink scotch and soda, Don's drink.

He was powerful and commanding, certainly nothing like my ex-husband. He often sent a cab to pick me up and would give me the keys to his black Lincoln Continental to drive home. His was a fantasy world like in the movies.

Don warned me early in our relationship to never betray him. I didn't know what that meant at the time, but I did find out later.

My friend Barbara was dating a guy by the name of Halcian, one of Don's associates. She was in love with him and believed he felt the same way about her. But after several months of dating, he stopped calling her.

She was devastated and begged me to talk to him. He said we should talk in person, not over the phone. Man, I was dumb!

A few days later Halcian picked me up and we drove to a bar that Don had never taken me to. We walked into the bar and three of Don's associates greeted us with knowing smiles. Halcian had set me up by making it look like I betrayed Don. My mistake was not telling him immediately what had happened. He didn't call me again.

After trying to reach Don for several weeks, I finally got through to him on the phone. We met, and he was cold, refusing to discuss anything. When I tried to explain, he just said, "Well, everybody has a story." He wouldn't explain what that meant, and I never saw him again. Don taught me a lesson: Be careful who you trust.

———

The next few days passed quickly. Friday arrived for the party. Senicqua and I met in the parking lot as prearranged and laced one of the cartons of eggnog with a hefty amount of rum. Then we filled in the "o" in "nog" on the special carton with a black pen for easy identification. We walked to the jail in semidarkness, thanks to the short days of winter. Thank God we got through the sally port with minimum scrutiny.

"I can hardly wait until the party," she said. "We'll give the special eggnog to those who really deserve it."

We rode up in the elevator laughing, anticipating the day, and walked into the FOP offices to deposit the perishables in the fridge. Our party was scheduled to begin at lunchtime with the potluck. Ron planned to let the staff go home early. "I'll stick around in case of emergencies," he said.

"See you later," I called out to Senicqua. I barely got into my office and seated before the phone started ringing.

Ernie's voice came on the line quickly. I felt a sense of panic.

"Tera's been in a car accident." My heart sped up before he could continue.

"She's going to be okay, but you should come home."

"Oh, my God! What happened? Is she in the hospital?"

"No. She's at home. I don't think she's hurt seriously, just scared. She needs you. She was rear-ended driving to school."

"I'm on my way."

"I'll stay with her until you get here."

I dropped by Ron's office, let him know what had happened, and rushed to join the traffic on the freeway to drive home, praying my daughter was all right.

CHAPTER 27

YOU FUCKING BITCH

January 1, 1982 arrived and I was scheduled to work the day shift. Deanne had spent the night with Richard, and Tera attended an all-night party at a girlfriend's house. Since the girls were both gone, I invited an overnight guest.

I stood in the shower longer than usual, trying to wake up. Larry spent the night with me and after washing my back, had gone to the kitchen to make us breakfast. The smell of the bacon and eggs cooking made me slightly nauseous. We'd been up late celebrating New Year's Eve, and my head was throbbing. Hopefully, the jail would be quiet today and give me some time to study. The Boards were only a few weeks away.

I dried off in slow motion, pulled on blue jeans, a black sweatshirt that had "Mornings Suck" written on the front in white letters, and joined him in the kitchen.

We lingered over coffee quietly and made plans for the weekend. He owned a small four-seater airplane and a house on the ocean at Pismo Beach. I enjoyed his company; but he didn't make me laugh. And I wasn't ready to try a third. Even though David had married Cece, we still met for lunch occasionally.

The freeway traffic was sparse and I made record time driving to work, parked easily, and walked to the jail.

I'd decided to make the rounds of the hospitalized inmates in 7100, check on the high profiles to make sure they were stable, and then hide out in my office to study.

After dropping off my purse, I walked down to the deputy's booth to let them know I would be available for the day if anyone needed me—but prayed no one would. I made a detour to the hospital kitchen to get a court-line for lunch later and a john wayne, pulled open the heavy fridge door, but found the pickings were sparse: some juice and two little cartons of milk. There weren't any sandwiches or cookies. One tired banana languished on the counter. It reminded me of the joke played on Bigtits.

It hadn't dawned on me that this was a holiday and all the courts would be closed. No need for the kitchen staff to make court-lines. I ferreted about and found a box of raisin bran cereal in an individual carton that became its own bowl. Not much, but that might hold me in case I didn't want to go down to the ODR.

People probably think all psychologists are serious. Not true! Not this one, anyway! At cocktail parties, I usually tell people I'm the roto-rooter lady. If they find out that I'm a psychologist and ask me if I'm analyzing them, my stock answer is, "I only do it for the money."

When I was younger, older psychologists intimidated me. They seemed so smart, to know all of the answers. I was afraid to even hope to ever be so wise. Now I know that no one has the answers for other people's lives. We each have our own answers, and a good psychologist simply helps you to determine what they are, and to trust them.

Sherry was right; no one paid attention to our pilfering from the kitchen anymore. The big scare was over. Have to admit, it was more fun putting something over on the system. Juggling my bounty, I headed down the hall.

"Hey, lady, how about a cig?" I swirled around to see an inmate peering through the tiny window in his cell door.

"Sorry, no can do."

"You fucking bitch."

I got back to my office, closed the bottom half of the door, dropped the box of cereal into the desk drawer for later, and pulled out my materials. After I got everything organized, I reared back in my chair with a textbook on personality theories in one hand and a cup of coffee in the other. I let out a deep breath and thought about how relieved I would be after I passed, and would then be free to start my own private practice.

"Let me out of here, you bastards!" someone was screaming out in the hall. "Let me go! You can't keep me! They're gonna kill me. Don't let them hurt me. Mary, Mother of God, help me. My brain is on fire; I'm burning! Ahhhhh! Help me, please someone help me. You mutherfuckers, help me!"

I came up out of my chair and made it to the door in record time. Across the hall four deputies were struggling to get a gurney out of the elevator. A hogtied duster lay on his stomach, screaming and spitting at the uniforms, his face blanched white and the veins in his neck popping out. He thrashed from side to side, against the sides of the gurney, almost rolling off. The deputies were oblivious to the frantic inmate's desperate pleas.

"Did you get any last night?" the taller deputy asked.

"No. And I spent a hundred and a half bucks on the bitch. I took her to dinner and dancing. Shit, I did the whole thing and didn't get nuthin'," the deputy at the front of the gurney answered.

"You mutherfuckers! Someone, please save me! They're going to burn me. Somebody gotta help me."

"When we got back to her place, she didn't even invite me in for a cup of joe. Just said thanks and that she'd see me around. Driving home, I tossed her phone number out the car window. How 'bout you?"

"I don't want to brag but...." another deputy joined in.

The screaming inmate drowned the uniforms' voices out as they moved on down the hall toward the hospital.

"Let me go, let me out of here! You mutherfuckers! I want to go home. I want to ahhhh...." *Shit, that duster wasn't the only one that wanted to go home—so did I!*

Guess the day wasn't going to be quiet after all.

"Pelto, we need you in the hospital, cell 7102." A uniform stuck his head in my office and told me they had just brought a perp up from 4500 and put him in four point restraints. I'd just settled down again and reopened the textbook.

"Give me a few minutes and I'll be down there." I put the book down and got to my feet in an attempt to stretch out the cramp in my right calf.

"You'd better find yourself a perfumed hankie before you see this ding. He's a mess," the deputy said as he stepped back from the office door to leave.

"Wait! What happened?"

"First, this ding pooped his pants, then the crazy bastard reached down in his briefs and grabbed a handful of it and smeared it into his eyes, stuffed some chunks up his nose, and finger- painted his face brown. His cellmate called the deputy over and told him what happened."

"Have they hosed him down yet?"

"No, they didn't get a chance. That crazy ding tried to gouge his eyes out. Took two trustees and two deputies to take him down. They barely got him into four points before he did some real damage to himself. That asshole laid a brown scratch on the deputy's hand. Cut right through his surgical gloves."

"Will he be okay?" I asked.

"Hope so. He's mad as hell. Had to go down to the nurse's station to have it dressed and get a tetanus shot, praying he doesn't get AIDS."

That adam henry was brought up on our elevator, now it was going to smell like feces as well as urine. That's going to make for a great ride!

After the deputy left, I checked through my phone messages and finished my john wayne. Then I figured I might as well go down to the hospital and get the interview over. I picked up the clipboard and the Intake Forms, and walked back down to 7100. Turning into the first row, I read the numbers on the cell doors, looking for 7102.

"Hey, lady, I need a phone call."

I kept walking.

"You fucking bitch! Did you hear me?"

I kept walking. Hopefully, the interview wouldn't take long. I just needed to enter him into our system and make sure he didn't need more treatment than the FIP team could provide. He might have to be shipped out to a state mental hospital for extended treatment.

Upon finding 7102, a deputy unlocked the cell for me. The uniform had failed to mention that the inmate had finger-combed the shit into his hair. He was disgusting looking as well foul smelling. I stood as far away as possible. A nurse had given the man Haldol IM, but it hadn't taken effect yet.

"You fucking bitch, I ain't answering none of your questions. Look, cunt, if you want to help me, get me a fucking phone call."

"Yeah, sure thing," I said. Unfortunately, he didn't get any more cooperative as I went along. Luckily, I managed to glean enough attitude out of him to know he wasn't suicidal. I finished the interview and asked a passing deputy to lock the cell door.

"Babe, can you see a couple more dudes?"

"Sure." *I'd love to!*

I ended up seeing four more inmates in the hospital area. By the time I reached the end of the first corridor, the inmates had called me a fucking bitch five times. Some happy New Year's Day this was!

Turning the corner leading to the last hallway in the FIP unit, I stopped abruptly and waved my arms wildly to maintain my balance and keep from falling face down on top of a large body lying in the middle of the corridor. I let out a loud yelp and started shaking as my mind flashed back to high school, Jay and my foray into the embalming business. But this time it looked like I might fall on the corpse instead of the other way around.

The body was covered with a yellow sheet, and I couldn't detect any movement. Dead? My heart skipped a beat. I backed away from the body and took a deep breath, not wanting to believe what I was seeing. The door to the cell stood open, no one was in there. Maybe this was a jailhouse prank. The body might spring to life at any minute and grab my leg. After the banana-fake-penis episode with Nurse Nancy, I knew the deputies were more than capable of anything. They enjoyed playing jokes on us.

I turned toward the deputy's booth and met a deputy walking toward me.

"Hey, sweet thing, you got the duty today?"

"All day long."

"What happened, Sam?"

"We're not sure. Found him dead as a doornail at the nine o'clock rounds. From the look of that paunch on him, I'd guess he bought the farm after having a heart attack."

I stood looking down at the shrouded bulk lying on the cold concrete floor.

"Well that poor bastard's out of his misery," I said.

"He's out of his, but you should see the pile of paperwork that asshole has made for me. The least he could have done was to buy it on someone else's shift. Come on down to the booth later, we got some good eats there," Sam said.

It looked like I'd be spared the food in the ODR.

"By the way, could you see a guy in 7124? We brought him up last night. He's depressed and we're afraid he might try something. I'll open his cell for you when you're ready."

"Is he in four points?" I asked.

"No, seems okay now, but we still have him on a suicide watch. You'll have to talk with him in his cell."

"I'll be back shortly."

As I turned to walk away, I glanced back over my shoulder, down the long corridor. The hallway was empty; the body had already been taken away. It was as if the man had never existed—all that was left of him was the paperwork.

I walked back toward my office, ordered a john wayne from a passing trustee, and told him to deliver.

I unlocked the office door, dropped the key in the desk drawer, and slumped down onto the chair. It was only ten-thirty and I had a pounding headache. Gonna be a long day.

The trustee arrived a few minutes later, walked into the office, and sat the cup of hot coffee on the desk.

"Sorry I forgot to bring you some cookies. You want anything else?" He reached down and adjusted himself.

"No thanks." He read the flat expression on my face.

"You okay, Dr. Pelto? You don't seem yourself. You upset about the drug thing?"

Eager to talk, the trustee dropped into the chair beside my desk.

"Drug thing?" The inmates are better informed about the machinations in the jail than Hedda Hopper, the busybody gossip columnist who wrote about the movie stars in the late '70s.

"Sherry and Bobbie are under surveillance. The "Man" thinks they're bringin' in drugs, sellin' to the homeys. Deputies go through their desks almost every night lookin' for evidence. They been searchin' their cars, too." He watched my face.

I moved uneasily on the hard wooden chair, attempting to conceal any clues to my feelings. It was hard to know if the allegations were true or not, but this perp didn't need to know if I had doubts. He might construe anything I said or did as an acknowledgment of their guilt.

"Trustee, I would like a plate of cookies, I'm expecting a guest. Thank you for getting them right away."

He gave me a blank look, stood up, adjusted himself again, then turned and walked out of the office. I wondered if this excessive adjusting was some type of comment or if he had the crabs.

Oh shit, I hoped the girls hadn't done something stupid.

I wasn't in the mood to study, so I grabbed the morning edition of the Times, which I had crammed in my briefcase. I pulled it out, held up the front page, and read a headline: "Man Held in Fire at His Psychotherapist's Home," by Ronald L. Soble, Times Staff Writer.

A man awaiting trial on charges of attempting to rape his psychotherapist and assaulting her with an ax was arrested Thursday on suspicion of setting a house fire in which she and her husband were sleeping.

William Clark, a 37-year-old insurance underwriter from Canoga Park, was booked on additional charges of attempted murder and arson after he walked into the West Los Angeles police station, accompanied by his lawyer.

Clark's bail is set at $1 million.

The victims of the fire were Ava Gawronski, 32, a psychiatric social worker who suffered second- and third-degree burns over 70% of her body from the 4 a.m. Wednesday fire at her West Los Angeles home; and her husband, David, 35, who was burned over 90% of his body.

Both were in critical condition in the burn treatment ward of the Brothman Medical Center in Culver City. Their 8-month-old daughter was rescued unharmed by a neighbor.

I was enraged! Not only at this man, but also at the men I saw who committed the senseless murders of innocent people. Someone should set that asshole on fire. Make him pay for the suffering he'd caused. He should be put to death!

There was enough evidence to show that even with this ultimate punishment hanging over someone's head, it wouldn't prevent them from their hideous acts. It would however, certainly deter them from harming someone else. I had to get out of this place. I might start screaming and not be able to stop. The year remaining to obtain the retirement wasn't worth staying. As soon as I get licensed...

CHAPTER 28

THE WEDDING

The night before Deanne and Richard's wedding, the nuptial party gathered for the rehearsal. It was cold outside and the wind was howling so hard around the patio that it was impossible to stay out long enough to walk through the ceremony. Instead, we walked through it inside the building. The kids were counting on me to arrange perfect weather for their wedding day, and right now that didn't look promising. Unfortunately, the inside area wouldn't be large enough to accommodate all of the guests. Obviously, if it rained, their wedding day could be a disaster.

Returning home from the rehearsal, I watched the forecast on the ten o'clock news. It didn't predict rain. My muscle tension relaxed a little.

After fighting to get to sleep, I downed a Valium and two glasses of wine. I dreamt that a howling wind was lifting Deanne up and carrying her away from me. Frantically, I ran after her, trying to rescue her but was unable to. I woke up in a cold sweat, my heart pounding. The wind had subsided and there was no evidence of rain.

Pulling back the drapes the next morning, I saw heavy clouds hiding the sun, and rain was spotting the bedroom window. My heart sank. Why had I ever made such a crazy promise to the kids? I had assured them that it would be a nice day.

Between eating breakfast and getting dressed, I watched the sky. The rain had turned to a light drizzle. My parents were staying with me and Dad pushed me to stop worrying and trust everything would be fine.

Thank God, the rain stopped two hours before the ceremony and didn't start again until several hours afterward. By the time we headed for the facility, the sun was breaking through the clouds and the wind had subsided. And by the time the guests were arriving, the patio was dry. The weather was just cool enough to enjoy our formal clothes. What a relief!

The wedding was well attended, the bride and groom were beautiful and handsome, and the ceremony went off without a snag. Ron Kline and his wife attended and commented on how beautiful Deanne looked.

Ernie and I walked our daughter down the aisle and the groom's parents did the same for their son.

My new son-in-law hugged me and said he'd never doubted it would be a perfect day. He was impressed with my power—now if only I could keep him impressed.

The wedding and reception had gone perfectly in every respect. My relationship with Larry hadn't. We had a fight over a trivial matter and he left right after the ceremony. My parents left a couple of hours later.

The newlyweds had a flight to Hawaii for their honeymoon and left shortly after the reception. Tera left with her boyfriend and I was home alone. I walked down to Deanne's bedroom and pulled the door shut gently. I would decide what to do with the room some other time. I already missed her.

CHAPTER 29

THE PSYCHOLOGY EXAM

The incessant ringing of the telephone jolted me out of a sound sleep. I didn't open my eyes; instead, I pulled the pillow over my head, trying to drown out the noise. The sound was probably part of my nightmares. I suffered with them through most nights, tossing and turning in an uneasy sleep.

It was four-thirty in the morning, still dark outside.

I was tired, having stayed up late again last night, studying. The psych Boards were being given in less than two weeks and I was already panicking.

The ringing continued, making it impossible to ignore.

I fumbled around for the phone with a bad feeling in my stomach.

Suddenly, I was nervous. Reaching for the phone, I had that uneasy feeling you get when the doorbell rings and a man is standing there with a telegram in his hand. My father always said that nothing good happens when you're awakened in the middle of the night.

After some hesitation, my mother's familiar voice came on the line. She sounded strained as she began to speak. Then she spoke quickly, as if she wouldn't be able to finish telling me what had happened if she didn't. "I'm sorry to have to tell you this, Vonda, but your father is dead." The words spun around inside my mind. I was unable to comprehend what she had said.

"What did you say?" My voice sounded strange.

"Dad is dead."

"What happened?"

She continued, telling me that she had awakened to find the bathroom light burning and Dad gone from their bed. She lay awake, waiting for him to return. After some time, she became concerned and called out to him; he didn't respond. She started looking for him frantically and found him lying on his back on the bathroom floor.

"He looked like he had gotten tired and couldn't get back to the bedroom before falling asleep," she said. "He had placed his eyeglasses above his head and had his arms laying at his sides. I couldn't figure out why he had gone to sleep on the floor. I tried to wake him up. Called his name. Shook him. He didn't respond. I finally realized he wasn't able to, and never would be able to again." Tears welled up in my eyes, my throat constricted, and I couldn't find words to respond.

Mom said she had called the paramedics and they were on their way.

My mother was unnaturally calm; blessed shock had rescued her from the tremendous pain. Her mate of fifty years was gone.

I could picture my father laying on the pale blue bathroom tile with the starched, white eyelet curtains covering the small window located above the bathtub. Tears blurred my vision as I got into a sitting position, now fully awake.

Dad had reached seventy years of age in January, much too young to die. I rocked back and forth, trying to comfort myself. I hung up the phone after I assured her that I would be there as quickly as possible.

I pulled on blue jeans and a sweatshirt, suddenly cold, and met Tera in the hall walking toward me.

"Mom, what's wrong?"

"It's granddaddy. He's gone."

As she dressed, I called Deanne and Richard, and within an hour we were driving to Mother's house located five hours away.

The funeral was held a week later after our relatives arrived from Texas and Arizona. Dad was buried in the local cemetery, which is located alongside a busy freeway. Dad joked that when he was buried, the trucks driving by would probably keep him awake. He was a good, loving man and didn't deserve to die at such a young age.

A few days later, I went to Sears and walked through the men's department where Dad bought his overalls and noticed a man that looked like him. I was sure it was Dad. He hadn't died after all! Someone was playing a terrible trick on me—it was all just a hideous joke! They had hidden him, and when I went home to Needles he would be out in the garden working on his tomatoes. I so wanted to believe that fantasy.

The psychology Board exams were given a week later. I attended them. Don't know how much of the test I completed. It didn't matter. Nothing mattered. During most of the test, I sat staring into space, wondering what was important in life.

The instructor called time and told us to hand in our tests. I didn't respond. I was numb. I looked down at the open booklet and didn't care that it was incomplete. It didn't matter to me. My father was gone.

I still miss him.

CHAPTER 30

WILLIAM BONIN:
I LIKE ANIMALS

It was Monday again. I got up late, didn't have time for breakfast, and rushed out of the house and drove to work. I was having trouble keeping the tears back. But I didn't want to stay home alone. I needed to distract myself.

The traffic was light, making it an easy drive. I pulled into the prized upper parking lot, flashed my counterfeit pass, and walked to the jail's entrance.

Stepping off the elevator on the second floor, I walked by the Trash Bag Murderer's cell on the way to my office. Eli and his roommate were sitting on their beds, opposite each other, clad in white underwear, playing chess. The board and pieces for the game were fashioned from playing cards pasted to bottle caps with toothpaste, pages out of magazines, and toothpicks.

"Do you play chess, Doc?"

"Never did learn."

"How can you have a Ph.D. and not know how to play chess?"

"Too busy going to school and raising kids."

"Can you pull me out today? I gotta talk to you. I'm going crazy, still waiting to go out to Chino. I can't stand this uncertainty. My time on the stand finished a long time ago but the attorney hasn't told the man to release me. Nobody understands how hard this is. I'm 'bout to lose it and do somethin' stupid."

"You going out for an evaluation?"

"Yeah. It'll be good to get out in some fresh air. The food's hot, too. Sure tired of cold mashed potatoes and warm ice cream plopped on top of a slice of white bread. Supposedly, the treatment is better. Not like here where the trustees spit in about everything they give me."

Ken Bianchi had complained about the same indignities.

"They give you psych tests out there, I guess to see if you're crazy. Shit, I don't know what kind of stuff the shrinks want to find out, and I don't care. Anything is better than sitting in this cell all day. Guess they'll make the decision where to ship me out to, to do my time."

"How do they decide which prison to send you to?"

"Depends on what kind of skill the facility needs. Like if you're a carpenter, they'll send you to a prison that needs one. Or if you're an electrician, or whatever. If you're sick, they'll send you to a hospital-type place first and then ship you off to a place to serve your time."

"Eli, I can't make any promises until I see what else is on my agenda today. But I'll try to call you out."

Short-timers often get so agitated when they can see their release dates coming up that they do stupid things, like pick a fight or even try to escape.

An inmate hid in an outgoing laundry basket underneath the clothes. Before the guard noticed he was missing, the basket was loaded in the back of a truck. The inmate might have gotten away except he couldn't wait to have a cigarette. As soon as the truck pulled away from the jail, he lit up. Poor dude had nothing but bad luck. He dropped a match on some of the bed linen and accidentally set them on fire. He panicked.

The smoke started billowing out the back doors of the truck. The driver didn't notice it but another motorist driving along the freeway did. The Good Samaritan pulled up alongside the truck and motioned the driver to pull over. When they opened the back doors, they found a red-faced inmate coughing and trying frantically to stomp out the fire.

The Sheriff's Department was called. They arrived, picked up
the escapee, and returned him to jail. Too bad because the inmate
was a short-timer with only a month left on his sentence, to which
the court tacked on additional time.

I understood his feeling of wanting to escape. After Dad's
death I realized how fragile life is, and how much of my precious
life's energy was being used up everyday just trying to survive
working with the psychopathic inmates. I was loosing myself. I
was loosing my soul.

Driving into work this morning I decided that I should make
a special trip down to see Bonin, fearful that he may have become
suicidal. His sentence had been handed down after the two month
trial and I knew by now the shock he had initially felt would be
worn off. Even though he plead guilty, I was still surprised at
how quickly the trial was completed. At the sentencing hearing
the seven man-five woman jury recommended that he be put to
death.

Now the time had come for me to face my own feelings about
the death penalty. It had taken me many months of struggling
with my early religious training, but now I knew how I felt. Bonin
should not be allowed to live!

Judge Keene ordered that Bonin was to be moved out of the jail
and transported to San Quentin State Penitentiary where he would
be placed on death row until his execution.

I didn't feel ready to see the Freeway Killer yet, so I walked
down to the hospital kitchen and picked up a court line and a coffee
then went back to my office to return some phone calls. I took a bit
of the dry sandwich and was chewing it when the telephone began
to ring.

"Doc, this is Jerger down in 1750. Can you see Bonin this
morning? He didn't want any breakfast. He didn't even want his
freeway time he's always demanding. Something's up."

"Ten o'clock work for you?"

"Works for me," he said.

Bonin's probation report arrived in the morning mail and Lupe had laid it on my desk while I was down at the hospital kitchen. I wanted to read some of his early history before going downstairs to see him, to try and understand some of the factors that made him into a vicious killer. Bonin was the instigator of the killing spree and his four co-conspirators were influenced by him.

I set my coffee aside, picked up the report and began reading.

William George Bonin, the Freeway Killer, was born on January 8, 1947 in Willimantic, Connecticut, growing up in an intact family, sandwiched between two brothers. He was physically abused by his father and neglected by his mother. I skipped over the rest of the personal information.

Bonin had confessed to strangling twenty-one boys and was convicted of torturing and raping fourteen. His killing spree lasted for more than two years. And he was under police surveillance when he killed Stephen Wells, his last victim.

The lives of many people were impacted by his crimes. I'd learned that children reared in homes with overly strict, abusive parents turn out to be very similar in later behavior to children who are raised in permissive homes where little discipline is practiced. As teenagers, both of these groups have difficulty with authority figures and act out inappropriately.

I took a sip of the second john wayne the trustee dropped off and continued to read Bonin's report.

His early criminal behavior involved petty theft, robbery, and grand theft before he graduated up to sex perversion, kidnap, torture, and finally murder. In all, he was suspected of killing forty-four boys.

During the period between November 17, 1968 and January 12, 1969, he was observed driving a vehicle, which had been identified as the one used in a series of assaults on young hitchhikers between the ages of 12 and 17. He offered money as an inducement to get the young men to go with him and consent to engage in oral copulation. After he drove his victims to an isolated spot, he used handcuffs to restrain them and then sodomized them. On one occasion, a 14-year-old was choked and on another occasion, the defendant struck a 17-year-old with a tire iron.

On January 28, 1969, he was arrested for a 288 sex perversion, a 207 kidnapping, and a 286 sodomy on a minor. He was found to be an MDSO and the authorities sent him to Atascadero State Hospital for treatment from January 27, 1971 until June 11, 1974.

For several months in mid-1975, he was seen weekly in private psychotherapy sessions. Later on in the same year he was involved in private counseling at the San Antonio Southeast Mental Health Clinic in Long Beach. *Was doing therapy and being a psychologist all just a bunch of bullshit? Maybe my life has been a waste of time.*

On October 11, 1975, Bonin was arrested again, and pled guilty to molestation charges.

On January 23, 1976, he violated his probation and was sent back to prison, and was incarcerated until October 11, 1978, when he was paroled.

On March 14, 1979, Bonin committed his first murder. He picked up Ronald Gatlin, age 18, in Van Nuys, at approximately eight-thirty in the evening and drove to an isolated area. He tortured the boy, then sodomized and killed him. Gatlin's nude body was found the next day in Duarte, California.

The autopsy revealed that the victim had puncture wounds to his neck and right ear. The coroner stated that "apparently an ice pick had been used to cause the wounds." Gatlin's neck exhibited signs of ligature marks. The death was ruled a homicide. Death by strangulation.

I'd met with Bonin many times and looked for some type of psychopathology but hadn't found any. Thinking of the horrible crimes he had committed made it difficult to believe anyone in his right mind could be so vicious.

"Vonda, you got time to go down for a john wayne?" I was engrossed in Bonin's report and was startled when I heard her voice. Sherry was standing at my doorway.

"Wish I could, but I'm on my way down to see Bonin."

"Have you seen Johnny Wadd yet?"

"Saw him a few days ago."

"Did you get his autograph?"

"No, sorry; I forgot." Actually, I was embarrassed about asking the porn star for it.

"What's he like? I've seen his movies and they're a hoot. Shit, he can't act worth a damn, but with those jewels, who cares."

"He's interesting, bright and quick."

"Is he as sexy looking in person as he is in his films?"

"Yes, he is." I smiled.

"Did you get to see everything?"

"Sherry! It's Magic Fingers that gets that privilege. I'm not that kind of doctor."

"Boy, some girls have all the luck. What did your girlfriend think about meeting Bianchi?"

"She couldn't concentrate on the play, said she just kept thinking back to shaking hands with the Hillside Strangler. And the sound of the cell doors clanking shut and the urine smell in the elevator. She didn't have much to eat in the ODR, either. The best thing is, she doesn't tell me it's no big deal to work here anymore. In fact, she told me she doesn't know how I can stand it."

"So I take it she's not coming back for another visit? Next time, get me an autograph from Holmes," Sherry said as she walked out of the office.

"Catch you later," I said.

I glanced at my watch. Time to go down to see the Freeway Killer.

I picked up a notepad, a pen, then pulled my office door shut behind me and locked it securely.

The elevator transported me down to the first floor. Bonin would remain housed in High Power until he was transferred to San Quentin.

"Stranger in Paradise" was playing. That's a joke!

I got off the elevator, walked the short distance to 1750, and pounded on the metal door, using alternate fists while trying to get a deputy's attention. Finally, a deputy peered through the small window, recognized me, and opened the door.

"You down here to see Bonin?" the deputy asked.

"Yeah."

"Couldn't have happened to anyone more deserving." The deputy gave a thumbs up toward heaven as we walked to the booth. "Occasionally, justice is served," he mumbled.

I nodded my agreement.

"I'd like to see Holmes, also. Is he around?"

"Holmes is in court, probably be back before lunch."

"I need to check Bonin's log first." Sure as hell don't want him killing himself, my ass would be grass. Recording an inmate's daily behaviors was one of the least favorite duties the deputies had to perform, but they gave me a lot of information.

"Let me know when you're ready to see Mr. Bonin, Doc, and I'll pull him out for you."

"No problem."

The deputy unlocked the door to the booth and stepped aside to allow me to enter. I walked straight to the file cabinet, pulled Bonin's log out, poured some coffee, grabbed a maple bar, and sat down at an empty desk.

I took a sip of the coffee and began to read the log. It noted signs of restlessness, problems sleeping, and poor appetite. It also noted that Bonin was withdrawn and isolating himself. He even refused to leave his cell daily for the twenty minutes of freeway time—time he had demanded in the past. The deputies said he liked to go down to another inmate's cell, unzip his pants, and push his woody through the bars for a blowjob.

Bonin's grooming and hygiene had declined. He refused to take a shower or change his clothes, all signs of depression; he might need to be transferred to the inpatient unit on a suicide watch. I would make that decision after evaluating him.

I finished reading the log between bites of pastry and swallows of coffee, then signaled the senior deputy that I was ready to see Bonin. I walked to the interview room—a room that had become as familiar as my own office upstairs.

Waiting for the deputy to return with Bonin, a sense of dread came over me. I had resolved my ambivalence about the death penalty, but we had developed a relationship over the last year, and he had come to trust me and let me see his vulnerable side. *Did we as a society fail him?* If his parents had taken him to therapy when he first started having trouble at age nine, would that have made things different? Or kept him at home instead of putting him in a County facility? Or if he hadn't been raped by several older boys? If all of these things had been different, would he be at this juncture in his life, or would it have turned out differently? I wished I had the answer—not only for him but for other kids I would see in the future.

It was too late for Bill. He'd committed unforgivable acts and would have to suffer the consequences. He'd made his choices.

Within a few minutes, the deputy appeared with Bonin following behind. Bonin's stride was slow and deliberate with his shoulders slumped forward, his head hanging down.

I wondered if he felt guilt or remorse for his deeds. Or was he only sorry he'd gotten caught? I would soon get my answer.

The Deputy pulled out his keys, unlocked the door to the cold, windowless interview room, and flipped on the switch that ignited the overhead fluorescent tubes. The bright light was unable to dispel the gloominess of the interior space.

Without instruction, Bonin pushed the door open, walked to the raised chair, and slumped into it. I walked to the desk chair, trying to conceive how Bonin must be feeling. I settled down onto the chair and waited for the deputy to cuff Bonin's arm. After he had finished, he glanced in my direction and left quietly.

I scrutinized Bonin's face as he looked around the room. His eyes slowly studied the walls as if he were seeing them for the first time. After he thoroughly inspected the room, he turned back to face me.

Silence hung in the air like a hangman's noose. I waited for him to speak, tapping the underside of the desk, trying to relax. Finally, after some time had passed, Bonin spoke, his tone angry.

"I've been sentenced to death! Sentenced to die by lethal injection."

"I know." I felt like I should say something more, but I didn't have any words to comfort him.

"This doesn't seem right. I really couldn't help myself. The urge to kill was too strong."

I sat rolling my ballpoint pen back and forth under the palm of my hand.

"I know I pled guilty, but they could have just given me life without parole. I don't want to die!"

I sat quietly, alternating between scrutinizing Bonin's face and looking at the ugly mustard-colored wall behind where he sat.

"Guess I'm in shock or somethin', 'cause none of this feels real."

Bonin dropped his head down to rest it in his free hand. The hum of the air conditioner was the only sound that penetrated the silence. After several moments Bonin raised his head and his eyes were glassy with tears.

"It kinda feels like all this shit is happenin' ta somebody else, not me. When the jury called out those verdicts, I jus' sat there - it was like I was in some kinda fog or somethin'."

His voice had changed to a monotone. His face was flat, devoid of expression. I remembered seeing Bonin on the Friday night newscast after the death penalty sentences were read. His face wore the same expression. He appeared to have dissociated, much like I did when I sat for the State Boards.

Bonin looked out at me with empty eyes.

"Dr. Pelto, did you see Billy Pugh? I'm worried about him. He's real scared. Guess you already know he did some of the murders with me."

"I know. I'll talk with him."

"Bill, I read your probation report. You had a long history of picking up boys, having sex with them, and then letting them go. You didn't kill for many years. What changed? What made you start killing?"

"I met Vernon Butts. I admired him 'cause, shit, he had it all together. Everybody liked him; it was cool having him like me.

Made me feel real important. I never had no friends. I was shy
and uncomfortable around everybody, and I couldn't make it with
girls. One time I got my courage screwed up and tried to ask this
here girl out for a date. She wouldn't give me the time of day. It
really hurt me when she jus' laughed while I stumbled 'round. I
made up my mind right then that I'd never let a girl hurt me like
that again."

"I read where you were married for a short period of time."

"My mom pushed that. Didn't last long, big mistake." He
looked away with a frown.

"My teeth was bad, all crooked. I wouldn't smile 'cause I was
embarrassed. I was a homely kid, and jus' never fit in.

"Vern hung 'round with this here other guy named Jim Muir. I
think he's still out there somewhere doin' his thing, killin' kids."

Were the authorities aware of this man? I wondered.

"Vern told me that he and this here guy would go off for a
whole day with a kid, take him up to the L.A. sewer system to play
Dungeon and Dragons, and then kill him. It sounded real excitin',
listenin' to him talk. He never tole me how many kids they'd killed
before I come along. God, I miss him. I still can't believe he hung
himself."

"Did you believe his story? That he'd actually killed someone?
Maybe he said that just to impress you."

"Sure, I believed him; why not! Hell, Vernon didn't need to
impress me. He was on the inside."

"Did he ever tell you about any of the killings?"

"Tole me how he and this other guy rammed an ice pick into a
kid's ear. He described it, I mean all about it. Said it only goes in so
far before it bounces off some bone inside. I guess he musta done
it 'cause otherwise he wouldn't have known what would happen.
I almost was gettin' a boner when Vernon was describing some of
the stuff they would do. He was really somethin'. We'd sit and talk
for hours." Bonin was smiling, remembering "the good old days."

The room felt hot and stuffy. Bonin's body odor was
pervasive.

"One afternoon Vern and me picked up a kid, had sex with him, and then strangled him. After I did that one, then it was no big deal. Besides, then I didn't have to worry no more 'bout the kids identifying me.

"People don't know what goes on out there. You just watch, one of these days they're gonna be in for a real big surprise."

"What kind of big surprise, Bill?"

"There's still a group of guys down in the South Bay that meets jus' to play the Dungeons game. They're inta all kindsa sex stuff and sadomasochism, too. They're not gonna stop with their fun and games. You watch and see."

I shifted in my chair. *Should I tell the authorities, or did they already know?* I glanced over at the doorway and saw the edge of a deputy's shoulder protruding through. I was glad he was listening.

"Bill, how come you let some of the boys go and killed others? How did you make that decision? You moved Jim Munro in shortly after you met him, and didn't harm him."

"Sometimes, I jus' got frustrated over things, felt horny and restless and wanted to scream. I'd get tense and think I was gonna go crazy if I couldn't get some release, like my head would explode. So I'd go out huntin'. Killin' helped me ta mellow out. At work, I'd think 'bout what I was gonna do when I got home, and that would help me get through the day. It was like pressure in my brain needin' to go gamblin' or gettin' drunk. I had to do it."

I sat quietly, listening to him. I didn't get sick to my stomach anymore.

"One time I picked up this sixteen-year-old kid and took him back to the house. We partied a while, then I headed to the john to take a leak. When I come back to the bedroom, I caught him goin' through my billfold. He'd lifted a hundred. I asked him about it, he denied takin' it. I said, 'Well, I think you did.' Kid kept sayin' he didn't. Shit, I wanted to kill him, but I couldn't 'cause too many people had seen him with me. Figured they'd link me to the kid if he turned up dead. I was so damn mad at that asshole. I was boiling' inside. But I couldn't off him. Couldn't take a chance on getting caught. I dropped the turd off and then went out looking for someone to kill."

Bill had become animated and was using his free hand for emphasis.

"Dr. Pelto, I had to do somethin' to release the tension. Ya gotta understand what it was like. I felt like I would explode inside. What else could I do?"

I didn't answer him. But a lot of alternatives flashed through my mind, for instance going to the gym. Thank God, not everyone takes the same course as he did.

"I went up to Hollywood Boulevard and found this kid to pick up. I tole him the story about the kid stealin' my money and how mad I was. I tole him straight out I was gonna kill him. That maybe it wasn't fair but I had to do it."

"What did the boy say?"

"At first he didn't believe me, he thought I was jus' jerking him around. Then he began to cry, beg me not to kill him. Didn't get much more time to say anythin' 'cause I killed him about five seconds later."

"Did you feel better after you killed him?" I was working hard to keep my voice flat.

"Felt a little better, helped me get rid of some of the pressure inside my head."

"Any sympathy for the boy, when he screamed and pled for his life?"

"Nah. I didn't feel nothin' for him. See, I wasn't thinkin' about his feelings."

"Was it like killing an animal?" I asked. He shook his head from side to side.

"Nah. That kid was like an object, a thing. I got more feelings for animals."

Bonin was worse than an animal. Animals don't kill for revenge or sexual excitement. They kill with a purpose.

"When you killed a boy, did you think about his family grieving for him?" As soon as the words came out of my mouth, I knew the answer. Bill shook his head from side to side as he answered.

"Nah. I didn't feel nothin' for him or his family. I didn't think about any of them." Bonin didn't hesitate before answering, but seemed frustrated that I didn't get it. He felt no guilt, remorse, or sadness, the normal human feelings!

"Nothin', no ma'am. Hell, I didn't feel nothin'." He began to fidget around in the chair.

"Bill, if you hadn't been caught, would you have stopped killing?"

"Nah, there weren't no way I could have stopped myself."

"Do you think any type of therapy would have kept you from killing in the first place?"

"Shit, I been through all kinds of that talk therapy. That stuff's a bunch of crap. All that bullshit don't do nothin'. Most of those therapists don't know their ass from their elbow. I learned that psych jargon and parroted it back to them. I knew what they needed to hear."

My God! Was I one of those stupid therapists? I sure as hell felt like one of them right now.

"Do you think you wanted to get caught on some level? Like you deserved to be punished?" Many theorists believe people feel they deserve punishment and make mistakes in order to be found.

He looked at me, eyes wide open, as if I was totally out of my mind.

"That's a bunch of bullshit. You're kiddin' me, right? I wanted to get caught and wanted to be punished? That's some stupid idea. Shit, that sounds like some do-gooder social worker's theory. I'm just sorry I wasn't more careful. But I did get away with it for quite a while." Bonin's face broke out in a big smile.

"Well, they caught me, but you're gonna be real surprised. This ain't over, you watch and see. There's a lot of guys still out there, killin'."

Will the killings ever stop?

He turned his dead eyes to the wall and repeated, "Nah, I wouldn't have stopped killin'."

The deputy uncuffed William George Bonin's wrist and lead him out of the claustrophobic room. The enormity of his crimes blanketed me like a cold shroud and made my body feel stiff and resistant to moving.

Finally, with great effort, I stood up, stretched, and tried to touch my toes, then gave up the idea and walked back toward the main part of the module.

CHAPTER 31

JOHN HOLMES—
IN THE BUFF

"**O**kay, boys, bend over and spread those little pink cheeks." The senior deputy's voice bellowed out the order. "Gotta make sure you homeys didn't bring anything back from court you weren't supposed to."

The deputy was pulling on rubber gloves. Initially, I wasn't sure what was happening. Of course, I knew about strip searches but had never been present at one.

John Holmes, the King of Porn, and Angelo Buono, the Hillside Strangler, were bent over, directly in front of me. In the buff! Their blues lay in a rumpled heap over to the side of the room. The two men had been returned from court on the noon bus and were being put through the customary search. The rectum is a favorite place used by the inmates to hide everything from drugs to guns.

These searches are necessary to protect the deputies. A deputy was killed by an inmate who had hidden a gun and escaped from custody. The inmate jammed a gun up into his body cavity before being taken out of jail. While he was being transported to court in the back of a patrol car, the inmate dislodged the gun from its hiding place and when the car stopped at a traffic signal, the inmate raised the gun and shot the deputy to death. He jumped out of the car and took off running down the street. It took several weeks before he was recaptured. I never heard how he got out of the patrol car or how he got his cuffs off. Guess the "how" didn't matter.

I quickly stepped back out of view and waited until the Senior completed his search, hoping no one had seen me. Then I thought to myself, *Now, Vonda, a nice girl wouldn't go out there with these two naked men.* Then I thought, *What the hell! I don't feel like a nice girl anymore.* Working in the jail for the last two years, I'd become accustomed to being called a fucking bitch, and telling people to fuck off. I didn't feel like a psychologist—I felt like a street fighter trying to survive in a battle zone. Cussing with the deputies was all part of my life. My world had become distorted. The majority of my life was spent with killers. Oftentimes, it was difficult to believe some of the men were murderers because they were so nice to me. Even though I knew most of it was manipulation, it still felt good when Ken told me I worked too hard or John told me I was attractive. Except for my two children, there was no one else in my life that seemed to care about me.

I was no longer that young girl raised in the church. I didn't fit in with the PTA ladies or the Women's Club anymore. I was different. I had heard and seen things that most people are barely aware of; I didn't fit in on the outside.

I looked back at the Wadd and decided to move in for a closer look.

John looked even longer and leaner standing there without his clothes. His body was almost hairless and it was evident that the filmmakers hadn't needed to use any trick photography or enhancements. Angelo, on the other hand, was short and skinny with a lot of body hair. He was a sharp contrast to Holmes in every way. Buono had a tattoo on his arm, but I couldn't make out what it said, and didn't want a second look.

"Okay, boys, you're clean. You can suit up," the deputy said.

With his announcement, I walked slowly back out into the module. The deputy finished pulling off his gloves, walked over, and dropped them in a wastepaper basket.

"John, I understand you wanted to talk with me today," I said, now standing two feet from him. If I stood any closer, I could get pregnant! Wait until Edi hears that I saw Johnny Wadd in the nude.

"I really do." His voice was full of seduction and charm.

"I have some time now."

My face burned as red as my hair—not with embarrassment, but with excitement.

"I'll be right in. After all, I'm not catching a train anywhere," John said.

I glanced over at Buono; he gave me an icy stare and turned away. He pulled on his blues quickly, irritated by my presence.

John, on the other hand, was preening and seemed to enjoy the discomfort the deputies were feeling as they watched our exchange. John looked at me and winked.

"Yo, homeboy, get back in your blues." The deputy reached out and patted John's bare arm to get his attention.

I returned to the interview room to wait for him. Boy, if the girls could see me now.

A short time later, John walked through the door into the little office, went straight to the barber chair, and stepped up into it. He knew the routine. The deputy followed closely behind and put John through the usual ritual of cuffing his wrist to the chair.

"Good to see you again, Dr. Pelto. How's tricks?"

"How did it go in court today?" I asked.

"My attorney said we're going to meet with the prosecutors next week to try to work out a deal.

"The D.A., Coen, says he has to see what I got to offer before he will consider talking a deal. But shit, I know what they're gonna want." John pulled his mouth tight. "They're gonna want me to testify against Eddie Nash and Gregory Diles in exchange for immunity from prosecution. If Coen thinks I'm gonna say anything, he's gotta think I'm crazy or stupid. No way in hell would I do that. I'd rather take my chances with the jury system than with Nash and Diles."

"John, it sounds like you're between a rock and a hard place." I immediately regretted using that cliché.

"When they picked me up in Florida, I admitted to Detective Frank Tomlinson that I had engineered the murders back in July."

"The ones at Wonderland Avenue?"

"Shit, I didn't have no choice."

"Why not?"

"Nash threatened to kill me. I was scared. He is evil. He got my address book and wrote down the names of all my friends and family. Eddie told me if I ever talked he would have them all killed. Shit, man! I won't ever talk. Even if I was dead, he would seek revenge against them."

John was agitated. He tapped his fingers noisily on the arm of the chair.

"How did the murders come about?"

"They were in retaliation of the robbery. Eddie figured that I had something to do with his stuff getting stolen 'cause I was over at his place all the time. Told me he'd kill me if I didn't tell him who did it."

"Did you believe him?"

"Yeah, but I swear I didn't know he would kill anybody. I thought he would get his stuff back and then ream them a new asshole. Dr. Pelto, trust me—I'll never say who did."

John was visibly shaking.

Out of the corner of my eye, I caught a glimpse of a deputy standing in the doorway. "Everything okay?" I smiled and nodded. The uniform stepped out of sight, but I figured he was still listening.

Holmes' face looked strained.

John and two other men had a deal going with Eddie Nash. They would steal all types of merchandise, trade them to Eddie for drugs, and then sell the drugs to get cash on which to live. They got into a bind when they started using the drugs themselves and not having enough left over to sell.

Holmes admitted that it was his idea to rob Eddie. He knew where Eddie had the drugs and cash hidden. One night, John met with the guys at Wonderland and drew a floor plan of Nash's house. Early on the day of the robbery, John went to Eddie's and made sure the sliding door was unlocked. The plan worked like a charm. The guys broke in, got the drugs, some jewelry, and a bonus of ten thousand dollars in cash.

"Did you go to the Wonderland Avenue address with Eddie?" I asked hesitantly.

"I took him over there, but I swear I didn't know he would kill anybody.

"I had to set it up for him. I may have been there, but I swear I didn't kill anyone. And, Doc, trust me—I'll never say who did," he reiterated.

"My attorney is arguing duress as my defense. Eddie threatened my life. I didn't have any choice. I had to let Eddie know where the robbers lived."

Nash and Diles were considered suspects in the murders but, due to lack of evidence, had not been charged. They picked Nash up on drug charges; that's all they could hold him on.

"They've postponed my trial until April twenty-seventh. No bail. I don't know how long I'm going to be stuck in this shit hole." John tapped his feet furiously on the metal plate of the chair.

"That Eddie is a coke freak! He snorts about a million bucks up his nose a year," John said angrily.

"By the way, did you know I have a new film coming out? It's called Exhausted. Those publicity guys say I had sex with fourteen thousand women. They exaggerated! It was only thirteen thousand eight hundred and seventy."

It was hard to believe that John actually knew the exact number of woman he had sex with, but I didn't question him. What did it matter?

Later in the afternoon I tried to compute how many liaisons that would be per day or per week, throughout his thirteen-year acting career. At 37, Holmes had to have been very busy. I figured he was exaggerating.

"You know, Doc, most women make even a strong man go limp. When we do a film shoot, I have to concentrate on one part of her to keep the Big Guy standing at attention. Like, if she has pretty breasts or hips or skin, things like that. I have to ignore the rest of her."

"You seemed to have engineered a system that works for you."

"I like talking to you, Doc, because you're an intelligent woman."

"Thank you, John." I figured he was playing me to spend more time out of his cell, but it sure as hell beat being called a fucking bitch by some of the other inmates I saw.

"Some of the girls I work with are really beautiful, but they have nothing between their ears. They're a real turnoff for me. You ask them if they like Kipling, and they ask what group he's with. Dumb, really dumb!" John had crossed his legs and was wildly swinging his right one.

"How are you feeling?"

"I'm a little down. It's the shits being in that cell all day. It really helps when you call me out.

"By the way, Billy Pugh has a crush on you," John said. "He wanted to write you a poem, but I think he chickened out. He said he likes to talk to you. I told him I have a crush on you, too. He said he would step aside and let me have you." John watched for a reaction.

I couldn't keep myself from smiling. This was all such a game. All this mock male competitiveness. So many of my conversations with the inmates were pure manipulation—nah, they were pure bullshit.

"Do you enjoy reading?"

"Yeah, but I like to fuck more." He enjoyed trying to shock me. He didn't know I was way past that point.

"You're a real attractive woman, Doc. And, anytime you want a free one with the Big Guy, you can have him. You can have him right now. Just push the door closed. Man, he sure would like to come out for a spin." I had to work hard to keep a straight face.

"Mr. Holmes, that's not a possibility." I had to admit that Big Guy was an apropos name. And I was excited by his offer. What was I thinking, if only for a moment? John Holmes is on trial for bludgeoning four people to death. I'm a psychologist. I could understand how some of the female staff got involved with inmates. These men were our world. Staff members have been charmed into helping inmates escape. These inmates become like suitors and fill both their need and our need for a relationship, no matter how inappropriate it is.

I walked to the door, found a deputy listening outside, and asked him to return Holmes to his cell. After the cuffs were released, John stepped down from the chair, stretched, and turned to me before leaving.

"Dr. Pelto, thank you for seeing me. Would you please see me again real soon?"

"Sure. I'm down here almost daily. I'll call you out."

I was wondering: *What's a nice girl like me, doing in a place like this?*

CHAPTER 32

ANGELO BUONO:
TALK TO MY LAWYER

I followed Holmes out of the office, back into the main portion of the cellblock. My mind was reeling. I had just seen John Holmes, the Wadd, in the buff! I couldn't believe it. *And oh, my God, what I was fantasizing! Far fucking out!*

It was flattering that he found me attractive. It was hard being a woman and to not respond to his compliments. What in the hell was wrong with me? I was a professional. How could I ever entertain the idea of seeing Holmes outside of the jail? I spent more time and got more attention from Holmes than I did Larry. And he was by far friendlier than the FOP staff.

The conflict arose from being trained to work with people with a nonjudgmental attitude. I was taught to compartmentalize my mind. Separate out what a person has done and deal with him in an objective manner. The problem was, blocking out what they had done, made them human to me. Being a psychologist, a single woman, and a mother, it was difficult to maintain an appropriate distance from the inmates.

As I rounded the corner heading out of the module, I spotted Angelo Buono, now fully clothed, standing in the hall, talking to the senior deputy. Bianchi had painted a horrific picture of Buono, describing how he had raped a girlfriend's 14-year-old daughter, saying, "It was to educate her about sex the right way."

Just looking at Buono made my skin crawl. He had the look of a hungry snake with a gaunt face, black shiny eyes, and slicked-back, graying hair. I dreaded talking to him.

I addressed my request directly to the deputy.

"Would you take Mr. Buono into the interview room? I need to speak with him."

The deputy turned to me with an uncertain look, wondering if I really wanted to talk with this killer.

"I have to see him." The deputy caught my look, and remembered that was my job.

He turned to Buono.

"Okay, homeboy, you heard the lady."

The Hillside Strangler turned, glared at me, but didn't move. Buono clenched his jaws. He wasn't going to get an "A" on the cooperation scale. I didn't like the idea of spending time with him and knew the feeling was mutual.

"Come on, homey, move it." The deputy pointed his finger toward the door to the interview room.

Reluctantly, Buono started moving forward, shooting dirty looks back at me as he walked. I followed several paces behind, not wanting to chance being touched by him. Of all the killers I had seen so far, he was the most frightening looking.

I got across the small office and sat down beside the desk as Buono stepped up into the barber chair. He continued to glare at me with icy black eyes. The deputy snapped the cuffs closed, and looked back at me before he left the room.

"I'll be right outside if you need me."

"Thanks."

How in the hell did Buono persuade all of those woman to have sex with him?

Bianchi had said "there were girls over at his place every night, doing him. I couldn't figure out why they kept comin' back, 'cause Angelo treated them like dirt—called them whores, sluts, and cunts to their faces."

An article in the L.A. Times said a snitch named Steven Barnes told the jury Buono had admitted that he was responsible for the

Hillside Murders. Later, Barnes changed his story and said Buono admitted he killed some of the girls. The confession supposedly took place in a sheriff's van when Barnes and Buono were being transported to court. Buono's defense attorney, Gerald Chafe, said that his client "has never admitted to any of the murders" and that Barnes was "not a trustworthy person." I thought about what Komerchero had said about the snitch system not being reliable.

After the deputy left the room, along with my usual spiel about lack of confidentiality, I explained to Buono that I wasn't there to discuss his case or anything to do with it.

"Does my lawyer know you're talkin to me?"

"No, he doesn't."

"Then why am I here?" he demanded, glaring at me.

"I'm an employee of the county Mental Health Department assigned to the Forensic Outpatient unit in the jail. My job is to see if you are experiencing any problems that I can help you with." He gave me a dirty look. I was grateful he was cuffed to the barber chair and that it was securely anchored into the concrete floor. I double-checked its base to make sure the bolts were still in place.

"I don't need any help." His words came out in a snarl.

"Can I get a little information on you?" I needed to evaluate any suicidal potential Buono might have.

"Are you having any problems sleeping?"

"Ask my lawyer."

"What about your appetite? Any changes?"

"Ask my lawyer."

"Mr. Buono, I'm not here to cause you any problems or talk about your case. In fact, I don't want to discuss anything you're uncomfortable with. I'm only interested in your mental health. I want to be sure you're not in danger of hurting yourself." So he would be more at ease, perhaps I needed to start with information that was already in the computer.

"Could you tell me your birth date?"

"Ask my lawyer. Look, lady, I don't need or want anybody's help."

I was exasperated. But I had gotten enough attitude that I knew this alleged Hillside Strangler wasn't suicidal and I had covered my butt. I figured if you looked up the word "asshole" in the dictionary, you would find Angelo Buono's picture beside it.

"You through, lady? I got nothin' else to say to you."

I was convinced. I would make routine checks of his log and avoid any further contact with him.

God, Angelo was amazing; he had gotten four women to marry him and had eight children with them. It wasn't clear whether he bothered divorcing one wife before he married another one. He beat the holy shit out of his wives and scared them half to death if they didn't obey him. Buono was a brutal and depraved man. Thank goodness, he wasn't suicidal. I wouldn't have to see him again.

A deputy released Buono and I returned to the second floor, feeling irritable after the encounter with him.

After picking up some coffee, I returned to my office and pulled out Bonin's report to continue reading. I would think about lunch later on.

September 9, 1979, in the early morning hours, the defendant, along with Vernon Butts, abducted David Murillo, age 17. He was riding his bicycle on the way to the movies. They drove the boy to a secluded spot and then Bonin and Butts took turns sodomizing him. When they grew tired of him and were sexually satisfied, they bashed Murillo's head in with a tire iron and strangled him with a ligature until dead.

They drove to the Ventura Freeway off-ramp and threw the body out of Bonin's van. It was discovered on September 12, 1979.

On February 4, 1980, Bonin was picked up again—this time for a parole violation. He was remanded to the Orange County Jail until March 4, 1980. After a month of incarceration, on April 10, 1980, he was discharged from parole. Later that same day, he picked up Steven Wood, and sodomized and killed him.

He was involved in killing kids during the time he was on parole and checking in with an officer. The justice system had the

Freeway Killer incarcerated and didn't know it. *Well, that's the way it goes!*

Bonin teamed up with William Pugh on March 25 and May 29 and, together, they killed two more kids.

On April 29, 1980, Vernon Butts and William Bonin picked up Darin Lee Kendrick, age 19.

I put down the probation report and plucked the telephone receiver out of its cradle to stop the incessant ringing.

"You ready to go to lunch?" Sherry's voice came on the line.

"Youbetcha! I've been sitting here reading Bonin's probation report. Let's go see what creative things the inmates have done to our food today." I grabbed my office key, walked out into the corridor, and locked my office door.

A couple minutes later I heard the door to the FOP unit slam and heard Bobbie and Sherry's voices before they rounded the corner to the main hall.

However, as we walked to the ODR, I didn't join in on their banter. I was preoccupied with Bonin, who had been incarcerated many times, placed on probation and parole many times, violated probation and parole many times, returned to prison many times, given psychotherapy and then placed in mental hospitals for treatment many times.

"And he continued to kidnap, sodomize, torture, and kill!" I mumbled to myself, which made me question the value of incarceration and psychiatric care.

"Did you say something to me?" Sherry asked.

"No, just thinking out loud."

When we joined them at their table in the cafeteria, Deputies Johnson and Gonzales were already eating the roast beef, minus the lumpy gravy.

"Komerchero was finally shipped out to Chino today," I said.

"You mean Camp Snoopy? Real hard time!" Deputy Gonzales said sarcastically. "Tennis court, swimming pool, and lots of time out in the fresh air."

"He was afraid someone might attempt to kill him on the bus

ride out there," I said between bites of salad. "Since he's a high profile, do you think he was in danger?"

"He might've been," Gonzales said. "Any inmate who offs a perp like Komerchero gets respect and a lot of high fives from the other perps."

I hoped he would be okay.

"Did you hear that the Hefty Bag Company has contacted Komerchero?" Sherry asked.

I took the bait. "What for?"

"They wanted him to be a spokesman for their products. Their slogan is going to be: You slice and dice, we'll bag and ship. Money back guarantee if they leak."

"Yuk! That's disgusting," I said "But funny."

"Trustee, get me some coffee." Bobbie pulled out her cigarettes and lit one up.

"Me, too," Sherry said.

"Back to their safety, is there anything these guys can do to protect themselves? Do have to admit it saves the taxpayers a lot of money if they're offed," I said.

"Not much else they can do," Deputy Johnson said. "If one of these perps really wants to get someone, it's hard to stop them. They're real good at hiding shanks. They even stick them up their asses."

"That's got to hurt." I said.

"Yeah, and Magic Fingers loves to fix them up if they get cut."

"These perps haven't got anything to do all day. They're bored out of their minds. So they got time to think up new weapons."

I still didn't understand why in the hell they didn't keep these guys busy. I remembered what Jose had told me about the unions, and that they would be upset if they were put out of work. Still, it seemed to me that the inmates could be put to work doing something constructive.

The inmates take toothbrushes, hold them over a flame to soften them, and then sharpen the end by rubbing it on the cement floor. They also strip metal pieces from the ceiling and then rub them on the cement floor until they can shape them into shanks. Maintenance has to constantly do repairs. And they use razor blades to push into the softened ends of toothbrushes. When they get into fights, they can do a lot of bodily harm to each other.

After they go after each other, the deputies wait until they bleed out and lose consciousness. Then they go into the cell and haul the inmates up to 8000 where the doctors sew them up. Magic Fingers loves new faces.

"You guys ever afraid of getting hurt? You don't carry guns or nightsticks." I said.

"We carry flashlights, and they can be pretty persuasive. When things get out of control, we can use them." Jose said.

I'd heard of flashlight therapy, even seen the results of it. And I could understand the deputies being frustrated enough with the inmates to use it. It didn't make any sense to prepare the sheriff's personnel with extensive training with an emphasis on physical ability and then trap them in this vile environment for seven years after completing the academy. They're trained to engage in physical action and then not given a chance to use it.

"Enough of this jail talk," Sherry interrupted. "Johnson, tell us about the blind date Jose fixed you up with the other night. Did you get any kutchie?"

"Are you kidding? I wouldn't have fucked her with Jose's one-eyed monk."

"Come on, she couldn't have been all that bad," Sherry said.

"I'm telling you, she had a toilet seat ass and her kutchie was so puckered up, it looked like an old man's wrinkled, watery eye. Jose, you mutherfucker, don't ever do me another favor," Johnson said.

I pushed back my chair and stood.

"Thanks, guys, for a great lunch. I really needed a distraction. I've got to get back upstairs. Ron asked me to see Christopher Grinsby right after lunch. Thinks he might be suicidal."

"Wait up, Vonda, I'll walk back with you. I've got a bunch of perps to see. You coming, Bobbie?" Sherry asked.

"No. I can't face the rows yet."

We arrived at the elevator just as the doors opened, stepped in, and Sherry pushed the button for the second floor.

"Sherry, have they started transferring women into the psych hospital?"

"No. Why?"

"The other day I saw a very attractive woman walking down the corridor in 7100. She had on a tight T-shirt and a great set of boobs."

"Vonda, that wasn't a woman. That was Miss Victoria. He's in the process of becoming a woman."

"She's a man!"

"She or he—who knows what to call it at this stage? It's undergoing sex change operations."

"Geez, he's got bigger tits than I do," I said.

"He's taking female hormones. That's what made his boobs develop. Smoking pot also makes a man's tits get bigger."

I touched one of my breasts. *"What about me? Would it help my thirty-four C's?"*

"Little buckaroo, if that did the trick, we'd all be sittin' 'round smokin', big time. Shit! Some of these guys have better bodies than I do, and I've got a damn good one, even if I do say so myself," Sherry said.

Her sense of humor was great. She didn't take herself too seriously.

She told me that the deputies love the transsexuals. They give them tight shirts to wear, especially if they have a great rack. When the inmates come in through the reception center, they're asked their sexual orientation. If they're gay, they're asked if they're a stud or a queen. The deputies try to keep the studs together and the queens separate. Wouldn't you know, these studs often lie about their orientation to get put in with the queens? Then they party hardy.

"They be askin', 'You wannabe the wife or the husband? Wanna suck dick or get dicked?" Sherry said.

The inmates are not allowed to bring in make-up so they get it out of magazines. They rub the glossy pictures and get color off for rouge, lipstick, and eye shadow. And they use burnt matchsticks for eyebrows and eyeliner. These gays are very inventive.

"Have you noticed the tattoos? They apply them here in the jail, too."

"You're kidding." I raised my eyebrows.

"They use something sharp to cut the skin and then rub ashes into the wounds to make the designs."

"That's got to hurt," I said. "I can hardly stand getting a shot, and I pass out when the doctor wants to take blood."

"These tattoos are a macho thing; shows how brave these perps are. See you later," Sherry said, leaving me at the elevator on the second floor.

Shit! Christopher Grinsby was sitting on the bench, waiting to talk to me. I'd have to put off studying.

CHAPTER 33

RED HOT PANTS

Grinsby, a pale, effeminate 19-year-old boy accused of murder, sat quietly, fidgeting with the collar on his jumpsuit. It was wrinkled and he was licking his finger and pulling at it in an attempt to straighten out the stubborn fabric.

He sat perfectly straight on the chair opposite my desk and studied a picture drawn by an inmate hanging on the wall behind where I sat.

"Please, could we have some hot coffee? I've heard from the other men that you can get that for us, and maybe some cookies? It would be awfully nice of you."

Grinsby was soft and vulnerable, and would probably be raped before the week was over. It would happen when he went down to take a shower. The Sheriff's Department provided special modules for gang members, gays, and young or extremely vulnerable-looking inmates, and strived to make the pods homogeneous—but that didn't always keep them safe.

I remembered commenting to Ron, "It's a surprise that the county jail system seems so evolved and endeavors to be sensitive and protective of the men in custody."

At the time, Ron had laughed at me and said, "Don't kid yourself. They're no more sensitive than the inmates they have to protect. The Sheriff's Department just has to make sure nothing happens to these guys to interfere with the process of justice while they're waiting for their trials."

I ordered some coffee and a plate of cookies from a trustee. Sometimes I worried I might float away, drinking so much.

"Mr. Grinsby, Dr. Kline said you needed to talk with someone."

"Oh, please, call me Chrissy. I'm so scared, 'cause they've accused me of murder. I didn't do it." He reached up to smooth out his mop of hair.

"What happened?" An inmate decrying his innocence wasn't new to me, but it was my job to listen to them.

"Me and my friend Kenny had gone out to a club to dance. I was wearing my red satin hot pants and looked really cute."

I could see it.

"Well, anyway, we met this good looking stud as he was coming out of the club. He wanted to know if we would go with him to find this lady named Janet. What a body he had! Kenny and I didn't know either one of them, but it sounded like an adventure. Well, he called over a cab, and Kenny climbed in the front with the driver and I cuddled up with Ed in the back. By the by, that was the stud's name: Ed. Did I mention I had a darling little top that matched my hot pants perfectly?"

I could see that, too, but wished he would get to the point.

"Well, anyways, we were just riding around, then this stud, he just leaned up over the front seat to Kenny and told him to take his clothes off, right there in the front seat of the cab. Can you imagine? Kenny actually did it, too. Can you imagine? He actually took off all his clothes. I was so surprised." I wanted to ask what the cab driver was doing all this time but I didn't want him to prolong the story any longer than absolutely necessary.

"Next thing you know this stud tells the cabby to drive to the beach. Well, he took the next turn, I didn't really even know exactly where we were, but I guess we were going to the beach.

"Next thing you know Ed starts hitting Kenny, and then he puts his belt around Kenny's throat and starts choking him. When we got to the beach, he threw Kenny out of the cab."

"Was Kenny all right?"

"Well. That's just the thing. I don't know." Chrissy started to cry.

"What did the cab driver do?" I had some doubts about the validity of the story, and couldn't help but wonder why Ron wanted me to see this inmate. Later, I learned he was the son of a high county official. I was never told which one, and actually I didn't want to know.

"I don't know, everything's a big blur. I don't know if Kenny is dead or what. The next day, I tried to find out from a friend, who has someone on the police force, what happened. He said there weren't any bodies found dead on the beach.

"Later, this stud, Ed, tried to pick me up when I was on the street."

"Was this the same night?"

"Oh, no, no, no. It was a week or so later. At first I wouldn't go with him, but he was so persistent and so adorable that I finally gave in. Then one day he wanted me to meet him at his office. I thought he liked me and wanted to take me to lunch. So I went. Well, I couldn't believe it, he had these deputies there and they arrested me. He told them I had killed Kenny, can you believe that?"

I nodded my appropriate psychologist nod and said, "Uh-huh," thinking about being in my own practice.

"I almost raised my voice to the policeman when I said, 'That's a lie! That is a lie! I didn't kill anyone.' They arrested me anyways and I've been in jail for three months. I just can't stand it! I'm just simply going to go out of my mind. Last night when I came back from court, I just cried and cried."

The coffee arrived and Chris declined. Tears were running down his cheeks, but he managed to eat several cookies anyway. I had some of both, especially the caffeine. Actually, what I really wanted was to get the hell out of here and go over to Senicqua's office for a drink.

"They wanted me to lie and say that we had killed poor Kenny and put him in the trunk of the car, and then dumped him out at the beach. Of course I couldn't do it, because I didn't have anything to do with his murder. If he really was murdered. I kept telling them about the cab and that they had to find the cabby and he would tell them I'm innocent. They didn't believe anything about the cab and they wouldn't even look for the cabby. Now the real killer is going to get away with it and here I am, locked up in this place." *Another innocent victim!*

"Komerchero told me not to talk to other inmates 'cause a lot of them are snitches. He said these snitches get you to tell them about your crime and then they contact the D.A. and tell him what you said and make up a bunch of other stuff that's not true. They get their sentences reduced if they give the District Attorney something good on you."

I sat watching the activity out in the hallway through my open door. The deputies wheeled a screaming duster, tied down to a gurney, off the elevator and past the office; Ken Bianchi was making loving sounds into the phone's receiver, probably to the most recent woman to propose to him by mail; and Jim Munro poked his head through the doorway, mouthing the words that he needed to see me. I waved him off, motioning I would see him later. Next, a couple of uniforms walked up, stopped, and blew me a kiss, then pretended to hump each other. I wanted to laugh. *Thank God for some comic relief!*

"You know, I admit I'm gay, but I still have my standards. This black boy's in a cell next to mine. I told him a few things about myself, but then he started asking me all kind, of questions. I got so scared. I think he's one of those snitches, so I stopped talking to him.

"Well, one night I heard this loud banging. I looked up and I just couldn't believe my eyes. He had his big thing stuffed through a hole in the wall." He had my attention again. "Well, I told him I wasn't going to suck him off. My goodness, I'm not prejudiced about blacks, but I'm not going to suck his cock, either." At least this story was more interesting than hearing about his innocence.

"By the by, the guy over in the corner cell noticed you walk by and asked me who the good- looking redhead was with the great legs. I told him that you're the lady shrink and are very understanding."

I don't know why it struck me as funny that these two inmates were having this discussion about me. Sometimes I needed to remind myself they don't have any life except what they borrow from us.

"How are you feeling now? Are you depressed?" I asked.

"Well, I'm feeling terribly sad and miss my family. Now don't worry, missy. If you think I'm going to kill myself over this, don't worry. I wouldn't ever do that awful thing. I just keep thinking about my parents and how much they love me. They come to visit me all the time."

I summoned a deputy and asked him to return Grinsby to his cell. I didn't take a vote on his guilt or innocence; the judge and jury could figure that out.

I shut my door and walked over to Senicqua's office. I remembered telling Bianchi and Bonin that I would see them today. But, first, I needed to regroup.

"Have you gotten the results of your tests yet?" she asked.

"No, and it's making me nuts. How about a drink?" She pulled the bottle of scotch out of her bottom drawer and we each had a cupful.

"Shit, I can't concentrate on that crap. It doesn't make any sense, learning about a bunch of unrelated junk." I didn't want to talk about the test anymore. I had spent almost every night working on it and couldn't remember anything I read.

Just then Senicqua's phone rang. It was Central wanting her to bring some papers over to them. I walked her out of the unit and returned to my office. Glancing down the hall, I watched Sherry walk toward me.

"Come in for a little while and chat with me. What happened with the new DUI?"

"God, the Judge gave me five weekends picking up trash along the freeway and a hefty fine. I have to report in every Saturday and

Sunday at eight and stay until four. They will drive us out to the freeway to pick up trash. Guess it could have been a lot worse."

"Did Rod find out?"

"No, thank God. Bobbie covered my ass. She told him I was helping her paint her apartment. That little buckaroo saved me, again. That was one of the most embarrassing things that ever happened to me, worse than a pelvic exam. They strip-searched me, made me spread my cheeks, and then washed me down with quail lotion to make sure I didn't have any body lice."

"You showed the CHP your jail ID badge, didn't you?"

"I showed those fuckers everything except the tattoo on my butt. I dropped every name I know, too. I tried to explain to them that I was really tired from working the four tens and hadn't drunk that much.

"Well, guess I'd better get back to work."

"Wait a minute," I said.

I felt awkward talking to Sherry about the trustee's accusation, but I wanted to hear her side of the story.

"A trustee told a deputy that you and Bobbie have been bringing drugs into the jail and selling them. Have you heard anything about that?"

"Shit, yeah."

"Said you've been under surveillance for a while."

"It figures."

"Any truth to this?"

"No. That adam henry has a hard-on for me. I wouldn't give him a cigarette. He wants to get back at me, so he told this deputy a bunch of crap."

"The uniform believed him?"

"New deputy wanted to show how macho he is. If you ask me, he doesn't know his ass from his elbow. But I guess the department has to follow-up on any accusation."

"What about Gonzales?"

"He warned us about what was happening. But he couldn't do anything about it. A trustee told me they go through our desks at night after we leave. They've searched our cars, too. There's a lot of drugs in here, but we didn't bring them in. Shit, you can buy anything you want. Cheap, too! Even a good piece of ass."

"Gonzales told me the perp's girlfriends bring drugs in. How does a girl transfer them to an inmate?" I asked.

"She slips them into her boyfriend's mouth when she gives him a big smooch in the visitors' area. The girl stuffs the baggy in her mouth and then pushes it into the dude's mouth."

"Doesn't the deputy see what's happening?"

"God, Vonda," she started laughing at me, "haven't you been down to the visitors' area yet? It's a madhouse. The noise is deafening and the place is so crowded you can't bend over without getting pregnant." I conjured up a mental picture of the situation, and it wasn't a pretty one.

"There aren't enough guards to watch everyone. The visitors are running up to the guards with stuff they want to give their loved ones. They ask these stupid questions like 'Why are you holding my boy? He never done nothin' wrong.' The visitors distract the guards on purpose.

"Did you hear the other rumor about us? A trustee started spreading around that Bobbie and I are giving blowjobs in the elevator. That's his wishful thinking."

"Are you kidding?"

"Nope! I love this gossip. Let's face it: If we sluts did everything we get the wrap for, we'd never get any work done. Us sluts have our rights, too.

"Hey, thanks for the coffee and a chance to laugh," Sherry said as she stood to leave. "Got to get back over to FOP. I got a ton of paperwork to do."

"I'll walk over with you." I felt agitated and needed to move around.

I stopped short as we neared the FOP unit. "What on earth is that?"

There were two extra large sanitary pads taped to the door's window. They were arranged to form an X. A sign similarly attached underneath read "FOP's coat of arms." The crude sign was penned in red lipstick.

"What in the world is that?" I asked.

"That's a present from the deputies where Jose and Johnson work."

"Dr. Pelto, are you going to see me today?"

Kenneth Bianchi had walked up behind us, saw the artwork on the door, and began to laugh, but made no comment.

I remembered Bianchi saying he liked to fuck the girls first and not get sloppy seconds after Angelo had had them. And he didn't like doing it when they were in their periods. "Too messy!" he said.

"Have you heard from Komerchero since he got shipped out to Camp Snoopy?" Bianchi asked as we walked back into my office and sat down.

"No, but he remembered my birthday and asked his family to send me a card and a small brass tray."

"I'm surprised you haven't heard from him. He said he was going to write. I noticed you have some Camel Filters and Kool Filter cigarettes. How about trading them for a couple of my packs? I want to try something different."

"You don't need to trade. I'll give them to you."

"No, you don't need to do that," he insisted. "I'll trade you. I don't want to take yours without giving you some back." Ken held out the two packs of cigarettes. I refused to take them.

"Doc, you're sure stubborn. Give these to someone else who needs 'em. You'd be surprised what I get in the mail from all these women. Half of 'em want to marry me."

"I got a letter from Bonin," I said.

"He doing okay?"

"Yeah. He's through processing, waiting to be assigned to a prison to serve his time. Not sure which one yet, probably San Quentin."

"The newlyweds doing alright?" Ken asked. "I think they'll have a good marriage when they get through the adjustment period. I don't think people try hard enough in marriage. They split up too soon and don't give it enough time.

"I still haven't decided how I'm, going to testify," he said, changing the subject. "I swear I didn't kill anybody but I think I'll probably get convicted anyway. But at least I won't get the death penalty, and you never know what will happen. A lot of verdicts get overturned, and I could be a free man and out in the world again before you know it."

A cold shiver ran down my spine.

CHAPTER 34

JUST ANOTHER DAY
AT THE OFFICE

Not wanting to be reminded that she wasn't there, I had closed Deanne's bedroom door the day after her wedding. Although the house felt desolate with her gone, it was time to do something with the empty room—it was time to move forward.

When I opened my eyes this morning, the first thought that crossed my mind was the day in June twenty years ago when Deanne was born. That was a lifetime ago. Today, she was a married woman and gone from my home.

I walked down the hall and threw open the door, knowing that if I hesitated I would avoid going in, again. A dusty smell hung in the air and I could see tiny particles floating in the morning light. It was time to accept the fact that my oldest daughter had married and wasn't going to live in this room, ever again. Walking over to the well made-up bed, I sat down and thought about what an incredible woman she had become. But then, remembering the car accident she had in her senior year, she had also been the cause of many of my gray hairs.

She and a girlfriend had gone off the school grounds for lunch. As she pulled back out onto the street, an oncoming car broadsided her. I got the call at work, and the forty minutes it took to drive to the hospital was the most terrifying of my life. When I arrived, I found Ernie standing in the corridor. I rushed to him, putting my arms around him for comfort. He was totally unresponsive, like a statue. He looked down at me as if he didn't know who I was.

"Is she okay?"

"She has a broken leg."

I began to sob. "I have to see her."

After much pleading with the nursing staff, they let me into the ER where she lay, pale as a ghost.

The doctor wouldn't let me near her until he finished working on her injuries. Gratefully, however, I could hear her voice answering his questions. She was going to be okay.

She remained in traction in the hospital for six weeks and then another seven weeks at home in a body cast. Yet, Deanne still graduated from high school with a 3.95 grade point average.

One evening after work, I dropped by home, changed into blue jeans, grabbed a beer, poured it into a large colored glass to disguise what it was, and drove to the hospital to visit her. Halfway there, I had to make a sudden stop and the beer, which was sitting between my legs, spilled all over my crotch. Since there wasn't time to go home and change and still make visiting hours, I decided to make this into a game. I drank the remaining beer in the parking lot and then walked proudly down the long hospital corridor as if I were being crowned queen for a day, and watched people's reactions as they looked at my wet pants. Their expressions ranged from embarrassment for me to disbelief. What a trip! Deanne got a big laugh out of my wet pants, too.

Tera and I continued to have breakfast together whenever our schedules allowed. Most weekdays it wasn't possible due to me leaving for work so early. Tera was a flag girl in the marching band and was dating steadily. Most of the weekends she was out with friends and came home late. I dreaded the day she would marry and move away, too.

Larry and I were dating steadily, but I missed time with my children.

Monday morning and it was back to work. Tera, Deanne, and Richard were coming to the jail today for a tour. I looked forward to their visit.

I alerted the booth deputies that I expected guests and asked them to call me when they arrived. The two years of seeing me every day had broken down the barriers between us, although it still took me a while to get through the sally port. Overall, we had gained some mutual respect for each other.

I struggled with my office door lock, finally got it opened, and dropped my purse in one of the desk drawers.

"Hey, Doc, how you feeling today?" I looked up to see Bianchi leaning on my door. I avoided eye contact. I was not in the mood for his game playing. His superficial charm had grown thin.

"I've been meaning to ask how your mom's getting along. I heard about your father's death but didn't want to say anything before. I thought you might not want to talk about it," he said, reading the surprised look on my face.

"He's happy now," he continued, "and is looking down from up above, watching us. He can keep an eye on everything you do."

Being comforted by the Hillside Strangler gave me an eerie feeling.

"I'm fine, but thanks for asking. And you?"

"I'm okay. Are you going to bring the wedding pictures in? Weddings are a beautiful thing and it's good for people to have mates. You know, it's the nice girls that are chosen to be wives. Men always want nice girls, especially when they want to get married."

What in the hell is he rambling on about now?

"I had an argument with Eli Komerchero just before he got shipped out about what makes a nice girl. I contended that any woman worthy of marriage wouldn't sleep with you on a first date and he disagreed. He's a real adam henry and has no respect for women.

"By the way, I've got a couple more pictures for your walls." Ken handed me a picture of a rabbit and a caricature of Benny Goodman.

"Thanks," I said.

"Have you heard from Komerchero yet?" Ken asked. "You

might call his mother if you don't hear from him. Hope his sister answers 'cause she's the only one who speaks English."

"I haven't."

"I'm real nervous about the trial coming up, and I still don't know how I will testify."

Finally, when I didn't take the bait, Ken walked away. A few seconds later, I heard him drop a dime in the pay phone.

Bianchi had had one short marriage, and had a son with another woman he lived with but never married. I scratched my head, marveling at his words and opinions about nice girls and marriage.

"Got to get that inmate moved down to the other end of the hall. Isolate him. He's giving out free legal advice to all these assholes." The deputy's voice sounded irritated.

My ears perked up. An attorney had been moved into the corner cell formerly occupied by Ken Bianchi and was teaching inmates how to go pro per. It was fun eavesdropping.

"Yeah, but it was too late. He's already given out too much. Now a bunch of these slimes will be firing their public defender to go pro per.

"These assholes get their cases put off while they spend time with their cronies in the law library and don't work on their cases."

"Really pisses me off. They sit around and bullshit all day and talk to their girlfriends on the phone. Can you beat it?"

"No. Unlimited phone use, courtesy of us taxpayers."

"These guys really know how to jerk off the legal system."

"Then you know damn well when their trials come up they all start yelling for another public defender to represent them."

"Fuckers! They know how to eat up our tax dollars."

"Well, we'll make sure he doesn't teach anymore of these guys how to take advantage of the system."

I walked to my door just in time to see the two deputies walking toward the hospital area. I didn't recognize them but I thought, far fuckin' out! I wasn't the only one who resented these inmates taking advantage of us worker bees.

The kids arrived shortly and the deputy called to alert me that they were on the elevator.

I was excited about their visit. I wanted them to see where I worked and spend a little time with me. Deanne's marriage and job had kept her busy, and Tera was dating and involved in her school activities, which gave us little time to spend together.

When the elevator doors opened, I was standing in the middle of the hall smiling, waiting to greet them.

"Mom, that elevator stinks," Tera said, holding her nose. Yeah, I know.

We walked down to the hospital area and they peered in at the inmates. Some were tied down in four point restraints and some had their noses pressed to the window, yelling at me, calling me a fucking bitch. We went by Ken Bianchi's cell and found him laying on his bed propped up with a pillow watching Phil Donahue on TV. I waved to him and he came to the window to talk with us. I made the introductions all around. He was pleasant and charming, asking Deanne and Richard about the wedding and Tera about high school and did she want to go to college. *What a charmer!* We walked further and I pointed out Douglas Clark's cell, where he lay on his back, sleeping. Jim Munro was standing outside his cell, waiting to reenter when we approached him. He asked about seeing the wedding pictures. As we walked back to my office, I pointed out other rapist and killer's cells.

"Sorry, Mom," Deanne said. "We have to get out of here. This place stinks. I don't see how you can stand being here everyday."

Me either!

I rode back downstairs to the deputy's booth and kissed the kids goodbye. Their visit broke up my morning and meant more to me than they could know. I returned to my office, slumped down in my chair, stretched out my legs under the desk, and started to feel sorry for myself. Then I thought back to Tera asking if the elevator music was meant to sooth us or annoy the inmates. I'm not sure what it's supposed to do, but it sure bugs the hell out of me!

I realized I'd been pointing out the killers' cells to them in the same detached manner that Ron Kline had done to me on my first day in the jail.

CHAPTER 35

JAMES MUNRO:
THEY'RE NOT TREATING ME RIGHT

"Dr. Pelto." I looked up to see Munro hanging on my door.

"Are your daughters gone?"

I nodded yes.

"What did they say about me?"

"Said you were pleasant and nice to talk with." I stretched the truth. *Oh my God, I have put them in danger bringing them here.*

"They're sure cute."

"I'll let them know you think so."

"I need to talk about somethin' else."

He pushed open the office door without an invitation, walked in, and sat down hard in the chair closest to my desk. I felt irritated, and didn't want to listen to him whine and complain.

"Isn't it lunchtime, Jim?"

"Yeah, but I told the trustee to bring it in here. Got to talk with you right now," he said with emphasis.

Since the cafeteria would probably be closed before I could get down there, it looked like it would have to be a court-line and a john wayne.

"I got some more stuff I gotta tell you 'bout Bonin."

I leaned back in my desk chair and faced him directly.

"What's on your mind, Jim?" Maybe I could make this short.

"Guess you already know I testified 'gainst him. They gave

me a plea bargain if I'd talk. I ain't never been in trouble 'fore, so maybe I can get off light."

Munro had dropped out of high school at age 16 and entered the Army. After two months, he received an honorable discharge. I read his report carefully, trying to find out why the quick discharge, but it didn't explain how it came about. He wasn't bright intellectually, and maybe he was too easily influenced to be a good soldier.

"After Billy killed that Wells kid, I got real scared, figured he might do me in, too." Jim began to rock back and forth. "So I stole Billy's car and took off back to Michigan and bunked in with a friend. I didn't even call my folks for a while. Then that asshole, Vernon Butts, squealed to the cops that he seen me with Bonin the night he killed the kid. They come got me and brought me back to California to stand trial."

Jim stood abruptly and began to pace back and forth.

I leaned forward, rested my elbows on the desk, and reflected back to the first time I had met with James Munro. I was new and frightened of him. Now these killers wandered in and out of my office almost any time they wanted.

"Did you know Bonin would tell me all 'bout the murders when we got together? He got a big kick out of telling me that stuff. He said he'd stick the kids' heads down in the toilet sometimes."

Jim was watching and hoping for a response. I sat without blinking.

"He'd even butt fuck some of 'em after they was dead."

I still didn't respond. I wasn't going to be his reactive audience. Silence filled the room. Jim stopped his pacing and addressed me.

"Dr. Pelto, did you get the note me and Sammy wrote to you? We gave it to Deputy Smith last week to give you."

I didn't remember getting that note, but I did remember getting the five previous ones that had been slid under my door—each one filled with complaints about the deputies. I talked to Deputy George about Jim and Samuel's complaints. They had been griping about something or other from the day they got booked in. "Just ignore them," he suggested.

"That little adam henry started complaining of being lonely," Deputy George said. "Said he didn't have anyone to talk to. The D.A. needed him happy and cooperative. We moved him to a larger cell and gave him a companion. Everyone figured they were butt fucking but who cared, as long as Jim testified against his previous lover, Bill Bonin."

I turned my attention back to Munro.

"Jim, what's in the note?"

"We want to launch a complaint against Deputy Atwood."

"What's the problem?"

"That fucker is hound dog lazy. Jus' sits around with the other pigs and sucks up our juice and talks shit all the time. Those fuckers won't give us our phone calls nor nothin'. They don't pay us no attention. They rush us through our showers, hardly give us time to get the soap off 'fore they make us get out. They won't let us have forks. We ain't no animals. We can't eat that shit with spoons. We's got our rights and those fuckers can't treat us like that."

I wanted to tell him this ain't no fucking country club; instead, I put my hand up to my mouth and pinched my lower lip.

"Me and Sammy wrote this here letter to Lieutenant Chandler the other day. But we ain't heard nothin' back from him. You gotta talk to him, Doc. Tell 'em to treat us right."

He and Bonin sure as hell didn't treat Stephen Wells right when they killed him. Now he whined because he didn't get a fork to eat with? How many times could I say I was appalled or repulsed?

"The other day when I come back from the shower, I heard this here deputy say in a loud whisper, 'There goes the guy that likes butt fuckin'.'"

"Jim, I'll do what I can. Can't make any promises."

"Excuse me, Doc." The trustee had walked into my office with Jim's lunch. As he leaned down to set the tray on the desk, I almost yelled at him.

"Wait! Don't set it down. It's time for Jim to go back to his cell. He can eat his lunch there. We've finished talking for today."

Jim turned to me with a surprised look on his face.

"Wait, Dr. Pelto...."

"We'll talk again later," I insisted.

I wanted to see if I could make it to the cafeteria before it closed. I needed a break! I was disappointed the kids hadn't stayed for lunch. I didn't want to eat lunch at my desk.

With my office door closed, I became claustrophobic and with my office door open it acted like an invitation to the deputies and inmates walking past to come in.

On the ride down on the elevator, I recalled a discussion I had with Deputy Gonzales earlier in my jail career. I'd asked him how he dealt with the inmates and kept from reacting emotionally to the horrible crimes they committed. How do you maintain a civil attitude toward them? He, along with several other deputies, gave me the same answer.

"Don't delve into the crimes the perps were incarcerated for. It's the only way you can keep yourself from reacting negatively and wanting to kill them yourself. Some of these adam henrys should be hung up by the short hairs for what they've done. You just can't let yourself think about that stuff. Also, let me tell you, going over to the cop's bar to lift a few after your shift, really helps."

I had grown particularly tired of hearing James Munro whining. Each time he stopped by, the visual images of what he and Bonin had done to Stephen Wells came flooding back.

I worked hard to tune out the inmates' crimes. Trouble was, that's exactly what they wanted to talk about.

CHAPTER 36

ALONE IN A CROWD

The jail is an eerie place at night, with a discomforting stillness in the long hallways.

Overhead lights are turned off. Cells are darkened. Moving lines of inmates from one module to another down the semi-darkened halls has ceased; lone uniforms prowl about, checking and rechecking deserted staff offices. The elevator music is quieted.

Even though I was in the midst of six thousand male inmates and eight hundred male uniforms, the facility seemed deserted.

Ron dropped off a list of six Patton State Mental Hospital returnees for me to see tonight and suggested I see them in the Lieutenant's office on the first floor. The rest of the staff would have gone home by four-thirty. After months of arguing with the county personnel department about the value of flexible hours, they finally gave in and agreed to four ten-hour workdays with one day off. Now I wasn't quite sure how I felt about being left alone. Sherry would be working with me in the future, but she had called in sick today.

I sat rocking back and forth at my desk, looking over the list of names. None of them were familiar. My watch registered five o'clock—another hour before the inmates would be finished with dinner. My head throbbed and I felt a grinding in my stomach. Maybe something to eat would help my agitated state. I locked the office door and arrived at the elevator just in time to see the doors slide open. A trustee almost backed into me pulling the trolley out, filled with the inmates' meal trays.

"What's on the menu tonight?"

"Doc, I don't know if I'd eat down there if I was you. The homeys are serving mashed potatoes, gravy, stew, you know the lumpy surprise kind, and the fish that looks like it shoulda been buried a long time ago. Even a lot of tartar sauce ain't gonna save it. You're gonna wanna think 'bout somethin' else for dinner."

He was right, the selections didn't sound appetizing; probably not worth the long trip down to the cafeteria to confirm his diagnosis. There weren't many alternatives. Skip dinner; eat the dry cake I brought back from lunch and saved in the desk drawer; or go down to the hospital kitchen. I decided on a court-line sandwich, left over from this morning, and a john wayne. I stepped back from the elevator and headed down the hallway.

"Dr. Pelto, what are you doing here so late?" Ken Bianchi had hung up the telephone and was walking toward me.

"My hours have changed."

"Doc, it's not a good idea for you to work such long hours, you'll get overly tired. You work too hard already. You should be able to stay at home with your daughters and just relax."

"Thanks for your concern, Ken, but I won't be retiring for a long while." I was sure the Hillside Strangler didn't show his twelve victims this much concern.

"Oh yeah, you're divorced. I forgot that for a minute. I'm glad you're going to be around, 'cause I'd be awful lonely if you quit. That's selfish, I know, but I enjoy talking to you."

Obviously, the jail grapevine had been busy. I hadn't told Bianchi about being divorced. Come to think of it, he probably had learned my marital status and shoe size the first day I hired into the jail, which was two years ago.

I hated the fact that serial killers and other inmates knew so much about my personal life. My girls and I were vulnerable. But there wasn't any way to protect our personal information from these killers. I put in an alarm system at home, and we always had our car keys in our hands when walking to our cars.

Inmates were released daily and could write down our license plate numbers and run them through the DMV. They can find out our age, weight, where we live, and probably even what we dream about. Back in the early eighties there were no laws to protect us from this invasion of privacy. Now there are some laws protecting our identities.

The jail is a revolving door and when the inmates are booked back in, they bring the information with them. Sitting around in their cells, they are clever and bored. We are their soap box opera stars, our lives become their world; they listen in on our conversations and compare notes with each other. The trustees go through our desks and trashcans every night when they clean our offices. Deputies are supposed to supervise them; instead, they unlock our office doors and walk down the hall to flirt with the nurses.

"Doc, you look nice. Is that a new dress?" Bianchi looked tired as he leaned against the wall.

"Thanks for noticing."

"Mind if I come in for a little while?"

I struggled with the office door lock, finally getting the key to engage, turned the knob, and threw the door back against the wall.

"Come on in, Ken," I said without the irritation I felt.

"Just a second." Ken walked over to the trustee and asked for his dinner tray to be brought into my office. "Mind if I set this on your desk?"

"No problem. Eat up while it's hot."

"You kidding, Doc? Shit—oops, excuse my language—my meals are never hot. I feel lucky if the trustee hasn't spit in it or hidden a cockroach in the lumps. You wouldn't believe all the stuff I've found in my food."

"I thought that only happened to the staff's food. I never eat anything I can't recognize."

Bianchi laughed.

His meal looked far from appetizing. Stew, gray mashed potatoes, and a few pieces of wilted lettuce in a Styrofoam cup, no dressing. Two slices of white bread sat on the edge of the paper plate with strawberry ice cream seeping into it, turning the bread a pale pink.

Ken pushed the tray aside. "Mind if I smoke?"

I shook my head and he lit up as I pulled out my ashtray from the side desk drawer. I had just washed it.

"You know, Doc, I never have any personal contact with anyone anymore. When visitors or even my attorney come to see me, we have to meet in the room with that glass wall between us. We talk on those telephones. In the past, Alan Simon, my attorney, could meet me face to face, and he would always shake my hand when he left. You don't know how good that little bit of physical contact felt for me. My lawyer knew. He understood how important it was to be touched. I get so lonely and need someone."

He looked like he would cry. His face wore a mask of sadness and reminded me of the pictures of the children with the big round, sad eyes. I was momentarily drawn to him, that is until I remembered hearing all of this before.

Ken took a drag on his cigarette and watched me carefully.

I had learned to be on-guard with him. He was pleasant company and had been supportive after my father's death. He knew what to say to comfort me. And we had more in common than my friends in the outside world. We both knew how it felt to be incarcerated. But no matter how forlorn he looked, I had to keep reminding myself that he was a practiced psychopath who tortured twelve young women to death.

I looked directly at him and didn't respond. He lowered his head with a knowing smile. He knew what he was doing, and that his manipulation hadn't worked. He was playing a game with me.

"Ken, is there something on your mind you need to talk about?"

"No. I'm just bored and don't want to go back to my cell yet.

Since Komerchero got rolled up and sent out to Chino, there's nobody I want to talk to. He was fun to argue with."

I missed Eli, too. He had been pleasant company. Now that the filing was finished, I spent little time in the FOP offices.

"By the way, did you know that the Feds use your office at night?

I hadn't heard that.

"They sit in here, two—sometimes maybe even three—times a week."

"Federal agents?"

"Yeah. They got their feet up on your desk and shoot the breeze. Interview inmates in here. I hear 'em talking when I'm on the phone."

Oh, shit! Ken probably listened in on my conversations, too. I tried to remember whom I had talked with lately. It was emotionally draining being on alert all the time.

"Sorry Ken, I have to go."

"No problem, I'll catch you later." He picked up his tray and left through the open door. "Hey, don't work too hard," he called back over his shoulder.

With the amount of freedom these killers had, you'd think this was a country club, since they wandered up and down the halls or talked on the phone much of the day.

Shortly, I followed him out, stopped by the deputy's booth, and dropped off the list of inmates to be interviewed on my way to the hospital kitchen. Tonight it lacked the usual activity and raucous laughter. After rummaging through the semi-dark room, I came up with a stale court- line, two chocolate chip cookies, and a slightly green banana. I poured a john wayne and walked back down the now vacant hallway. No problem finishing my dinner before the deputy got the inmates called up. Even with the computers linked to the outer modules, it still took thirty minutes for the booth deputy receiving the inmate request to find him and have him escorted to the required location.

After finishing the court-line—which I inspected thoroughly

for foreign objects—and a john wayne, I went downstairs, hoping some of the inmates would be waiting.

I stepped off the elevator and walked the few yards to the Lieutenant's office, just as an explosion of laughter burst out from the open door. I figured someone must have gotten to the punch line of a joke.

"Have you seen the shrink? I hear she's got legs that go all the way up to her ass."

Loud laughter followed his remark. "She's coming down here tonight to talk to the grab and tickle gang." I hesitated, not wanting to go into a room full of uniforms I didn't know. There was nothing new about the deputies making comments about me. I was just tired tonight and not in the mood to handle them.

Since the hallway was deserted, leaning on the cold cement wall helped me gain my composure.

Finally, I walked into the brightly illuminated office. The walls were covered with yellow and brown torn plaid wallpaper, reminiscent of the fifties. Deputies sat at two wooden desks that faced each other and two more uniforms, still smiling, leaned against a counter that ran the length of the office.

"Excuse me, I'm Dr. Pelto. I'm here to see the MDSOs from Patton State Mental Hospital. Have any been sent down yet?"

"The sexual perverts? You mean the furry palm gang? Not yet," a young blonde deputy seated at a desk spoke up, as he threw a spit wad at one of the standing deputies. "We got word a little while ago that a couple of your wienie waggers are on their way." More laughter.

"Thanks. I'll walk down to High Power and see if there's anyone that needs to be seen." I really wanted to go down there to see how the King of Porn was doing after he was acquitted of the murders this afternoon.

After a couple of knocks, I was admitted to the inner sanctum of the cellblock and went directly to the deputy's booth to catch up on the latest gossip.

"Coffee, babe?"

"Yeah, make it a john wayne." I dropped down into a chair facing the window that looked out into the module, and leaned forward to stretch my back.

"You down here to see someone?"

"No, just checking to see if all the boys are okay."

"You hear about Holmes? I thought the evidence against him was pretty convincing. I'm surprised he got off." The other deputies nodded in agreement.

"Dr. Pelto, good news," John beamed as he peered through the open window. "The jury acquitted me! You got some time to talk?"

"Hold on, I'll be there shortly." I motioned toward the interview office located across from the deputy's booth.

I refilled my cup, poured another one for John, and walked across the corridor to where he waited by the door. He smiled as I approached and quickly took the hot coffee from me.

"Thanks! I rarely get it hot. By the time the trustee delivers dinner, the coffee is always cold. This is a good day, acquitted, hot coffee, and a shower later." I thought about how many things I take for granted.

The deputy got the door unlocked and followed us into the room to cuff Holmes' arm down to the sturdy chair.

On June 23, 1982, John Curtis Holmes' case had gone to the jury after a six-day trial. The jury deliberated fourteen hours over a four-day period of time, took five ballots, and acquitted the porn star of bludgeoning four people to death.

Ronald Launius, William Ray Deverell, and Joy Audrey Miller were each targets of the killers for participating in the robbery at Eddie Nash's house. David Lind was also a target, but he had left the house before the killers arrived. His girlfriend happened to be visiting and was killed. She was a mushroom, an innocent bystander. Susan Launius was also an accidental victim and the only one who had survived. She had come to see her estranged spouse in the hopes of reconciling. Her face and skull had been bludgeoned, and her neck cut. She had been battered so severely that she had little recollection of the murderers. "They looked like dark shadowy figures moving around me."

Neighbors were alerted to a problem when they heard her moaning, and broke into the house to find out what had happened. They discovered the bodies and called an ambulance and the police. Later they said that it looked like a blood bath had taken place, like someone had taken buckets of blood and poured them all over the house.

Holmes' attorneys were not optimistic about John beating the murder rap. The major hurdle they had to face was Holmes' confession to a uniform. He had admitted to being present at the murders when he was being transported back to California after his arrest in Florida. Later he denied saying anything.

"Have you heard the latest? They're talking about sending me to the Grand Jury, and holding me in jail until I tell them what I know about the murders. If they think I'm going to tell them anything, they're crazy. They either don't realize or they don't care that Eddie has threatened to kill me and my family. I swear I will never ever tell anybody who killed those people. I didn't know what I'd do if they convicted me, but I felt I'd have a better chance surviving in prison than I would if I said anything about Nash."

"You're really afraid of him."

"Yeah, but thank God, at least I don't have to worry about being convicted of murder anymore; people are even treating me like a human being again. They told me I looked relaxed even before the verdict came in. I said it was 'cause I was innocent and the jury could see it.

"I heard they picked up Nash on drug charges."

I didn't tell John that Eddie Nash had been in my office for coffee on several occasions. He didn't discuss the murders or mention John's name. He talked about his family and how he looked forward to going home to them. I knew more about him from overhearing his phone calls than what he actually told me.

"John, it's getting late, time for me to go back to the lieutenant's office to see the MDSOs."

"Can you see me tomorrow? I like talking to an intelligent woman."

"I'll check my schedule. Goodnight." I would make it a point to see him the next day.

Back at the lieutenant's office I found the blonde deputy standing in the hall talking with the inmates, and signaled him that I was ready to start the interviews.

"This way, ma'am, you'll have more privacy in here." He escorted me through the deputy's area and into the lieutenant's office.

I sat down on the cushioned chair behind the desk and picked up a picture of the lieutenant's wife and kids. I could see a strong family resemblance between him and his two young sons.

"Only three perps showed up. We weren't able to locate the rest of them. Guess the others are out for an evening stroll in the moonlight." The deputy laughed at the absurdity of his comment. "We'll keep trying to get the other ones, but I wouldn't hold my breath."

More likely they were at med call, a way to get some attention. Who knows, they might even like Magic Fingers and his KY.

I pulled up a chair close to the side of the desk for the interviewee, and then let the deputy know he could bring in the first inmate.

The deputy appeared shortly with Cedrick Bosley, Patton State Mental Hospital returnee. He dropped into the chair and extended his arms in order to be cuffed. The deputy touched his cuffs and then looked back at me. "Ma'am, I don't think these will be necessary tonight since we'll be sitting in the next room. Unless you don't feel safe and want me to."

"I'm sure I'll be fine."

"I'll leave the door open and, Doc, let out a holler if you need us. Relax, Cedrick, we're dispensing with the usual formalities tonight," the deputy called out as he retreated from the room. Bosley registered a surprised look.

Bosley was a short, squat man with fat fingers and a bald pate. His toothless grin revealed darkened gums, and he exhaled bad breath. He had a strong body odor and sported stains left from dinner down the front of his blues. His looks made my skin crawl.

Out of my peripheral vision, I could see him fidgeting around, shifting from one position to another. He seemed agitated, which wasn't unusual, since he didn't know me. I didn't pay much attention to what he was doing. I was preoccupied with getting his name spelled correctly on the county forms and writing down the information he was giving me.

The next time I looked at him, he was wearing a lecherous grin. Examining his face, I wondered what amused him; it wasn't long before I found out. As soon as Bosley caught my stare, he slowly lowered his head toward his lap; my eyes followed the movement.

The motion I had noticed earlier was Bosley unbuttoning his jumpsuit down to the crotch. He had reached down into his underwear and freed his fully erect penis. It now pointed proudly toward the ceiling.

Due to this unexpected exposure, my face flushed and I hoped Bosley didn't see it. I bit the inner portion of my cheek hard enough to distract myself, but not so hard as to make it bleed. I needed a little time to rehearse how I wanted to respond to him and his exposed member. In the most monotonous voice I could muster, I said, "I've seen it now, Mr. Bosley. Put it away before you catch cold."

Without a word, he winked at me and rearranged his clothing.

I completed the interview, stepped to the door along with the inmate, and signaled the deputy to send in the next man. Then I laughed quietly. *This job sure as hell isn't boring.*

I pulled out another Intake Form, ready to start the interview as soon as the next inmate was seated.

"What's your name?"

"Dwayne Washington."

I completed the interview and then asked if he was having any problems or if there was anything he needed.

He leaned over the desk as close to me as possible and said in a stage whisper voice.

"Ma'am, I don't mean any disrespect to you, but I jus' been wonderin' if you could get me a woman. I ain't had me a woman in a long time."

"Sir, get you a woman?"

"Lady, I jus' gotta have me a woman to fuck! I'm real bad horny and I'm hurtin' somethin' awful. Can you help me out?"

I must have been tired not to pick up right away on what he was asking.

"No, I'm sorry." I composed myself before I answered further.

"Our mental health department doesn't provide that type of service. Ask one of the other men what they do when that need arises. I'm sure they can give you some good pointers."

"Thank you, ma'am. I'll try that."

With that exchange, I sent him back out to the bench and waited for the deputy to send in the next inmate.

Well, Mr. Washington would have to do what most of the other perps did: cover it with a sock and beat it off. I left it up to him to find this information out for himself.

"Dr. Pelto, can you see an inmate in 7100 right away?"

I looked up to see the blonde deputy standing in the doorway.

"He should be seen this evening."

"Do you know anything about the inmate?" I asked.

"I don't have any of the particulars. A deputy in 2100 called about fifteen minutes ago and said he found an inmate hanging in his cell, had a noose tied around his neck and was barely-conscious, already turning blue. They transferred him up to the hospital; put him on a suicide watch, you'll have to see him up there. He's probably in four point restraints."

"Anyone else down here for me to see?" I asked.

"We got a couple, but they seem okay. Let me know if you're gonna come back down here tonight."

"Sure."

I grabbed my clipboard, pen, and Intake Forms, and headed toward the elevator to ride back upstairs, scurried down the hall to the hospital area, and checked the booth for a deputy to open the inmate's cell door. No one was around, so I circled the hospital area. Halfway up the far corridor of single man cells, I spotted a man dressed in a dark suit with shiny shoes, sitting in a doorway propped open by his metal chair. I realized he wasn't a deputy, but thought he might have a key to unlock the perp's door.

"Excuse me, I was wondering if you could open one of the cell doors for me? I'm Dr. Pelto and I need to see someone."

"Sorry, ma'am, I'm a federal agent, babysitting that inmate in there."

I peered in and saw the inmate sleeping peacefully. "What's the problem? He looks pretty harmless."

"Don't let his looks fool you. He's a bad actor. I gotta wait 'til that adam henry passes some baggies filled with coke. The asshole swallowed them when we made the bust. Can't make the charge stick until we get the goods on him, or maybe I should say out of him. I'll be sitting here for as long as it takes." He stood abruptly and curtsied. "I feel like a lady in waiting."

"Sounds like a dirty job." I called back to him and thought to myself, I hope everything comes out all right—that's what my brother used to say.

I trudged down another hallway and finally found a deputy on my second round of the hospital corridors. After explaining my mission, he unlocked the heavy cell door to 7116 where the inmate was housed.

"I'll be wandering around the halls if you need me," he said.

I entered the cold concrete room slowly. It was stark in its simplicity, with a metal cot anchored in the concrete floor and a steel toilet and wash basin combination. A young man, who looked barely old enough to shave, lay on the hard bed, clad in white underwear.

His sandy colored hair fell halfway across his soft face; his slender body was curled into a fetal position. He was quietly sobbing.

I introduced myself. He didn't respond. His face was tear stained and his eyes were red and swollen.

"I want to die."

The boy was soft, just the type the tougher inmates liked. I sat down on a chair provided by a deputy.

"Do you want to talk about what happened?"

He turned his face and looked directly at me as if becoming aware of my presence for the first time.

"Who are you?"

I explained that I was the shrink, there to help him. He raised himself slowly, in obvious pain. Struggling to obtain a sitting position, he wiped his eyes with the back of his hand.

"You're not going to tell anybody what happened, are you? I'm real embarrassed about it."

After I gave him my assurance, he took a deep breath and seemed to relax a little.

"They caught me in the shower."

"Who caught you?"

"Three black guys.

"When I walked into the shower room, I looked all around and didn't see nobody. The guys in my module warned me about watchin' out for the black guys, they told me the niggers like to butt fuck us whites. But I never thought it could happen to me. I never been in jail before. I got thirty days for not payin' my child support. I can't do it! I'll die in here!

"I had just stripped down and lathered up. Shit, man, it was the best I'd felt since I got booked in.

"I was standing there relaxing, with my eyes closed, pretending I was back home in my own shower. The water felt good. Then I heard some guys talking real loud behind me and looked back over my shoulder. These guys were standing by the door, but I figured they was jus' comin' inta the shower."

He began to sob again and had to compose himself before going on.

"There was three of 'em. Three big, ugly, black niggers. They must have seen me headin' down the hall with my soap and towel to get cleaned up. I was expecting my mom to come for visitors' hour this evening.

"All the sudden the biggest one yelled out at me.

"'Yo, cracker, let's see you wiggle that cute little ass of yours.'

"I wasn't sure what he was sayin' to me. I said, 'What?' Then he turned to the other two guys. 'Hey, homeys, you ever seen a white mutherfucker as sweet as this mama's boy? Shit, man. I bet this little sissy never had anything as good as I got here to shove up him.' Then that nigger, he turned back to look at me.

"'Baby, is you still a virgin?' The three of 'em started walking toward me. I was so scared I almost pissed myself. 'Has you ever had a real expert pack your poo for ya like I'm gonna?' the big one said.

"My mind was whirlin', trying to think of some way to get out of there. I could hardly talk 'cause I shook so bad. I was cold and my teeth were chattering."

I reached up and massaged the back of my neck in an attempt to ease the tightness.

"Hey, guys," the young man continued, "I got some money over there in my pants. Take it. I know it ain't much, but my mom is comin' this evening and I know I can get some more from her. Please, please. I'll give you anything you want. Please, just let me go."

"'Man, I ain't had me a fresh one in a long time.' I think it was the shorter one that said that. 'Have you, fudge packer?'

"They ignored me, kept coming at me. Oh, man, I was scared. My heart pounded and I wanted to throw up. I started beatin' cheeks for the door, didn't even bother getting the soap off, jus' grabbed a towel and run like a scalded dog. I thought if I could make it to the hall, I could yell for a deputy to help me. Before I even got close to the door, they come up behind me.

"'Hey, sweet meat, where ya think you goin'? Leroy, you ain't gonna let our pump get away, is ya? This party is jus' gettin' started.'

"Two of 'em grabbed me. Dragged me back inside. 'Yo, white trash,' Leroy said, 'you ain't goin' nowheres.' I never heard the other two guys' names, but I'll never forget their faces. They was sweatin' like pigs and I felt their hot breath on me, fast and hard. After they got me back inside, two of them bent me over the bench. They threw my clothes on the floor. I remember thinkin' that was my clean shirt and it was gettin' all wrinkled; stupid thing to think about."

I felt hot. Waves of nausea washed over me. Suddenly I was back in the house in Laguna Beach being raped. I was shaking all over, and having problems listening. I stood up and took several deep breaths. I can't deal with my own issues right now.

"They all took turns shoving their cocks up me. I don't even know how many times they got me. I was praying to pass out. It hurt so bad, I was afraid they was tearin'me up inside. I tried to call for help. They tole me if I didn't shut up, they would give me something to suck on."

Tears rolled down his soft cheeks.

"I didn't want to cry, I tried not to, but it hurt so bad I couldn't help myself; they called me a mama's boy.

"Damn the guards, why didn't they just let me die? Don't you see? I can't face anyone now. I'm not a man anymore."

I felt a lump in my throat.

"I'm so cold." He shivered and lay down again, curling back up into a fetal position. He wasn't allowed a sheet or blanket for fear he might tear it up and fashion a noose.

He would have to deal with this the rest of his life. He might be better off dead.

I summoned a deputy who was walking by and asked him to send a nurse. She arrived shortly, and I stepped out of the cell to explain what had transpired. She gave me a blank stare as if I was speaking Vulcanize to her. I searched her face, waiting for a reaction. There wasn't any. I tried to process her lack of response. In railroad parlance, she was an old head. She'd worked in the jail over fifteen years, way too many, and had burned out from feeding on the daily diet of cruelty and inhumanity. I identified with her, and realized the same thing was happening to me.

She left and returned with some medication from Magic Fingers. She handed the inmate a paper cup full of water, a tranquilizer, and then departed swiftly without a glance back at me.

I stepped out into the hall and fell in step with Deputy George. I had to get out of there.

"George, did you hear about the kid they just brought up to 7100? He tried to kill himself."

The elevator arrived and we stepped into the smelly car.

"Yeah, I heard three 02s got him in the shower. Those 2s just love those little white asses. When we get news of a knifing, it's usually the Mexicans. If it's a rape, it's the blacks; and if someone is curled up sucking his thumb, trying to hide in a corner, it's a white."

"I've heard. What will happen to the men who raped the kid?"

"What do you mean?"

"Will they be charged with rape and punished?"

"They're already in jail serving time."

"In other words, nothing?"

"You got it."

These rapists wouldn't be punished for their crimes, just like the two attorneys that had raped me.

"By the way, Gonzales got some hot tips on the ponies running on the third race tomorrow night. You up for them?"

I couldn't collect my thoughts. *How many rapists get away with it?*

"Hey, Doc, you in there?" He reached out and patted my shoulder. "The races?"

"Yeah. What time?"

"Sherry got a new radio, reception is much better. We'll meet at her desk in the bullpen; first race is at seven o'clock so you need to be there by six-thirty to get your bet into my bookie.

"See you later," he said.

"Yeah." He left me when the elevator doors opened on the first floor.

I stepped back into the elevator, pushed the up button, and pulled the office key out of my pocket. I felt shaky and exhausted. I couldn't handle talking to one more inmate tonight.

I walked straight to my office and telephoned the deputy and let him know he could dismiss the rest of the MDSOs. He assured me none of them were in crisis and could be seen tomorrow. I wanted to go home so I locked my door and headed back to the elevator.

Trudging toward the car, I looked forward to putting on a Carol King tape, setting the car on cruise control, and leaning back in the leather seat to try and relax. The motor started easily. I shifted into drive and headed toward the Santa Ana Freeway.

As I turned onto the roadway, I had to stop abruptly. The news on the radio indicated that a multiple car accident with injuries was up ahead.

Two hours elapsed by the time I turned onto my street. The dashboard clock registered ten-thirty. I was so tired I wanted to scream, and knew it would only be eight hours before I'd have to face the inmates again.

Turning onto the driveway, I threw on the brakes to keep from hitting Tera's car, blocking my entrance into the garage. Tears welled up in my eyes. My vision was clouded, making it difficult to pull back out onto the street and park the car. After getting the car reasonably close to the curb, I shut off the motor, leaned forward to rest my head on the steering wheel, and began to sob loudly.

My body felt heavy and refused to move. All of my anger and frustration became focused on Tera's car. The jail had won! I couldn't take it anymore. I was burned out. I hated the inmates. I hated the deputies. I hated the staff. I hated the other drivers. And I hated myself and what I was becoming.

I found Tera sitting on the couch in her pajamas, with her feet propped on the coffee table, sipping a coke and watching "All in the Family" on TV. Suddenly, I was enraged. I exploded. I was out of control, and Tera became my target. I screamed at her.

"Get up off your ass and move your fucking car right this second! You're inconsiderate and self-centered. You know I'm tired. Why in the hell did you park in my spot? Goddamm it, I had to park on the street."

Her face had the startled look of a deer caught in an oncoming car's headlights. She didn't answer but jumped up, ran to her bedroom, returned quickly with her car keys, and pushed me aside from where I still stood, shaking in the entryway. When I heard her car motor roar to life, I walked into the dining room and watched my daughter back her car out of the driveway. I was overcome with guilt and couldn't stop the tears. I hated myself.

Tera returned shortly and went to her bedroom without a word to me. I didn't try to stop her, knowing it wasn't a good idea to talk with her anymore tonight. I went to the kitchen, uncorked a bottle of red wine, took a glass from the dishwasher, grabbed the mail off the dining room table, and went to my bedroom.

The correspondence I had been anxiously awaiting arrived from the State of California Behavioral Science Examiners. I'd taken the exams in June and waited three months for the results. My hands literally shook when I held the letter with its official seal stamped in the left-hand corner. A notice that could change my life. In very polite but official language, the form letter said, "We regret to inform you that you have failed the California State Board Exams. Please contact the agency to obtain information regarding the next scheduled exam. The phone number is...." I didn't give a shit what the phone number was. I walked over to the bed and sank down on the soft mattress, dropping the letter on the floor. Ernie was right: I wasn't smart enough to become a psychologist.

My dream was never going to happen. I was going to start screaming and never be able to stop.

I poured a glass of wine, swallowed it, quickly poured another one, pulled out the Valium from the bathroom cabinet, shoved several into my mouth, and washed them down. I fell into bed without eating and cried myself to sleep. I was tired. I needed to sleep without the nightmares, and didn't care if I ever woke up again.

CHAPTER 37

CADBURY

I felt ambivalent about finding myself alive the next morning, relieved that Tera wouldn't have the trauma of finding my dead body, but not wanting to go on with my life. I wanted out! I didn't want to go on. I couldn't face telling everyone I had failed again.

The fight to get up, feeling lousy and hung-over, was overwhelming. The pills and booze ingested the night before had taken their toll on me. When the alarm blasted, I reached over and pushed the snooze button a couple more times and went back to sleep. This was stalling, and I didn't give a shit. The alarm signaled again that it was time to get up. Reluctantly, I swung my feet over the side of the bed and sat up. My head was throbbing. Shit, it was already seven-thirty; I was late for work. I stumbled into the bathroom, washed my face and took a couple of aspirin, hoping this effort would help. My eyes were puffy and stared back at me with disgust from the bathroom mirror. They felt even worse than they looked. In the back of my brain was a vague recollection of a beauty expert talking about some vegetable you're supposed to use on your eyes to reduce the swelling, but my brain was too fuzzy to remember which one.

After a shower, I pulled on blue jeans and a soft sweater, for needed comfort, and considered taking a mental health day off. But I knew that wouldn't help. I needed another job. Over two years had gone by, but it felt like a hundred. Passing the State Boards was still hanging over my head and I would need five months to become vested for my retirement—if I decided I could last that much longer. At this point, I really didn't care.

I didn't know if I had the strength to start studying again, and it didn't matter—I had to pass the exam.

Nothing mattered except Tera's feelings and how badly I had treated her. I oozed with guilt and shame for screaming and cursing at her and wished this had been the first time. Unfortunately, it wasn't. Sadly, it was happening more often.

This morning I waited until I heard her moving around in her bedroom and then went to the kitchen to brew coffee and scramble some eggs. I needed to have breakfast with her, and didn't care about being late for work. My overreaction wasn't called for—her parking in the driveway wasn't an unpardonable sin!

I heard her footfall on the black slate entryway and tried to figure out what to say. She couldn't know or have full understanding of the stress that filled my life, nor was it her "job" to do so.

As soon as Tera came to the kitchen door, I stopped scrambling the eggs, turned the flame off beneath the skillet, and turned to face her. She hesitated, seemingly unable to move. Her eyes were puffy and her face tear stained, matching mine. She looked fragile standing in her pink nightshirt with her long blond hair hanging loose, still uncombed. While sobbing out my apology, I closed the short gap between us and put my arms around her. I knew there wasn't any justification for my behavior, but I tried to explain my outburst and hoped, after her visit to the jail, that she had a better understanding of my stress level. She apologized, too. She explained that she knew I was stressed and promised not to block the driveway again. We both cried and hugged each other. In my heart, I knew she didn't know how fragile I had become.

The next months passed slowly—much too slowly. I drank more and tried relaxation exercises, but neither effort helped. My doctor told me my ulcer had worsened and prescribed more medication for it. He also strongly advised me to stop drinking

Fuck him and the horse he rode in on.

Relentlessly, I interviewed for other county agency jobs; there was still nothing available. In spite of the difficulty I was having concentrating, I pulled out my books nightly. I would have another chance at the Boards in a few weeks.

Bonin's, Munro's, and Komerchero's trials were completed and they were transferred out of the jail to prisons. There was still no time to study at work because there was a constant flow of Patton returnees for me to see.

Passing through the gate into the sally port this morning, the deputy almost caught my arm in the closing gate. Carrying a briefcase, a purse, and a coat over my arm, I was moving slower than usual. Trying to juggle everything through the narrow opening the deputies had allowed me took longer than it normally did, and the gate started to close before I made it through. Sometimes I thought the deputies played a game with the gate. They wanted to see how little they could open it and how quickly they could close it again without catching someone in it. But, then, perhaps that was just my paranoia.

I dropped my purse, yanked my arm back, and yelled at the deputies. They apologized and sent the gate in the opposite direction. I grabbed my purse off the floor and headed for the elevator.

"Jack the Knife" was playing. I didn't hum along.

"Doc, the Wadd wants to see you." I'd barely gotten into my office when Gonzales walked up to my door and leaned on the bottom half. "Johnny, The Wadd, Holmes has a crush on you! He's always asking to see you." I hesitated looking up at him. I didn't want him to see my puffy eyes.

"*Bullshit!*" The words flew out of my mouth before I could stop them. I was in no mood for kidding. Get a grip!

"And by the way, I heard you saw alllllll of him." I raised my head slightly and watched his grin turn into a bawdy laugh.

Sherry, the big mouth.

"He's on a hunger strike, won't take anything except water

or coffee with sugar," Gonzales said. "He refuses to eat. Shit, he's really pissed off at the Grand Jury. Can't say I blame him. They've already extended his stay ninety days. He's not gonna talk, no matter how long they hold him."

"Heard they moved him to the psych hospital, but I haven't had a chance to walk down to see him," I said.

"They rolled him up last weekend and put him in 7113. The docs got worried about him. Except for his boner, he doesn't have any extra meat on those skinny bones."

"Very funny," I said tonelessly.

"Babe, you OTR? Where's your sense of humor this morning?"

"Bad night," I didn't look up from the desk, "fighting with my daughter."

"That's why tigers eat their young, I've heard," Gonzales said.

"John's lost fourteen pounds in the last few weeks," he continued. "It's the old CYA —nobody wants the hassle of him killing himself. Too damn much paperwork."

That's the way it was: too much paperwork. My mind flashed back to Vernon Butts' suicide and how saddened I had felt. Butts did me a favor: His death got me the job.

"Holmes already looked like a prisoner of war to me," I said, trying to sound softer.

"You got time to see him this morning?" Gonzales asked again.

"Sure." *Maybe he'll cheer me up.*

"I'll break him out for you, just a little present from me, sweet cheeks."

"He's not confined to the cell?"

"You kidding? He was on the phone outside your office half of last weekend. You ready for him now?"

"Yeah, thanks," I replied.

Although Holmes had been acquitted of the murders on Wonderland Avenue, he had not been released from custody. The Grand Jury kept extending his incarceration, trying to force him into disclosing the names of the men who were involved in the Wonderland Murders.

While waiting for Gonzales to return, I pulled out my compact and reapplied some liquid make-up under my eyes, touched up my eyebrows, and put on fresh lipstick. With the little improvement in my appearance, I felt more relaxed. I didn't like the inmates being able to read any emotion on my face.

Gonzales appeared shortly with Holmes, pushed the bottom half of my door open, and walked in. I took a deep breath and stood up.

Without being asked, John sat down in the padded chair positioned beside my desk. He leaned back and stretched his long legs forward, almost touching my chair in the tiny office. It was exciting to have this sex symbol to millions of women so near, and without shackles.

"What, no cuffs?" John looked up at the deputy with a questioning expression.

"Nope, we're less formal up here." Gonzales said as he walked out of the room, pulling the bottom half of the door closed.

What he did next was totally unexpected and caught me off-guard. Standing outside Holmes' line of sight, Gonzales leaned his elbows on the bottom half of the door. Then he formed an "O" with the thumb and index finger of his left hand and pointed the index finger of his right hand and began to push it rapidly back and forth through the opening, all the while shaking his head back and forth, indicating that sex was a definite no-no. I got the message and couldn't contain myself. I started laughing out loud. John gave me a strange look, but didn't say anything.

I looked at his relaxed posture and realized I'd never seen anyone in High Power that wasn't cuffed securely to the barber chair. I hadn't thought about it before, but it was true. Here, alone in my office, I saw the killers everyday without any restraints. Actually, I felt much safer with the high profile killers than with the psychotics housed in 4500. The dings routinely hit and harassed the guards.

"So, this is your office. I often wondered where you were located. Hey, is this an old cell?" John turned around and perused the room.

"Can you beat it? I have my very own cell."

"Nice pictures. I like the cartoon characters."

"Ken Bianchi asked some of the inmates to draw them for me—thought they'd class up the dingy walls a bit."

"Bianchi, now that's one asshole that deserves to die after what he did to those women. He and his cousin Angelo are real mutherfuckers."

I agreed with his appraisal.

"Even though most of the ones I work with are ball busters, I like women."

He sure as hell doesn't mind using them when it suits him.

"What's this?" John stood and walked over to examine the little house closely.

"Jim Munro and his buddy made it for me."

"This is very clever. Did you know I like to design jewelry?"

"How are you getting along?" He was more fun, but I had a long list of Patton returnees to see.

"Not good!" He resumed his chair, extended his long legs, and began kicking the side of my desk.

"I understand you're on a hunger strike."

"I'm ravenous! I've lost weight almost everywhere. Except the important place, thank God." He smiled and looked down at his crotch.

"Shit, I want to get this all behind me and go back to work."

"Are you worried about your career?"

"Hell no! And that fucking Grand Jury can keep me until hell freezes over. I won't ever say who was involved. Eddie would have me killed for sure."

"How are you sleeping?" I asked.

"I dream of food almost every night. Last night this big chocolate candy bar chased me all around the cell. It almost caught me a couple of times, too."

"You're body needs food. You can't afford to lose much more weight."

"Doc, I really think I could make it if you got me a Cadbury candy bar. In fact, I'll marry you if you get me one." John's voice was filled with phony sincerity. "Could you please, please?" he begged.

John looked down at the concrete floor, shuffled his feet back and forth, and extended his lower lip, pretending he was going to cry.

I didn't respond. I needed time to take a vote with myself. What would be the consequences if I got caught? I knew it was crazy to even consider his request.

"Excuse me, Doc." Deputy Rodriquez was standing in the doorway. "I got some of your MDSOs out here."

"Sorry, John, we need to stop."

He pulled himself up from the chair and turned toward the door.

"Can I come back here to see you?"

I assured him that he could.

A few days later I called Holmes back to my office. He had just learned that he had been held over again by the Grand Jury. His incarceration was now up to a little over one hundred days.

"John, I have a surprise for you," I said after he was seated. With that, I handed him a folded magazine with two Cadburys inside. He opened the book just far enough to see what was there and looked back at me with a broad smile.

"Doc," he stood, walked around my desk, bent down, and kissed the top of my head, "you've saved my life." Then he returned to his chair. For the first time in a long time, I felt warm inside. He was so grateful I wanted to cry.

"Did you hear about the letter Eddie sent me?" John asked.

"What did it say?" I had heard, but I wanted to give him a chance to tell me about it himself.

"He told me to tell the truth. Can you believe that? He wrote that he'd forgive me if I snapped out of it and told the truth. He was whining, saying the government was crucifying him because of my accusations. That asshole's full of shit!"

"Do you think he will try to get to you?"

"Shit, yeah! A trustee said Eddie offered a deputy fifty thousand bucks to get into my cell. He's got lots of money. Probably find some hungry deputy to take him up on his offer. I'm a sittin' duck in here. Eddie said he just wants to be alone with me for five minutes, and I don't think he wants to buy me a drink."

We both laughed.

"I'm not safe in here. And if that fucker thinks I'm gonna sit around here and let him get to me, he's crazy. I'm gonna talk to the Grand Jury.

"Doc, I've really liked talking with you. You've helped me get through this. Do you like steak and lobster?"

"Yes."

John's blue eyes were twinkling. *What are you up to now?*

"Vonda, I'm gonna call you as soon as I get out of here."

He knows my first name? But of course he does!

"I want to take you out to the best steak and lobster dinner in town. Do you have a favorite place you like to eat?"

Oh shit!

"Thanks, John, but I don't think my husband would like that." The lie rolled off my tongue so easily, it surprised me.

"Doc, you're not married," he said.

The grapevine!

"Well, I guess I should have said my fiancé."

John rose to leave, folded the magazine, and put it under his arm.

"Vonda, it's been fun with you. See you later."

What if he really does call me? What in the world would I say?

CHAPTER 38

HOLMES HITS THE ROAD

A week later I looked up from my study books to see a smiling John Holmes casually leaning against the doorframe to my office.

"Yo, Pelto, how you doing today?"

"I'm good. Thanks, John."

"You know, you saved my life."

I smiled back, mouthing "It's our secret."

Holmes' hunger strike had ended and the doctors believed he was stable enough to return to 1700 where he would be housed until his release.

"Remember, Doc, I'm taking you to dinner as soon as I get sprung from this shit hole." John winked and turned away. As I smiled at him, I became aware of a slightly queasy feeling in the pit of my stomach.

The idea of him being released made me feel sad. He was a pleasant diversion from the dreariness of the jail.

Let's face it: In order for me to work with the inmates in a nonjudgmental way, I had to put aside what they had done. But there's a danger in doing that. When these barriers broke down between us, I became more vulnerable and more easily manipulated.

"Come on, John, time to go." Two deputies stood beside him, waiting to escort him back to his module.

After Nash's threat, John talked to the Grand Jury and it earned him his release. John decided he would be as safe out on the street as he was in jail and, no doubt, it would be a hell of a lot more comfortable.

The idea of having dinner with John was very tantalizing, but...?

Eleven-thirty; might as well go downstairs to the ODR and face the mystery food.

Well, this job can't get much worse, I thought. Little did I know what was waiting just around the corner.

CHAPTER 39

BIG MISTAKE

"Vonda, wait up." Ron stepped off the elevator and walked toward me. "Have lunch with me, need to talk to you about something." We walked in silence down to the ODR and after collecting our food, he directed me to an unoccupied table at the far end of the cafeteria.

"The county has offered me a position outside the jail. I'm going to take it."

"You're quitting?"

"I'm burned out! Can't stand working with the dregs of society anymore."

I can't deal with this job without his support!

"I plan to leave in about a month. Your internship's finished; all you have to do is pass the Boards. You'll get your license and be out of here. I'm sorry the county is still frozen and you can't find another job."

Me too!

"I hate the thought of you leaving. Even after I failed the test again, you were so patient with me."

"Vonda, don't fault yourself. Your father had just died. It's no wonder you didn't pass. By the way, how's the studying going?"

"Slow. I get home so tired that when I read something, it doesn't stick with me. All that interests me is watching soaps and drinking wine. When I'm not studying, I feel guilty and when I am, I feel discouraged and bored."

"I remember how that was!"

"Ron, doesn't it help you to get out of the jail and attend the meetings over at Central?"

"Those damn meetings are so full of bullshit, they aren't any relief. Paperwork is overwhelming and the assholes that come up with all of the new forms just don't have enough to do. Most of them have never worked in the real world. Let's face it, their elevators don't go up to the top.

"Vonda, you're frowning."

I took a bite of salad, realizing I had developed the same creases that appeared on his face. I had been so busy trying to survive, there wasn't any time to realize what was happening to me.

"It will be very difficult without you to talk to. Who's going to be taking over the FOP unit?"

"That's what I want to talk to you about. You've been my assistant for the last couple of years and know the ropes; you could do a good job. You interested?"

I ordered a chocolate ice cream sundae, a john wayne from the trustee who was removing the dishes from our table, and tapped my foot nervously, grateful my rubber-soled shoes didn't make any noise.

With my low frustration tolerance for bullshit, not to mention my lack of political savvy, sitting through administrative meetings would be pure hell for me. Ron was watching me and must have read the hesitation on my face.

"You want some time to think about it? You don't have to give me your answer right now."

"It would look good on my resume," I said.

"Vonda, whatever you choose to do, I want to warn you about Pat and Alicia. They run into my office and tattle any time you come in late or take a long lunch hour. Be careful of them, and who you trust. Always watch your back."

Unfortunately, at the time, I lashed out at Ron, telling him he should have told the women to go to hell. I've always been sorry for not thanking him for the warning instead. But, as it turned out, telling me about the two vicious women was a gift. It had never occurred to me that they were going behind my back. I did my job and was oblivious to them.

After a nice sendoff party, Ron left right on schedule. Little did I know that turning down the job would be my descent into hell!

CHAPTER 40

LIVING HELL

I had some vacation time saved up and decided to take a week off, starting the Monday after Ron left. I couldn't face the jail without him and needed some time to adjust to the change. Also, the Boards were coming up again in a few weeks.

Larry stood by, waiting for me to give up on getting my license and just marry him. It was tempting. Then I took a vote with myself and decided against it. That would be running away, giving up my dream. I would pass those fucking Boards, even if it took me fifty tries.

I returned to work the following week with a sense of dread. I picked up a john wayne and secluded myself in my office, hoping to get in a little study time. Just after I started reading about how the tongue differentiates between sweet and sour tastes, the phone rang. It was the new supervisor asking to see me.

Walking into his office, I immediately noticed a change. It had taken on a different look and feel. It felt cold and rigid. A nameplate sat prominently displayed in the middle of the desk: Richard Kushi, LCSW. He was a social worker. Inmates' files sat neatly arranged on one corner with Intake Forms lying neatly beside them. Not like the friendly mess Ron always had. Kushi's coat was carefully hung up, and there was a distinct smell of Chinese noodles in the air.

I sat down carefully, sensing the worst.

After very brief introductions, Mr. Kushi launched in.

And my life changed drastically.

"Vonda, I'm changing your work hours back to five days a week. I want everyone to adhere to regular hours. Also, from now on, everyone will be expected to adhere to a half-hour lunch."

Oh shit, this is going to be worse than I thought! There wouldn't even be time to have a relaxed lunch in the ODR, and forget about going out to lunch!

Richard rambled on about several other changes in the paperwork and new procedures to see an inmate. Meanwhile, I was working diligently to tune him out.

"There will be some other changes; I'll let you know about them later. That's all for now. Do you have any questions?"

What else are you going to change, you jackass?

I almost ran out of the office, picked up another john wayne, and went to my office, thinking about getting a hot fudge sundae, my favorite comfort food, on the way home from work.

I've never been good with authority, so this was going to be the worst!

Needing to talk with someone to try and reduce the sick feeling in my stomach, I locked my door and called Edi.

This social worker was the new boss! He was much taller and younger then me. I felt unnerved. The chemistry wasn't good between us. I wasn't impressed with him—but, then, he was impressed enough with himself for both of us.

Luckily, Edi picked up on the third ring and had time to talk.

"Oh shit, I feel a sense of doom. Ron should have warned me that this guy was a social worker."

"Vonda, you're just being paranoid."

"Remember, I've had one of those as a boss before. It was in my first job. I'll never forget her."

"You're first degree was in social work, wasn't it?"

"But I don't fit with them, we're too different. They're so fucking controlling. When I worked there, I was constantly on edge, fearful of being fired. Three months later she called me into her office and fired me. She didn't give me any clear reason, just said, 'You aren't working out.'"

"I remember. You were really upset."

"I called Mother, in tears. True to form, she said, 'Just pray about it, sweetheart, and it will work out for the best.' Actually, she was right. I went back to waitressing, and after a few months I landed the job at Orange County Mental Health."

"That was good."

"Well, I did learn one thing in that job. You can catch crabs from a toilet seat. The whole female staff caught them. We all assumed that a patient had infested us, but who knows for sure.

"Thanks for listening. Gotta get back to work."

"Let's have lunch soon," Edi said.

A couple of days later Richard called me back into his office. The hair on the back of my neck stood up. Panic! It was the kind of fear you experience when you're a kid and are called into the principal's office.

I stalled as long as possible before walking down to his office, and barely got seated before he started talking.

"Vonda, from now on all of the high profile inmates will be seen by one of the psychiatrists."

The two psychiatrists assigned to the FOP unit dropped by when they weren't involved in their private practices for the sole purpose of adjusting psych meds. They didn't spend more than five minutes with each inmate.

"I don't understand, Richard. I was hired to see the high profiles to help avoid another suicide like Vernon Butts. I have built relationships with these men and we haven't had any more problems with them."

"Vonda, this is for your own protection. You might get called to court to testify in their cases. We need someone who's qualified."

We both knew that was bullshit! In my almost three years there, I had never been served with a subpoena.

I was a psychologist, not an idiot, and more than capable of handling myself in court. His decree was a slap in my face! Walking from his office, my glands were shooting out acid, setting my ulcerated stomach on fire.

"Hey, Doc." I turned to see Munro walking toward me. "I gotta talk to you about Branson; he isn't going to let us take our shower today."

"Not now, Jim."

I got to my office, unlocked the door, walked in, and slammed it shut. It was time to leave this job, regardless of the consequences.

Ken Bianchi was the most upset with Richard's mandate.

"He can't do that," Ken said. "I need to see you! I get so depressed that I might try to kill myself!"

I told Richard what Ken had said.

"If his attorney requests it, you can continue to see him."

He was treating me like a child, who had to ask daddy for permission. In this case, though, the child had more education than daddy and had spent three years establishing a rapport with these inmates.

Ken immediately contacted his attorney, who shot a letter back to Richard giving the required permission. However, even after the letter arrived from the attorney, Richard continued to refuse Ken's request. I found myself in a strange position. I liked and trusted the Hillside Strangler a hell of a lot more than I did this new supervisor.

After that, I would walk down to Ken's cell and chat with him through the door, careful not to let Richard see me.

The following Friday morning, Richard walked into my office, slammed his fist firmly on my desk, and announced that he would fire me if I didn't get my license on the next try. It seemed to me that he took particular delight when he told me this. There was no memo from the personnel office, so I didn't know if this was really true. My paranoia was at an all-time high.

I couldn't let myself feel anything. I had to go dead inside to survive from one day to the next.

The State Boards were to be given the next day and my anger toward Richard was draining my energy. This was not the time to give my power over to the dragon. This was the time to concentrate on passing!

The next morning I showed up on time in downtown Los Angeles and immediately started the relaxation exercises I had been working on for weeks. My stomach felt sick and I was burning hot. *Vonda, this isn't life or death. The world won't come to an end if you never become a psychologist. But, shit, I did want it so badly!*

The test booklets were passed out, I did my breathing exercises, reading the questions carefully, and finished the test within the allotted time. Now it was in God's hands. Waiting for the results was always the worst. If I was in luck—or maybe I should say smart enough, I don't know for sure which—I would pass and be eligible to sit for the orals, which are given a couple of weeks after the written test results.

I slept most of Sunday, exhausted and not very hopeful. I didn't even have breakfast with Tera. There was no reason to believe that I had succeeded this time. But I sure was praying a lot. Mother even put me on her prayer chain with the other church ladies. It doesn't hurt to get all the help you can.

CHAPTER 41

FACING THE DRAGON

Monday was upon me again; time to face the dragon. Calling Richard a dragon helped me maintain my sanity. It was my private joke. My silent mantra became: Don't let the dragon get you!

Richard was an expert at demeaning me. From the beginning, he introduced me to the visitors that toured our unit by my first name. The new male psychologist in the FIP unit was introduced by the title of "Doctor." When I called this to Richard's attention, he said, "You must be one of those women libbers."

The next blow came when he called me to his office and said, "We are short staffed and I need you to start walking the rows every day with the rest of the staff on 4500." My worst nightmare had arrived.

I thought back to what Sherry had said: "When we walk the rows in 4500, the dings fill cups with urine and throw it at us. They throw feces, spitballs—anything they can get their hands on."

"How can you stand it?" I had asked.

"Little buckaroo, it's a job and I need the money. But you never get used to it. Those dings are really cocksuckers!

"Some of them lie on their bunks nude, and jack off while we stand there trying to talk to them. Others start beating their meat when they see us coming down the catwalk and try to shoot it at us as we walk by their cells. It's disgusting and degrading. And it doesn't matter, 'cause it's our job. It's real hard to handle all the things the dings come up with."

On my first day walking the rows on 4500, I was scared. Sherry sent me up to the second tier, while she walked the rows on the floor. After a little while, I figured it must be a full moon because the dings were out of their fucking minds.

It was chaos! The inmates were throwing toilet paper spitballs and food out through their cell bars, and screaming and arguing with each other so loud I could hardly hear myself think.

One of the perps was jumping up and down while hanging onto the cell bars. The adam henry was as naked as a jaybird, not even wearing socks. Another ding was standing on his head in the toilet with his dong sticking straight out.

Suddenly I let out a blood-curdling scream.

The deputies heard me at about the same time Sherry did and came running out of the booth. They got to me before Sherry could get up the metal stairs.

When they reached me, I was shaking all over. Words wouldn't come, I just kept pointing down.

"Jesus, she's in a state of shock," Sherry said. "She's gotten tougher, and can usually handle anything that's thrown at her."

They had to lead me off the catwalk. It wasn't until we got back into the deputy's booth that I broke down. Between sobs, I told them, "I was distracted with all of the noise and commotion, trying to interview an inmate. He was sitting on the floor and I couldn't hear what he was saying. When I leaned down closer to the cell bars, the ding grabbed my skirt and pulled it through the bars. He held it with one hand while smearing pudding up and down my legs. Oh, God! He was reaching up as far as he could and I couldn't get loose from him."

"Are you okay?"

"I don't think so." I bit my lips to keep from throwing up. "Let me go, I've got to get cleaned up." Sherry followed along behind me, half running to keep up. We got back to the FOP unit and I ran into the bathroom, barely making it into the stall. Sherry helped me wash up. I didn't think I would ever get the shit off me. "I hate this place."

I asked Richard to let me out of walking the rows. "Vonda, that's not fair to the rest of the staff. We're short and need everyone out on 4500."

My work record went to hell. After a day off, I returned to work and was immediately called into Richard's office. A Patton returnee that I was assigned to see had committed suicide; he was housed on 4500, and Alicia was seeing him. Richard was mad as hell at me, holding me accountable for the death.

The tormented inmate was probably better off collecting his reward, whatever that was. *Oh, my God, I had become a psychologist to help people. Now I didn't give a shit. I didn't give a shit what made the killers do what they did. I just had to do my time.*

CHAPTER 42

FATE STEPS IN!

Fate has always played a big part in my life, often stepping in at the most unexpected times.

Returning from lunch a few days later, I stumbled on the raised lip of the elevator, dislocated my kneecap, falling to the floor in pain. Injuring my knee wasn't new—it had also happened to me while attending college and working as a waitress. It happened one Sunday afternoon while cleaning house and scrubbing the bathroom floor. Rushing around, trying to get the house cleaned, I forgot the floor was wet and slipped and twisted my leg. No one was home at the time to help me, and I lay on the floor, hoping to pass out when I couldn't get my kneecap to slip back into position. I couldn't tell how much time was passing, but I knew I had to have someone help me and started screaming. Thankfully, a neighbor heard me, broke into the house, and called an ambulance. The doctor in ER put a tube cast on my leg that extended from my ankle to my ass, and put me out of work for three months.

We had barely enough money for food, and couldn't afford the luxury of health insurance. Now we didn't have any income. Anyone who says that getting Welfare is easy hasn't ever tried to get it. It's dehumanizing. After being interviewed by two real assholes that turned down my application, I was finally assigned to an older woman who understood the grave situation we were in. She okayed food stamps and aid to families with dependent children.

The girls hated to go to the grocery store. It embarrassed them. I didn't like it, either, especially when we ran into our neighbors.

"Vonda, are you okay?" Senicqua had seen me fall. She called a couple of deputies over to help me up and then drove my car to the front gate. After pulling myself together, she helped me limp to the car. Luckily, I had injured my left leg so I could still drive.

The orthopedic doctor diagnosed torn cartilage and said I needed arthroscopy surgery to correct the tear. He scheduled the surgery for a few days later. I called Mother and she was on the next train into Long Beach to help us out.

It was a weird transition from the jail back to normal life. I was different from other people. It felt like we had nothing in common. You can't get called a fucking bitch everyday and not lose your ladylike polish.

It was a relief to be out of the jail, but I didn't fit in anywhere. I couldn't handle going to parties, exchanging recipes, and talking trivia with other women. I felt isolated and could understand why policemen only hang out with each other. My thoughts were different. I was so aware of the "seamier" side of life. I was suspicious of everyone who walked anywhere near me.

My shiny illusions about people had been destroyed. People are naïve, unaware of how evil other people can be, and that they are capable of real cruelty. Given the right circumstances, almost everyone could harm others.

I knew the secrets. No one really knows what goes on in someone else's mind. A practiced psychopath can trick you into believing anything.

"Mom, what has happened to you?" Tera asked.

"I'm not sure."

CHAPTER 43

CELEBRATION, COME ON!

"Mom, are you awake?" Tera was standing beside my chair in the living room.

"What time is it?"

"'Bout four o'clock."

"I must have dozed off."

"I have the mail."

"Put it on the table."

"Mom, you might want to look at this. It's from the State."

"Don't know if I want to open it. You do it."

"'Congratulations, you have passed the written portion of the....'"

"Oh, my God! Let me see that!" I quickly scanned down the page. "'The orals will be given on the fifth of November. Call to schedule...'

"Oh, Tera, I don't believe it!" She came to me, put her arms around me, and we cried and hugged. Then I called everyone I could think of to celebrate.

Now it was just a matter of passing the orals, which would be held in San Francisco two weeks later. I flew there with several other fearful candidates and appeared at the appointed time. As I had predicted, the orals weren't as frightening as the written portion. Now it was the waiting game again.

It was almost Christmas and we were going to Needles for the holidays with Mom, my brother, and his family. Before leaving Long Beach, I gave our house key to Dionne, a neighbor, and asked her to check on my mail every day, in case the results of the orals arrived. They were due any day now.

It was the day before New Year's Eve when the telephone rang and my brother called out to me. I was scared.

Dionne's voice was on the other end of the line. "Vonda, a letter came for you; it's from the State."

"Open it, please." Suddenly I was hot and sick to my stomach.

After a silence at the other end of the line that seemed to last forever, Dionne said, "Congratulations, Vonda, you've passed!" I couldn't believe it. My life just opened up.

"Oh, Dionne, thank you! Thank you so much for calling!."

I had felt numb for so long, I didn't believe it would ever be possible to feel alive again. Now the adrenaline was pumping through my veins, and I could hardly catch my breath.

I hung up the phone and began to sob.

"Vonda, are you okay?" My brother ran to me.

"I passed! Oh, my goodness, I passed!"

After I healed sufficiently following the surgery, I began a private practice. A friend helped me get a job as a psychologist in a board and care home, which housed psychotic patients. With my new license in-hand, doors were already beginning to open. I figured if I did return to work, I could manage seeing patients in the evenings and weekends to continue building an income base.

I only needed two more months with the County to become vested in my retirement. I debated with myself as to whether it was worth returning to the jail to earn the eventual reward. When I thought about going back, the nightmares returned. But then again I had put in nine years and ten months to become vested. What were two more months?

My second entrance into the jail was much more difficult than my first. Unfortunately, I knew what lay ahead.

The gray concrete monolith loomed up in front of me as I walked the dusty concrete sidewalk. Dry spiky scrub and two straggly trees, trying to survive in the lifeless soil, lined the path. The windowless building grew larger as I neared the end of the walkway. I took a deep breath and strode forward to be swallowed up by this inhuman place of horrors.

After being admitted into the inner sanctum, I walked by the cell that had been occupied by Eli Komerchero and thought of the argument he had had with Ken Bianchi over what made up a nice girl. I smiled at the memory. There are two sides to people, even drug dealers and killers.

Richard had hired and given my office to another social worker and didn't have any intentions of giving it back to me. I would be sitting in the bullpen with the rest of the staff. They weren't any happier about the arrangement than I was. But that didn't matter. I could see an end in sight.

For the next couple of months, Richard and I pretty much ignored each other. I saw the Patton returnees in the hall outside of 4500 with a guard close by, and never walked the rows again.

One morning when the office was quiet, I phoned a deputy in 1700.

"I heard Holmes finally talked?"

"Yeah, and got kicked out a short time after you left."

I was disappointed and hoped the drop in my voice wouldn't alert the deputy to my feelings. I hoped John would call, if only to tell me how he was doing. He had promised to send me a full-size, signed poster. God only knows where I would hang it.

"What did Holmes tell them?" I asked.

"Don't know. It's all sealed, probably won't ever know. Enough to get him freed, though. He was an interesting dude," the Senior said. "Better than most of the perps we get in here."

"I know what you mean."

I fulfilled my final two months and set a wedding date to marry Larry.

Although Sherry and Jose never confessed to having an affair, they came to the wedding together, and brought a set of four-point restraints for us to have fun with on our honeymoon.

As a famous author once said: "He was raised to be charming and not sincere." After two-and-a-half years, Larry and I separated and subsequently divorced.

Three years later a friend asked me to attend a benefit to raise funds for a women's shelter. It was to be a Halloween masquerade party. She wanted to play yenta between her attorney and me. Jim Lia came as a Mafia don and I went as a southern bell, with a lavender dress billowing out over a hoop slip, lace gloves, and a picture hat with silk flowers.

It was love at first sight for both of us. We married five months later, sixteen years ago.

Deanne and Richard's marriage was going well, and she was pregnant with their third child. Tera had finished college, was married and pregnant with their first child.

And we all lived happily ever after.

P.S. Although I left the jail twenty-five years ago, I wasn't able to write this book until now.

Each time I would begin working on the manuscript the terrible nightmares would return. Finally I am free from them.

CHAPTER 44

WHERE ARE THEY NOW?

John Holmes was held in contempt of court by the Grand Jury for 111 days after refusing to disclose who the perpetrators were in the bludgeoning deaths on Wonderland Avenue. His was the longest term ever served for contempt. He finally disclosed some information and was released. His testimony has never been made public. Called "the King of Porn," Holmes died on March 12, 1988, at the age of 43, in the Veterans Administration Hospital in Sepulveda, California, of complications from AIDS.

I was never privy to Holmes' dark side, although I did learn of it. Even after being diagnosed with AIDS and banned from working in this country, he went to Europe and continued his movie career. He made several more films and exposed his female co-stars to the disease.

In 2001, Eddie Nash was arrested for the Wonderland Avenue murders and pleaded guilty to manslaughter.

James Munro, who testified against William Bonin in the Freeway Killings to escape the death penalty, was given a sentence of fifteen years to life with the possibility of parole. He is currently serving his sentence at Mule Creek Prison in Ion, California. He and I still correspond.

William Bonin was sentenced to die for the Freeway Killings in 1982 and died by the executioner's hand on February 23, 1996 in San Quentin, California. He died without remorse. His family didn't attend the execution and no one claimed the body, which the State cremated.

He had exhausted every legal appeal. His was only the third execution since California reinstated the death penalty in 1977, and the first one by lethal injection.

Arthur Jackson wouldn't allow his attorney to plead him NGI. He denied that he had any mental problems. He refused any medication or therapeutic help. Jackson was sentenced to twelve years in jail for attempting to kill the actress. Saldana was unhappy at this light sentence and fearful he would continue to stalk her when he was released. He served his sentence and was deported back to England.

Yehuda Avital, the Trash Bag Murderer, is serving a life sentence for two murders.

Elihua Komerchero and Joseph Zakaria, also Trash Bag Murderers, served their time and were deported back to Israel.

Kenneth Bianchi had a callous disregard for life and was sentenced to life with possibility of parole, and is serving time in Walla Walla, Washington.

Angelo Buono was sentenced to life without possibility of parole and has died of a heart attack.

Douglas Clark is sitting on death row, awaiting execution in San Quentin Prison, California.

CHAPTER 45

MY THOUGHTS

Nome of the serial killers I worked with exhibited any psychotic symptoms. I would classify them all as psychopaths, someone who is callous, devoid of empathy, lacks remorse or feelings of guilt.

Having the ultimate power over life and death made them feel strong and reduced their feelings of inadequacy.

I believe there is nothing a therapist, even Freud himself, could have done to stop these killers.

There are three indicators of sadism in children: cruelty to animals, wetting the bed into adolescence, and setting fires. Destruction of property can also be a predictor of aggressive behavior in adulthood.

Most serial killers are white male, often clean-cut, and look like the boy next door. Don't ever believe that you can pick out a killer or child molester by their looks. Even psychologists can't do that.

I don't believe serial killers or child molesters can be rehabilitated, and they should never be allowed to return to society. I also don't believe that the death penalty is a deterrent to a killer, but it does keep them from committing another murder. We *do* have a right to be protected.

Probably being abandoned or abused as children plays a large part and contributes to their abhorrent behavior. But many people suffer sexual and physical abuse, and they don't become killers.

Just like you were born with certain characteristics, I believe these killers are born that way. They lack a conscience or empathy for other human beings. There is something missing in their genetic makeup—that's what allows them to torture and kill so easily.

Bottom line, albeit perhaps a bit too simplistic: We need more research to improve our ability to spot serial or mass murderers at young ages.